# BEAT ZEN AND THE ART OF DAVE

# BEAT ZEN

## AND THE

# ART OF

# DAVE

## DAVID MCNAMARA

THOMAS CLARKE PUBLISHING

*Beat Zen and the Art of Dave*
Thomas Clarke Publishing

First published in 2015 by Thomas Clarke Publishing

Thomas Clarke Publishing
Perth, WA 6009
Australia
Phone: +61 408 995 770
Fax: +61 8 93868352
Email: thomasclarkepublishing@gmail.com

National Library of Australia
Cataloguing-in-Publication entry:

Author: McNamara, David Winston,
Title: Beat Zen and the Art of Dave / David McNamara.
ISBN: 9780994487407 (pbk)
Dewey Number: 796.51092

# ABOUT THE AUTHOR

As an author, artist, pilgrim and wayfarer, David McNamara has been spinning tales of adventure and yarns of fiction for more than 15 years. Originally from Perth on the remote west coast of Australia, David's enchantment with movement was sown at an early age. But a European gap year in 1998 hooked David on backpacking, and independent travel soon turned into a Beat Zen way of life. The more places David visited, the more eager he grew for longer adventures and more remote destinations – trekking through the Andes, the Alps, the Himalayas and the Amazon; traversing the Mosquito Coast, the Trans-Siberian, the Silk Road and edges of Mesopotamia; sailing on Egyptian feluccas and Panamanian catamarans; crossing glaciers in Pakistan and deserts in Africa; visiting ancient archaeological sites around the world including Ciudad Perdida and El Mirador, surviving South East Asia hedonism, highway bandits and police corruption; hitch-hiking across Mongolia, Tibet and Tajikistan; and road tripping around North America.

Along the way David came to realise that journeying across vast continents via river, road, trails, rail and sea is not that different from overlanding it through life. With fortitude and passion, David's innumerable budget backpacking odysseys across six continents produced its own inevitability in 2011 with the release of his first book, *Loves, Kerbsides and Goodbyes*. David has since completed his eagerly awaited second travel memoir in which he's continually discovering new places and cultures, and meeting new and fascinating people. David continues to live a life on the open road, gathering material for a third travel book while working on two books of fiction. When he's not seeking out an untold story, he's heading towards an unknown destination over the horizon – enjoying being lost in the spaces between places.

# CONTENTS

*"The weight on my back reminds me that I'm free."*

## CHAPTER 1

# THE LEAVING PHENOMENON

I hadn't heard of the *Leaving Phenomenon* when I left my home-town in 1998 to go backpack around Europe. But I guess the mystical forces don't care whether you know them by name or not. It was the first time ever I was getting on a plane, heading to the other side of the world — and in less than three weeks before I departed I met a girl.

I was still living at home, working part-time at a local video store — covetously saving for the trip. Alice appeared on a quiet Sunday evening to drop off a video that a customer had returned by mistake to the video store she worked at. Our introduction could have been a film. I do concede I was watching an excessive amount of movies at the time. I enjoy the memory more now since the march of time and progress has laced the scenario of two rival video stores with a bygone sense of charm, like *Be Kind Rewind* — and maybe in a few more years following the extinction of DVD libraries, music stores and book shops the Capraesque story will decay further into something overly sentimental and outdated.

Alice has just turned 18 or maybe she is still 17 years old and is in her first year of university studying architecture. She is comely and spirited with hoisin eyes behind high school bangs.

She talks for what seemed like an inordinate amount of time and way longer than what was civil.

Do I make a move? Ask her out? Get her digits? Do I fuck!

My solitary pick up manoeuvre at the time is a curt salutation such as 'Hi' or worse still 'Hiya', which lingers awkwardly with false expectation something constructive *(like my name at least)* will follow. I don't regret this — weird is better than boring right? It takes me time to realise chicks weren't necessarily listening to much of what I said anyway.

After Alice leaves and before closing I clear the returns bin and find a video belonging to her video store. If Eros was finally speaking to me after 20 years of incoherent, interpretive godspeak I'm listening. The following night after work I drive by her video store to return the favour. I can see through the shop front windows that she's working. We organise to meet up two days later and she kisses my face off like sushi grade octopus. We meet up again the next night and again she kisses my face off.

Our introduction feels like an augury that's turning sour due to my imminent departure. Three pseudo dates later we're perched with legs over the edge of a wooden climbing frame on playing fields near to where we lived. I finally muster just enough gumption to come clean and admit I'm going away.

'I'll wait for you.'

Her words also come from a film script — and I consider Alice is probably watching an immoderate amount of videos as well. But unlike a Hollywood promise or malediction projected on the big screen through a delirium of conviction, Alice's vow is so earnest and quiet and too real it scares the celibacy back into me.

'Ummmm.....' is my immediate douchebag response while I stall, trying to think up more douchey words to crap on equivocally about how I was going away for some time. My airline ticket is valid for a year, and I presume a year won't be enough time, which is why I nominated the return on the day it expires.

I repeat how I don't know when I'll be back, muse out loud over how never is longer than forever but both are fucking long. Then I garnish it with some shite about how it's not you it's me to complete sounding like a total tosser.

'I'll still wait for you,' she replies.

Alice could have been *it*. In some ways she was some kind of *it* in that moment. She had just committed something of herself. Under a hue of retrospection Alice represents the first genuine romantic episode of my semi-adulthood — and it didn't court the attention of others, or rely on compounding the word *like* as the only way to convey emotional substance. But I'm only 20 years old. Time has no value. And I'm blind to Alice's courageous virtue and vulnerability — too young to see how rare and precious it is. I tell her not to wait forever. I didn't really know where I was heading — just that it would take a lot of time.

A week later and on the eve of my departure I find time to say goodbye to Felix, my best friend from school and university. He lived with Gemma, whom I bonded with over acoustic guitars, lo-fi tunes and the predisposition to shun public performance for the reassurance of lounge room venues. Gemma has blushing brown eyes and the enviable pale nacre of a British complexion. Her drollery often dipped into self-deprecation and hinted at a jaundiced past from a cruel relationship. But when her fiery, sardonic marrow broke free of her modest facade, she was captivating and lively company by contrast.

We talked, we drank — we spun aspirations of our futures about the lounge room, only to hear them tangle and fall as we enumerated the stark realities of life obstructing our dreams. The cynical truth of the world passed down by our parents. The three of us agree never to shy away from the proverbial precipice in life — to always seek out the visceral feeling of teetering on an imaginary edge, replete in the blissful validation that comes from risking a large measure of comfort and contentment to create or invest in something unique and profound.

This was not hard for me. I was about to exonerate myself from my family, friends, and hometown for the first time in my life — to embark on an inaugural journey across the globe. It was a defining moment of independence, marking my life as something that now belonged solely to me. If I'd known at the time leaving shit behind took care of so much other shit I probably would have done it much sooner. But I had just met Alice and was about to leave her as well. And her existence exacerbated the queasy, indigestible mixture of fear and excitement in my gut.

The blunder of nerves invoked by goodbyes and departures dulls over time. But backpackers don't easily lose the emotional upheaval of forgoing friends, family and a stable life for the risk and rewards of the open road. Trepidation and impatience adorns all but the weary traveller on the eve of an intrepid new adventure. It's our endorphin that elicits an unrepentant urge to plan and book the next trip shortly after returning from one.

I later wondered if this emphatic rivalry of exuberance and apprehension is why I'm giving Gemma a back massage past four in the morning. When discussing the *Leaving Phenomenon* once with a group of backpackers, someone likened the allure of an about-to-depart traveller to the aura of someone entering a new relationship after a long drought — where a rousing sense of reinstatement and confidence, capped by their unattainability, transforms a person into a walking aphrodisiac to all and sundry.

I keep looking at my watch. It's now 4.09 am. I have to be at the airport no later than 11 am and I haven't packed so much as a sock or toothbrush. A feral timbre of nerves is crying out for me to end the night — desperately trying to peel me away from the promising situation to curb the likelihood of missing my flight. But an authoritative voice deep down in my loins — the voice of Isaac Hayes keeps telling me something is about to go down. So because of Isaac Hayes I stay put.

A quarter past four.

My fingers tire and I stop. Gemma turns around and looks up from the lounge room floor. I know she means to kiss me, but I'm pretty shit at bridging carnal spaces. I leant on nightcaps, not herbal tea for these tasks. So I let Gemma's seniority prevail, expecting her to join me back on the couch.

Instead, she pulls me down on top of her on the carpet. The feel of her body beneath me is soft and supple like her kiss — unlike my anxiety which lurches in a large recess of my brain. It refuses to quit, torturing the moment's purity by erecting a Babylonian list of all the items I need to remember to pack — simulcast with lively debates about the quantities:

*Socks — three, maybe four. What about jeans? Do I need jeans? What about casual wear? Definitely a shirt and tie for job interviews — should I pack a belt? Is two ties too many? What about emergency food — packet soup maybe. Vegemite!*

The lists quickly ascend to a towering height that grows unstable under the strain of my memory, starts to sway then tumbles like building blocks. Yet this only stimulates my mind further to pick up all the fallen blocks and start over *(repeatedly)* again, and again. With Gemma willingly taking my weight I still find it impossible to surrender to the moment. Acknowledging this makes it all the more infuriating and impossible. I then utter words that I still can't quite believe that I would ever say.

'I can't, I should go.'

How can my own words betray what until then had been my lifelong lustful ambition — to be in this position, with a girl who wants me? I don't even know if we are going to do what I said I couldn't do — it's that absurd. And what's worse is while I try to figure out why I am so intent on sabotaging my libido's legitimate claim I've started a new packing list:

*Vegemite, Vegemite, Vegemite — don't forget Vegemite! Defi-nitely two ties — it'll save money and time when I get to London — forget the denim, it weighs too much. How many tees are too many? What about those snack tins of baked beans mum has in the pantry? Passport! Don't be a dickhead and remember your passport and ticket! Will baked beans cause a problem with French customs?*

I'm not sure why Gemma stressed this was a "no strings attached" affair. Maybe like me she had also never been in a situation before where a complete fuckstick was abnegating a beautiful, delectable unattached sexual experience. I say something equally clichéd about not wanting to damage our relationship. Why was I doing this? I don't even really know what I'm saying — because if our friendship was a body I'd fuck it right now too if it would let me.

'No strings attached,' Gemma repeats.

I know I've escorted myself irrevocably down a path *(to my own personal horror and self-retribution)* from which I can't recover. Gemma understandably gets upset and pushes me off her as she sits up.

'Well why did you fucking stay here till four in the morning giving me a massage?'

I have no answer.

I also don't want to admit that while on top of her I've gizzed into my t-shirt — an irrepressible fuck you in response to my mutinous words. And as I notice the stain seeping through from my navel, it's fair to say that the indignity of premature ejaculation is a compounding factor in forgoing unforgettable, commitment free sex — and partly the reason I make a hasty goodbye.

With barely an hour of sleep I wake in a panic to pack. In 1998 two hours is the recommended allocation of time given to airport protocol and procedures. Packing takes over four hours. I haven't even left the house and I'm already living in the margin, eating into the half-hour drive time when I jump onto the family computer and sign up for my first ever email account with Hotmail. By the time I'm sitting on a pint of VB in the departure lounge I'm wallowing in an emotional hangover. I had unleashed a phenomenon that my young Catholic bones were not yet ready for and with a mixture of relief and regret I boarded the plane.

On the backpacking stage it's hard to deny fate and destiny are major players cavorting along the open road. It's a veritable selling point of budget overland adventures. Shoestring travellers may not gamble with their hard earned savings, but we love to gamble with choices determining the direction of our journey, and to a larger extent our lives — goading fate into giving us a peak at the seductive mystery behind it all. Backpackers continually provoke serendipity with games of luck and chance. We flirt with the ground and skyline in supplication for a sign when choosing an onward route. It's not hard to imagine a supernatural corollary when the daily sequence of what to eat, when and where to get a drink, whether to stay another night, *(and if not where to go next)* results in a propitious encounter with a gorgeous Belgian backpacker that evening by a hostel bar — it's also an entertaining game to play:

*Yes, she is alone.*
*Yes, she would love to have some company sightseeing tomorrow.*
*Yes, by the power of Neptune it is still 241 happy hour at the bar.*
*Yes, of course I would love to know more about her over a beer.*
*And my sweet lord, yes! I am happy to assist if the beer starts to make her feel too bloated.*

Jung's *Synchronicity* is alive and well when global maps become game boards and travel guides the instructions to your life. Ruse or not, it's no more evident than with the *Leaving Phenomenon,* which acknowledges the auspicious connections and romances that befall travellers just before they are about to leave on a long journey. And it's a favoured subject feeding the nimbus of backpackers around bamboo fires — where fantastical stories of happenstance are exchanged.

Strict itineraries smite these forces. Time is what's needed — time out in public to simply hang about and be noticed. Some would argue a traveller's free spirit and liberty encourage the divine elements to gravitate closely and orbit conspicuously around us. In the backpacking world where outcomes are indentured to the handful of decisions regulating a backpacker's day, it gets easier to see the tricks of chance and coincidence. Destiny too reveals herself demurely — as if vision of her translucent design is rewarded to the early risers who worship the new day and hedonists who stay up so late they spot her silken dew-laced trap in the fleeting morning light.

Travel guides do help corral backpackers along a thin allure of must-see sights across vast tracts of continents. So random encounters become commonplace. And what is first treated with incredulity is quickly branded routine and passé. There's a perverse irony to the effete disregard which calcifies around the recurring magic and madness of budget backpacking — especially since a major push for many shoestring travellers is to be unfettered from the daily cycles of devastating monotony. But most of us are creatures of conformity and habit *(even travellers who often don't see they are simply exchanging a rigid form for a more fluid one)*.

I returned to my hometown a year later. I saw Alice again — and again she could have been *it*. But time and circumstances had changed the equation. And like me, she wasn't looking for anything serious. We were "out of sync". They were her words, not mine and maybe a product of the nineties, which were about to end with Y2K and *The Matrix* trilogy fuelling pop existentialism on the cusp of a new millennium.

Feeling the incorrigible pull to leave as soon as I returned I made plans to relocate to Manchester early in the New Year. I spent the next five months working to save for the trip. Friends held a farewell party in my honour two nights before I was due to depart. While recognising my promising courtship with destiny and the open road, I wasn't deluded into thinking the *Leaving Phenomenon* would appear each time. I didn't saddle departures with expectation it would turn up to deal out a full house of fortuitous prospects. This was because biblical spells of abstinence blessed the prolonged periods I spent living and working to save for my next adventure. So by way of contrast meeting someone new on the threshold of leaving always felt all the more extraordinary and magical. And I liked the fact these moments boldly appeared on the eve of travelling to somewhere new and unknown, as opposed to the diminutive manner good fortune lightly spices domesticity. It vindicated my vagabond lifestyle. And although repetition under any auspices of divination tends to nullify its significance, my version of the *Leaving Phenomenon* and I had a pretty good understanding — primarily because I didn't seem to have much luck getting punani any other way.

The house party for the most part was a respectable affair, which relocated at a reasonable hour to a forgettable neighbourhood nightclub. Soon after we arrived a girl I barely knew dragged me into dark and furtive corners of the club and kissed me with wet lips and ardent tongue. She then grabbed my hand and led me off the dance floor, past all my friends and out of the nightclub like she had done it before.

I awoke the next morning and found my way home. During the course of the day spent procrastinating over what to pack, a thick miasma of small-town innuendo settled in the gaps between phone calls of final goodbyes from friends. Only later were intentions made clear. And realisations often occur too late to make much of a difference anyway. But somehow I ended up as the unwitting hostage in the moral of a hackneyed sitcom episode — where I was a Dwayne or Dwight, the incorrigible one, morally lost and unsure of the transgression I'd committed while a prudish cast closed rank on me, adamant that what I did was really bad.

I didn't give a shit.

This wasn't a cavalier reaction to the salacious rumours and murmuring disapproval. It also wasn't due to the aureole of complacency shining over me as I was about to get on a plane to another hemisphere, deliberately to escape this hometown incestuous *Dawson's Creek* shite. The reason I didn't care still remains — I really liked Faye. She was Ashtanga yoga fucking hot with a wry turn in her expression that always signalled a mischievous change in the colour of her eyes.

A year passed before I saw Faye again. I messaged her when I returned home briefly for my brother's wedding. She admitted she was smashed the night of my going away party and barely remembered me. We hooked up anyway like we were strangers who couldn't help feel we'd met before, and we covered the gap with booze and late nights. We hung out in her bedroom and listened to *Eternal Nightcap* by The Whitlams. Each time she sat on top of me and curled her legs around my back, she apologised by saying, 'Do you mind?' while reaching for the bottle on her bedside table. The sharp snap of the plastic lid punctured the silence and fractured the sexy manoeuvring. One of us always made the other giggle and it became a ritual of sorts.

I didn't know how long I was staying or where I was going, which is the prerogative of someone in their early twenties. Faye kept asking me to stay the night while I kept making excuses why I couldn't. I used my brother's wedding as an excuse to buy an around-the-world ticket. I arrived a month early for the wedding and decided afterwards to backpack around North America. I hoped it might provide some abstruse answers to life before returning to England for work. Since our time was defined by my imminent departure Faye and I didn't complicate it with talk about feelings or the future.

When I next returned home I was in an insolvent rudderless funk after an attempt to relocate from Manchester to Dublin failed. I contacted Faye. Maybe it was the remnants of my charm, or a brief flirtation with the *Arrival Phenomenon (the* Leaving Phenomenon's *lesser known cousin)* which elicited an invitation to her shared house. We surrendered to a nostalgic evening drinking red wine and playing music. I awoke the next morning to the timid chill of autumn and scent of sandalwood burning. I looked across at Faye, who was still asleep. Careful not to mistake the thick ligament of wine stuck in the back of my throat, somewhere between my head and my heart I detected an unsettling strength of affection take hold that Faye was all colours of amazing.

The short drive home stiffened my resolve to clarify this stirring. Not through any specific action mind you. My mind found early morning revelations all a bit too hard to contemplate — which is why I relied on showers, coffee and sunshine to make sense of a new day. I did decide however to at least acknowledge my feelings. This commenced with feeling painfully foolish and cursing myself for ignoring the possibility of Faye for so long.

I left to travel north on a weeklong fishing trip with my Dad and when I returned a "Dear John" letter was waiting in the mail. I knew it was one even before I opened it. It wasn't by my instincts. On this occasion I recognised the handwriting. Then I noticed the postage stamp and thought how funny it was Faye used the postal service to send a letter which she could have delivered herself via a short drive or long walk. I even joked to myself saying, 'Wow, she must really not want to see me.' Then I opened the letter and realised I was right. In the letter Faye wrote:

' I don't think I want to catch up with you
again (so I'm not going to call you).
I made an effort to let go and move on from
things at the end of last year and so
seeing you again now seems strange...

*I want you to know that I've enjoyed
what we had together at different
times over the last couple of years –
thank you for those times...'*

I thought of Gemma and the "sure thing" I managed to fuck up two years ago. In spite of a backpacker's arguable appeal when departure is imminent, Gemma seemed to capture the basis of the *Leaving Phenomenon* — hooking up secure in the knowledge two people know exactly where they stand. It's not always about one-night stands and casual sex — not that I consider there's anything wrong about physical intimacy without expectation. My heart loves seldom and skin loves to touch. However, I grew up in the nineties with the repressed sexual guilt of Irish Catholicism compounded by the rampant AIDs epidemic — where underwear *(no matter how unwarranted)* incubated the seeds of pestilence and death. So for me this kind of liberation took time. Now it's a carefree pushbutton app with swipey-right, swipey-left gestures.

The result I suppose is I take meaning from every bit of nakedness — because I'd find it a bit boring otherwise. But they're still just moments — and moments are reflections of transience. So when you're not around, where there isn't a yarn of time to knit all the shared memories into a collective history moments expire before they can breathe, stretch, bind and evolve into something more enriching and meaningful. An imminent outbound plane, train or bus disables any thrill or wonder that this time it could be something special — that a connection is worth exploring to hope and see if it germinates into an enduring relationship of substance.

It often makes me wonder. What elements in life, and in love do our choices preside over outcome? Fate versus coincidence; destiny against chance. It's a debate as old as words for those who need chaos or an anonymous god. But in a conventional world, it's fair to say the dalliance of divine intervention or chance moments can be harder to discern. Romance is buried under the mandate of rigid agendas and strict schedules — motes of luck seldom rise to intervene. It can be a fun game to play in hindsight — joining the dots — moments of forgetfulness or tardiness which tickle and bend stricture with a minuteness of providence. But it is much better suited to the realm of fiction. So how's love coping on the open road, and in the high speed world of throwaway dating and artificial connections; compatibility based on advanced search algorithms; Facebook walls plastered with platitudes and verisimilitude; Tinder hookups and breakups; Instagram selfies of fresh new love; and vengeance in the lovelorn fingertips of anyone with wifi access?

I grew up influenced by the swashbuckling heroes of the big screen — appreciating that an Austrian goodbye is preferable to a German one, and loving a princess when she's your sister is a bit fucked up but when it's Princess Leia it's understandable. So I find it hard to ignore the hubris of commercial romance. Beyond the dynamic shifts in mobile technology and how we interact we still grow up embalmed in a cinematic sense of soul mates and star-crossed lovers from Hollywood's reboots, remakes and reimaginings of romance and true love. They beset DVD collections and megaplex cinemas full of poor mutable young fuckers and sentimental souls from the West to the Eastern edges of black markets. Even hardened travellers succumb to nostalgia's loved-laced yearnings on remote overland journeys — where solitude and disconnection rouse quixotic delusions of romantic rendezvous and reunions with old acquaintances.

Under the impartial spell of retrospection I can easily convince myself phenomena of ill-fated love or love at first sight is all a mechanism of lust and loneliness. And the ceaseless regurgitation in trite paperbacks and Valentine's Day blockbusters is simple profiteering from a false aphrodisiac. But then I consider a *Before Sunrise* connection on an overnight train from Rome to Bologna, a Bohemian dawn splitting an absinth fuelled embrace, a punch drunk bunk bed romance, a note in red ink left on my hostel pillow that reads 'Jun 21st Munich @ Vordsadt Cafe 9.30pm ☺ If I don't go to Budapest it would be fun,' an unfulfilled Mont Saint-Michel encounter, hedonistic Manchester hookups, a Canadian Greyhound overture leaving Winnipeg, a torrid Cuban affair, a seaside fuck on the Dalmatian Coast, a provocative train station goodbye in Tomsk, an email address hidden in the back of a copy of *Clockwork Orange*, a gur in the wilds of Mongolia, the roll of a loaded dice, a moon slung beach in Goa, a tantric St Kilda fling, a last minute couchsurfing acceptance to Charleston SC and the best impromptu birthday celebration since I was nine. And with all the other random and furtive moments caught by askance glances, sweet and conflicted goodbyes and ebrious, kerbside connections I steadily become unsure about what I believe.

# CHAPTER 2

# BACKPACKING BAPTISM OF FIRE

I first arrived in London, the European capital for indigent Antipodean dossers in 1998. After three and a half months backpacking around the continent I was drawn there like most roving Australian backpackers — a careenage promising free accommodation from vague relatives and friends of friends. However, soon after I found myself knee deep in all the same shite I was trying to escape from by leaving my hometown.

It was no secret the generation of adventurous young Aussies before me had established England and Europe as a college graduate's rite of passage. They ushered a fresh sense of popularity and libertine pleasure to budget travel on fleeted vessels named after Thor Heyerdahl's famous Norwegian raft, the Kon-Tiki. Yet unlike its namesake, which was derived from an older translation of Viracocha *(the Inca sun god),* any semblance of anthropological and cultural curiosity was zipped away in the fanny packs of Contiki's 18–35 year old clientele as they partied hard on tour buses around the continent — spreading the Antipodean beer guzzling legacy to beer guzzling Europeans.

Afterwards, many Australians and New Zealanders with European heritage lingered for years working in London while continuing to jaunt around the continent in a post-study malaise. Some of whom found roots and romance and never came home. In fact, by the time I arrived in Europe these ill-defined origins of the gap year were a mandatory experience for graduates. And many of the backpackers around me traipsed about in a more than vague fashion — as if they were being shepherded by a prescriptive urge to conform rather than any deeper yen to explore the Old World aesthetic. They did it quickly too — imbibing everything like they were downing a funnel at an underage *Superbad* party, before stumbling out the garage door of Europe, without experiencing anything real — just to get a high five of kudos and get on a jet plane and get the fuck back home.

It makes me wonder how much of the backpacking culture has survived from when I first strapped a pack to my shoulders 15 years ago. How's Marco Polo's legacy doing in today's world — when tomorrow feels like it already got retweeted yesterday? Never before has history been so personal and so comprehensively and flawlessly recorded. It's instantaneously captured to be shared, liked, pinned, tweeted, instagrammed and facebooked then forgotten. But with such a short expiry date, how is it affecting the crucial process of vetting what we collectively remember and what we forget?

Independent travel and the desire to regularly get away have never been stronger. And the growing popularity towards extended excursions abroad now sees trips of a year or more as something commonplace — distorting the difference between a vacation, a journey, a new beginning, and a new life. As antiquated notions of the annual holiday are superseded by infatuation to escape, whenever possible, I wonder how many of us recognise there is also freedom which can enslave. The contradiction which tinsels this eloquent truth is what first attracted me to Zen. I guess it's because long-term travel often conjures fanciful notions to aspirant travellers, backpacking dilettantes and vicarious Beat Zen buccaneers — when in reality *(like most things)* it is still bridled by its own set practices, sacrifices and trappings. So what is first thought as liberating can end up being a placebo of sorts.

It makes me question if budget travel today is all just an impertinent reaction to the superficiality of postmodernity. Or is there some deeper, more instinctive appeal against the erosion of real distance caused by globalisation and the affordable ease of air travel? I don't envy the conundrum tyro travellers must face attempting to punch outside the critical distance from their own societal views and influence — tethered to smartphone technology whilst traversing the noosphere in an expanding mist of global connectivity.

Alternatively, perhaps nothing has changed or evolved beyond the ancient and fabled yearning for one to escape his or her foreseen destiny. If I'm honest there was nothing particularly spiritual about my initial desire to get the fuck out of Perth. Fresh from university, and brandishing shiny and shrewd new analytical tools of psychoanalysis, feminism and semiotics, phallic layers of new meaning weren't lost on me as I sat at the back of a Qantas Boeing 767 listening to the Flight Captain's announcement from the cockpit. But I was too caught up exercising the prerogative of every youthful generation — to presume the tortured sense of disenfranchised angst belonged to me.

Of course escaping home and running away with a head full of fanciful delusions is how many parables and spiritual journeys begin. Most notably is the story of Siddhartha Gautama, the wealthy son of a tribal chief. Finding himself inexplicably dissatisfied with his privileged life, Gautama leaves his wife and child in search of answers on a journey spanning more than five years to eventually become the Awakened One, otherwise known as Shakyamuni Buddha. Looking back, I'm sure part of me wants to convince you I was after some enigmatic sense of resurrection when I left Australia. But I wasn't running away to find sanctuary in a *sangha,* or enrol in a *sesshin* to retreat from the world and engage in intense meditation. I was simply seeking anonymity. Yet in hindsight I can see how easily I fit the allegoric wayward son, which is recounted in the *White Lotus Sūtra* of Mahayana Buddhism — or if you prefer, the laconic reprise as the Prodigal Son in the *Gospel of Luke.*

I was travelling with Joel, another mate from university when I touched down in London. It was at the start of August and Britain was half-naked, celebrating a rare and resplendent Indian summer. We initially stayed in Muswell Hill with Joel's relatives. We both had extended families in London so we decided to divide our time respectively between our kin until we found a flat of our own. For a fortnight everything was fine. The revered late summer mutely disappeared. Leaves vanished from the trees, only to be resurrected as large sodden slabs of detritus covering the streets and parks. We got jobs at Odeon cinemas in Camden Town and Holloway Road, which loosely vindicated our media degrees because we convinced ourselves we were at least nominally working in the film industry. We also started looking for a flat, during which time we moved down to Islington to stay with my second cousin, who had just returned from a recent trip to Australia, where she stayed with my family.

At the time my cousin had a spare room in her semi-detached townhouse. We agreed to stay a fortnight since she could afford to leave the room unrented for this time. But the accord rapidly deteriorated within the first week. The kitchen suffered the most. Jaundiced sticky notes accumulated with each new day. It reminded us of the first hostel Joel and I stayed at in Nice, where laminated warnings in bold lettering lined corridors and decorated the rooms — much like the decor of Australian airport customs.

The situation became desperate. We also realised our uncompromising paltry budget put us in direct competition with the maelstrom of parsimonious students returning to begin first semester at North London University. It all seemed rather hopeless.

There were no civilised phone calls to discuss amenities such as the inclusion of a washer and dryer, or inquiries about the approximate cost and houseshare system for paying utility bills, landlines and a TV licence — no decorous retreat to crunch sums and calculate additional costs then debate whether it was affordable. The phone call quickly devolved into a primitive yawp:

'ISITSTILLAVALLABLE?'

When rarely answered in the affirmative a mad dash ensued across north London to get to the address and find out it had become occupied in the meantime.

Joel admitted a vague intention to ask my cousin if he could rent the catacomb where I was sleeping. It was upstairs at the end of the hall where I moved after a few nights to garner a small amount of privacy from sharing the front spare room. It had little faculty beyond a storage space and would have paired honestly against our frugal allowance for weekly rent. I didn't mind. I hadn't come halfway round the world to remain under the yoke of filial dependence and shack up with family no matter how close or distantly related. I'd also been backpacking solo around the continent on the fumes of the insolvent Australian dollar. To say I was selfish and thrifty is harsh but true. But until I left Perth I didn't realise how constant the pressure was to appease everyone around me, because *(like most hometowns)* everyone is in cahoots.

The remoteness of my hometown makes it a tricky place to describe — especially growing up there. Located on the south-west coast of Western Australia, Perth is the capital of a state that accounts for a third of the island continent. The dichotomy of growing up in a large city that feels like a small town, and rests between a vast ocean and ceaseless desert, encourages idiosyncrasies — of who we are and how we view ourselves in the world. Famously, white swans are our black sheep. And there is only two degrees of separation in Perth because everyone knows everyone, or at least knows your faults and fuckups — which you are constantly reminded of from the same tired old stories rehashed from the same people whenever they were predictably encountered in the same predictable places. Even the young, energetic demographic of Perth disguised in hepcat nonchalance and cool can't escape the big city in their small town boots. They fly to opposite corners of the globe to frolic about with other likeminded souls and engage in illicit affairs that are fierce and fleeting as holiday flings can be. And invariably, with phenomenal speed a litany of inconceivable connections uncovers these indiscretions through random friends of friends to respective boyfriends or girlfriends back home. It's called getting *Perthed.*

However, outwardly people of Perth understand the world is a big place because everywhere is far and expensive to get to — so distance is no big deal because like time it's all relative. As a result Perth people love to travel — and we travel a lot. I realised without family and friends to rely on *(where I was an alien and everyone around me was a stranger)* required a degree of prioritising my needs over those of others. My sense of compassion also grew, but being a foreigner for the first time in a foreign land edified the considerations I gave to my own wellbeing. And the satisfaction and self-respect from honouring my own needs was a liberating feeling — to realise this in no way made me a bad person.

By the start of our second week in Islington the proliferation of yellow square leaves on the kitchen table started to imitate the seasonal decay outside on London streets. The autumn colour could have evoked a warm breakfast ambiance if each message wasn't in a very unassertive British fashion explicitly telling us to fuck off. Hometown preconceptions started to mount like an old familiar weight. This was precisely the crud I was trying to purge myself of that had accumulated from growing up, shackled to the same sundry place, surrounded by the same people, same family all reinforcing each other's predefined roles. And the anonymity I sought, which I thought would be all too simple to find was proving elusive. It turned out the existing housemate was manipulating my second cousin — exploiting an imperialistic divide and inciting a manic fear us dirty colonial urchins would entrench ourselves like plantar warts and never leave. It was no surprise when the rest of my extended London family got involved. Under the auspices of concern for our wellbeing a campaign of extradition gained support. Regardless of Joel's intentions it was evident to me our short tenure was doomed and likely to end prematurely. With a healthy mixture of accountability, duty and good intentions the mother of my second cousin abducted us on the eve of the fortnight and made us stay at the family home out in Loughton — zone fucking six on the Central Line.

The large fully detached Victorian house evoked vestiges of Hampden House from Hammer Film productions I vaguely remembered watching as a kid. A short and formal vestibule greeted us. We stood in awkward silence with our cumbersome backpacks, facing the front door while Mother Superior unlocked a side door to the front sitting room. The ornate interior, adorned with antiques and pristine chattels was lifeless save for Mother Superior. Her husband *(my mother's cousin)* worked down in Portsmouth during the week. So he only commuted back to the family home on weekends. And with all the siblings grown up with families of their own, it was just Mother Superior and us.

After a polite chat outlining an unclear yet strict sense of governance, we were escorted to a bedroom at the top of the stairs. We soon realised all the other doors in the house were locked as well. The eerie custom fanned my morbid imagination — trapped in a residential maze of terror, fighting for my life with the only means of escape a master skeleton key hanging around Mother Superior's neck.

On our second night stay there, I mistakenly caught a Central Line service that diverted to Hainault. I fell asleep and woke up approaching Newbury Park. I jumped out in a drowsy panic. But it was the last service of the night so I couldn't get back to Leytonstone where the line deviated, or onward to Hainault which would at least put me closer to my provisional Loughton home. I was forced to navigate through a Stygian fog lanced by roaming foxes. I used the luminous maps on intermittent bus stops like breadcrumbs — and walked in moonless limbo, feeling hopelessly lost for an indeterminate time before my feet found the reassuring crunch of the horror house's pebble rock driveway. It was well after 2 am by the time I crawled exhausted into bed.

That was my last night in Loughton. The reason for this started with a brittle rap on the bedroom door which woke me at 7.30 am.

'David, can I speak to you downstairs please?'

The same sibilant request followed a knock on the door the previous morning. It resulted in a fustian inquisition about my future plans in London — the lack of which was a precise yet unexplainable motivation for my trip. Being of no relation, Joel avoided this ritual both mornings in pleasant slumber.

I stumble downstairs, eyes lacerated by sleep. Before I get comfortable Mother Superior launches into an elaborate proposal to loan me an unspecified sum of money. Inexplicably, she then switches to a tone of disapproval to ask why I was back so late. In a less than eloquent manner I try to convey the nature of my work at the cinema — minimum wage work, which fucking sucked. I mention overtime, late finishes and scrambling desperately along Holloway Road to catch the last tube service. I'm careful to avoid talk of my nocturnal pilgrimage the night before — but it's all a foreign language to her anyway and she returns to the topic of loaning me money.

I'm jaded by the unfulfilled expectation of sleeping in on my first day off after a week of double shifts. And Mother Superior's offer is sounding ridiculous as she outlines a strict contractual agreement of repayment. I knew I would politely refuse whatever she was going to suggest at the start of this pre-breakfast intervention. But then she starts patronising me *(and my parents)* by saying she will only give me money after gaining consent from my parents. The thought of Mother Superior calling my parents paints me in a rash. Flushed by a surge of lower middleclass pride I put an end to the one-sided negotiation by declining her offer, defiantly, respectfully. Wondering whether I should be insulted I walk back upstairs.

I can still recall the tantalising revelation on the landing of the staircase. It dawns upon me as my Han Solo inner voice says, 'Kid, you don't have to take this shit!' In Zen the term *kensho* describes a moment of awakening that can strike anyone suddenly, intuitively in everyday life. And while first insights can be powerful, life-altering experiences, Zen teaches us that without greater meditation and practice they don't lead to the Great Awakening called *Satori*. However, Zen is just one chapter in the worldly tome of mystic traditions. And what appeals to me about less orthodox teachings in all branches of religion is their collective veneration and testimony for profound experiences occurring in daily life. Bede Griffiths, who embodied religious pluralism as a Christian Yogi, encapsulated the vivid insights shared by many of us in his autobiography *The Golden String*:

> '*Any experience of this kind is probably not at all uncommon, especially in early youth. Something breaks suddenly into our lives and upsets their normal pattern and we have to begin to adjust ourselves to a new kind of existence. This experience may come, as it came to me, through nature or poetry, or through art and music; or it may come through the adventure of flying or mountaineering, or of war; or it may come simply through falling in love, or through some apparent accident, an illness, the death of a friend, a sudden loss of fortune. Anything which breaks through the routine of daily life may be the bearer of this message to the soul.*'

To this day I'm unsure how transcendental my *moksha* moment was on the staircase. It resonated like a mystery — getting louder as I became cognisant to a supreme faculty of movement and travel that was at my disposal — the convenient ability to exit any trippy mandala of controversy without commotion, consequence or retribution. But in a less than Zen-like manner it evoked *Robin Daffy Hood,* one of my favourite childhood Merry Melodies cartoons. Invigorated with the schizoid zeal of a cartoon duck, I reach the top of stairs reciting Daffy's call to arms:

*'Ho! Ha! Guard! Turn! Parry! Dodge! Spin! Ha! Thrust! Flee!'*

My memory paints Joel's face in consternation when I wake him to tell him the news.

'Fuck this dude – you can do what you want but I'm fucking outa here.'

I watch as he briefly considers his position. I would have loved it if he stayed to outstay another welcome. If we weren't out in zone six on the Central Line, or if he wasn't equally spooked by the accommodation I'm certain his dexterity for self-preservation would have contemplated the matter further. I inform Mother Superior that we're leaving. She insists on knowing our forwarding address. I lie and say we've found a vacancy at a north London hostel. I name a hostel I vaguely remember listed in the *Loot* and give a fake phone number. Standing on the driveway laden by our enormous packs, we're handed silver teaspoons in sandwich bags as parting gifts. The ceremonial goodbye adds to the terror and relief of leaving as Joel and I debate what we can only assume is some bizarre archaic symbol of British hospitality.

With nowhere to go we sniff out the hostel in north London. At a daily rate of £7 it's not entirely surprising to discover that the hostel is essentially a halfway house with no vacancies. We loiter on the side of a road, popped up by our packs like we're still backpacking *(which in the moment we kind of are).* Watching the autumnal shadows creep over the kerbside and across the street we decide there's no other recourse than to call Joel's relatives and ask if we can stay again for a couple of days.

In today's world, the pervasive integration of technology and connectivity can make it hard to imagine what life was like before mobile phones and the internet — like the city you live in where changes *(both big and small)* become imperceptible. And some dear readers might not have memories old enough to stretch back to an era of analogue phones, pagers, mix tapes, floppy disc drives, dialup internet and VHS. So you could be wondering why the fuck we didn't just google our way out of trouble and find another place to stay. Well, there was a time before cyberspace and touchscreens — and other technological innovation which has since revolutionised the way we travel.

In 1998 there was no Gumtree, Craigslist, Hostelbooker, Hostelworld, Hospitality Club, Couchsurfing or Airbnb. People relied on daily hardcopy classifieds like London's *Loot* and shop front handwritten adverts. We didn't even own mobile phones for fucks sake. We were homeless and out of our depth. And the looming prospect of another full week of working that commenced at 11 am the next morning accentuated our predicament. Joel and I both knew it was a bad call to return to his relatives, but without any other affordable option we dug into our pockets for change and looked around for the nearest payphone.

Beyond our tussle with north London students for dirt cheap lodgings, our chief impediment was born out of ignorance to the advance cost of rent in the UK. The practice of paying a month's rent in advance plus bond *(minimum one month's rent)* ballooned a £50 week room *(which was all either of us could afford)* to £400 or more *(which neither of us had)*. So Joel and I overloaded our working week with split shifts and doubles so we could afford a flat when we actually found one. As a result the only free time we had to search for accommodation was early in the morning before the cinemas opened.

Joel and I took turns waking up early to walk down to the shops and get the daily edition of *Loot*. However, on the first morning back with Joel's family it was easy to see the rules had changed. Previously we agreed on finding a shared flat. Yet when I woke I heard muesli munching, Loot-toting Joel on the phone and out for himself — shitting on any sense of kin and camaraderie as he called every single bed listing in north London. Self-interest had prevailed. In all fairness it was a reasonable progression given our utter failure to find a cheap two bedroom property. But the situation was absurd. We sat opposite one another at a breakfast table in a quaint middleclass London kitchen — ignobly taking turns on the landline to ring the same classifieds and competing for the same spare room.

The next morning it's my turn to get up early and buy the *Loot*. Taking Joel's lead I sit in the kitchen searching for fresh listings of single rooms in houseshares. Mother Superior 2.0 enters and broadly inquires as to how it's all going. Perhaps it's her genial tone I find disarming, or the aftermath of my own family dealings that's put me in a particularly susceptible mood. Yet I fear I'm too candid when outlining the difficulty of finding a place while working so much overtime because she doesn't respond. Instead she retreats in a very British manner to the adjoining dining room, conjures a weighty caesura then reappears *(side exit)* to deliver an apoplectic tirade disparaging me and my behaviour.

Her entire body visibly shakes as she hollers with bilious vitriol about how my shit won't fly in her household because I am not like Joel *(ergo I was of no relation)*. No shit, I thought finding the irony in no way amusing — playing the role of a delinquent who's getting ripped by a crazy-arse mother. It wasn't that I didn't appreciate her position. I probably was taking the piss — after all backpackers exist in the space between hospitable gestures and expired welcomes. But this didn't prevent an abject feeling from her less-than-fair aspersions. The rules had constantly changed on me, and my motives were no more self-serving than my best mate. But by way of implication I take all the shrieking to mean I'm not taking responsibility for my current situation — and blithely pissing all over the fulsome and fickle sense of British hospitality upheld by their household.

I admit at the time I was not yet acquainted with the myriad of subtle quirks of British etiquette that varied from that of Australia, and much harder to discern given our congenital history. London is brutal — especially for destitute backpackers. The capital's legendary status as a colonial mecca for overstaying welcomes with loose blood ties and friends of friends was well supported long before I arrived. I imaged Antipodeans' coarse sense of decorum straining proverbial bridges of local hospitality day and night — I could hear the timber creak and snap all over London, and the jovial afterglow of fractured amity regaled down at the pub with quintessential Australian humour and boorish contempt.

It takes time in the UK to appreciate the differences. British hospitality is a grand petrified structure, curated over the centuries by parochial adherence to tradition and protocol — as such the rituals are nuanced and convoluted. Most evident was it didn't tolerate spontaneity. You didn't just "pop around" unannounced to someone's gaff in Britain like you did Downunder. And you also never, ever turn up in London without previously securing a couch to crash on, because getting hold of Londoners in a personal emergency is futile. Everyone in London is constantly busy doing something, or equally nothing — and when they're not they're in a meeting or on the tube or in a shop and without cell coverage. Otherwise they'll happily blame the rain, or a single tube connection for their inability to leave their house. When you are rarely offered a lift home in England it didn't get you to your front door. It meant dropping you at the nearest arterial crossroad exigent to the driver's homeward route. And when the British made a decision based on decency it was adamantine and immune to debate.

Threat of asphyxiation stains the face of Mother Superior 2.0. A lilac glow bruises her complexion forcing her abusive spray to simmer to a thankful respite. I respectfully make my leave and head back upstairs. Ignoring a very real sense of déjà vu I can't work out how I'd managed to travel halfway around the planet, to a city of 20 million strangers *(which equalled my home country's population)* and still found myself at the nadir of all this antagonistic family bullshit.

Before I left Perth I already felt my own brief existence haunted me like a shadow — caged and chained to the moribund thraldom of my hometown. I was convinced without uprooting myself from all that I knew I would remain in a provincial kind of stasis — that protects you from change and freedom of thought which I so desperately desired. The compulsion to sever myself from the umbilicus of my hometown, from all the rhetoric and contretemps, to escape and become lost in another place was immutable. So as soon as I graduated I figured what better place to be an orphan lost in a crowd than the city of London.

Again on the stairs of my temporary abode a realisation I'm free takes hold. But in reference to myself it seems twice is the charm. The emotional distress accrued from over a fortnight evaporates into the eggshell wallpaper and oatmeal carpet, and a lenitive clarity spreads upward and outward from my bones to my pores. The art of escape awakens within me — how the simple act of travel can preserve individual freedom by extricating oneself from the tartar of life which builds up from chewing on one place for too long. The impulse to flee is so clear and glorious, the outcome so certain *(decided two steps ahead of me)* I feel like it is my own creation.

I don't know why I was developing a pattern towards having profound mystical experiences on stairways. But it's impossible to compare this intoxicating moment of lucidity with the mild epiphany that prompted Joel and I to do a runner from my extended family two days before. Over half a decade later, I still remember the first time I heard Bright Eyes *The First Day of My Life*. While I was never sure how much of Conor Oberst's dense lattice of lyrics and autographical references I was supposed to get, I felt I knew precisely what he meant when he sings the opening verse:

*This is the first day of my life*
*Swear I was born right in the doorway*
*I went out in the rain suddenly everything changed*
*They're spreading, blankets on the beach*

Reaching the top of the stairs I'm wearing a rapturous shroud incubating a new me that hasn't the time for introductions. I walk into our shared room. Washed clean in a chrism of resurrection, I tear off the shroud and wake Joel up so the nascent new me can reveal an impulsive and unwavering plan. I tell Joel I'd just got lambasted and that I'm going to make like a tree and leave. I think he appreciated my situation *(along with my reference to* Back to the Future*)* but was a bit too tired to consider it. I knew my disappearance would drive a thin maul of discomfort between Joel's family and him for a short while. But fuck them, I thought. I could be the anathema they would bond over. And I wasn't going to appease anybody's sense of decency after the shit I just got served made it abundantly clear I wasn't welcome anymore.

I was reeling with an inglorious sense of disbelief by the time I boarded the 43 bus service for Holloway Road. It's an arcane sensation heading to a full-time job with everything you own strapped to your back while hauling a very real sense of homelessness. To quote George Orwell from *Down and Out in Paris and London*:

*'It is a feeling of relief, almost of pleasure, at knowing yourself at last genuinely down and out. You have talked so often of going to the dogs — and well, here are the dogs, and you have reached them, and you can stand it. It takes off a lot of anxiety.'*

I thanked the speed of my own eviction, which left me numb standing outside the cinema three-quarters of an hour early for work. I only remember feeling slightly sheepish as I heaved my oversized pack through the narrow side door of the cinema. Intent on passing unseen, I quickly made my way up the ornate spiral staircase and through the "Staff Only" door. It led to a rear stairwell, at the top of which was the staff room nested in the rafters of what was a grand old Gaumont cinema before WWII. I stashed my backpack in the unassuming recess between staff lockers and pulled on my work-issue black polo shirt with an aquamarine underline around the collar. I walked back downstairs to clock in where I was assigned the upstairs cafe/bar for the day shift. Like the scullion Mr Orwell, I appreciated the worth of life experiences which I was sorely lacking. This was the seed of my design *(even if I couldn't put it into words at the time)*. It was the whole reason I was here in London. But as I setup for the day's trade I grew steadily unsure of the peripety I was drifting into.

When I left for Europe four months earlier I was aware of a well-established Perth network in south London. It included Ben, an old buddy who dated back to early school days. I had called Ben out of courtesy when I first arrived and we caught up for a pint on the Southbank. He recounted a familiar story of Antipodean infestation, brought about when he welcomed another mate, green off the plane to crash his couch. Ben's invitation multiplied like a germ. Within days he had five Aussie couch crashers who then interred themselves in his small second storey flatshare for three long weeks. He expressed regret over the timing. He had only just got rid of the larrikin army. And had the imposition not been so fresh in the memory of his two Fulham flatmates he would have insisted that I come and stay.

I decide to call Ben again on my lunch break from a public phone on Holloway Road. While the phone rings I realise I have no iota of what to do if I can't get hold of Ben — and the fact that in no way I find this alarming should terrify me, but it doesn't. It turns out Orwell was right. Having no contingency, no other option felt good. I was free falling, free and triumphant with a queasy sense of satisfaction, like that which comes from eating too much pizza. A convenient side effect is I have no appetite for a lunch I can't afford. When Ben answers the phone at his work desk I immediately chalk it up as a good omen. I tell him how bad I feel for putting him in such an uncomfortable situation but I'm desperate for digs for a few nights.

'All good Dave – it's been a while since the boys were here so everything's settled down.'

The relief is sublime. The word *relief* is a funny one, under-nourished and vagarious we're often compelled to quantify the feeling — prop it up with pillows of other feeling words like I've just done. But due to this day *(because of this moment)* I still consider the extract of sweet relief the most underrated emotion of human distinction — capturing the bravura of our existential uniqueness in the same manner usually reserved for sunsets over water and the awesomeness of humans in a crisis.

It's after 11 pm when I finish my double shift. I joust with London's metro to get south of Thames and arrive at Ben's just before midnight. He answers the door with irrisible eyes doused in sleep.

'Hey Ben–oh sorry dude, did I wake you?'

'It's cool.'

Ben escorts me upstairs while I fumble to express my immense gratitude.

'I really appreciate this man.'

'Shhhhhhsh.'

I forgot about Ben's unbreakable languid amble as he points to the lounge room.

'Couch.'

Passing the kitchen he again indicates.

'JD,' then as an afterthought adds, 'Coke's in the fridge.'

As Ben continues his sleep-driven shuffle down the darkened hallway to his bedroom there may also have been an inaudible 'goodnight' capped by the click of his bedroom door shutting closed. The cathartic release of finally finding myself in a place of unconditional hospitality is so overwhelming I realise I'm standing motionless in the lounge room with my 23 kilogram backpack still strapped to my back.

Abandoning preordained roles that fight to keep you in one place — and jumping the freight train of life to where the outcome is unknown is one of the great fundamental joys of solo travelling. And while the freedom for transformative self-reflection comes from time absorbed by long journeys, it begins with anonymity. And anonymity starts with escape. Anonymity is a new beginning — wiping the slate clean, and having the fortitude and freedom to be whoever you want to be without the imperceptible weight of suppression from those who think they know you.

I mix a stiff JD and Coke and collapse on the foldout sofa. I amuse myself with the irony that in trying to find anonymity I travelled to the other side of the world, passed a backpacking baptism of fire and burnt bridges along the way; and only discovered what I was truly looking for by crashing on the couch of an unassuming old school friend. As I close my eyes I see myself on a curtained stage relaying the moral of the story — while blood may be thicker than water, good friends are the fucking haemoglobin, and for what good families do they can really fucking suck.

Buddha discovered the *Middle Way* by revising the ascetic teachings he undertook as Siddhartha Gautama at the start of his spiritual journey. I too testify to the value of moderation, especially in the territory of consumptive practices. But I'm also a hedonist, greedy for the cornucopia of life experiences. Call me a picker, a poacher, a hypocrite, I don't mind because all of us are all these things. This is why I find merit in the strict abstinence and the abstemious traditions practised by major religions. I don't mean extreme anchoritic practices like that of St Simeon, which often serve the spiritual hunger of the individual. I'm also not suggesting that we should all be slumming it and deracinating people of privilege. But compassion creates understanding — and it's clear the world needs understanding now, more than ever. Having nothing reminds us all of our natural virtue and is one of the greatest and most humble lessons we can all learn from. Being poor also forces you to learn *(literally)* since you have to teach yourself to fix everything because you can't afford to get anyone else to do it.

I got a dream room in a houseshare three days later behind Alexander Palace in Muswell Hill — right around the corner from Joel's relatives. It was a shoebox that in a previous life serviced overnight staff working at what was a residential nursing home. Reincarnated, it now housed a tribe of six other Muswell hillbillies: a Kiwi, a Canadian, an Australian, two Spanish, and one local Londoner.

After a year in London I did the impossible — I'd saved to travel again. This time I went to Scandinavia, Eastern Europe and Turkey for two and a half months. But as soon as I returned I wanted to leave again. I'd had enough of London. I'd had enough of Holloway Road and the crusty, saccharine interior of multiplex cinemas. I'd had enough of living in an increasingly fractious houseshare with six other people. Every morning I woke desperate to get out of London and replicate the halcyon days of my summer spent in Europe somewhere else in the world.

Every day I remained in London the feeling compounded. I had a return ticket back to Australia that was about to expire. The answer seemed simple enough. But as soon as I got back I was snared by the doldrums of my hometown — choking on the city's inertia and stagnant effluvia, which had compelled me to leave in the first place. I knew escape was inevitable. I saw the new millennium in as everyone in my hometown did every year — getting wasted in someone's backyard under a muted sky and fell asleep in a whisky fog on a refuse couch on the front porch feeling dirty and content all at once. I then packed my bags and returned to England — to Manchester this time to join my best mate Felix, and his older brother Charles, a veteran expat who invited us both to stay with him *(which in Australian vernacular was a pad to crash for a vague extended amount of time)*. And for the good part of my twenties I lived there, unburdened in the company of old and new friends and allowed myself to turn into the person I wanted to be.

# CHAPTER 3

# ESCAPING THE HOSTEL KA'BEH

Thirteen years after my first overseas journey I'm in Cancún staying at the Hostel Ka'Beh, a downtown party hostel. There I meet Yail, an Israeli backpacker. She comes up to me and without introduction encapsulates the primal urge of backpackers by asking,

'What are YOU running from?'

While I remain a moderately spiritual person I guess until writing this now, my faith has remained unexamined — evolving quietly all on its own as a portmanteau of personal beliefs. To give an undercoat to my spiritual leanings I was raised a strict Catholic and as such my salvation never felt insecure. My middleclass Christian roots meant that nothing was hard fought or won — my ancestors had done all the fighting. My beliefs were handmedowns so I never felt anything protective or meaningful about them. My indifference matched my adolescent angst and mistrust — where I doubted an almighty benevolence as much as I supported a wrathful omnipotence. Unsurprisingly, my renunciation of Catholicism *(along with organised religion in general)* came at the liminal climax of teenage rebellion.

Looking back I would like to think my apostolic revolt was a reaction to the daunting prospect of adulthood — and the orgy of deceit and delight I was poised to enter. But if I'm honest the catalyst was a cliché much closer to home — my status as the middle child in a large Catholic family. The fallible designation of a middle child meant that I was already made to feel shit about just about everything, because just about everything is always my fault. Tired of all the soapbox sermons and indoctrination, I decided at some point I didn't need this pontificating and didactic shite from God too. If God couldn't make room for a chronic masturbating hellion of contradictions without dangling a carrot of afterlife glory before me then I had no room for a god either. Or in the words of Oskar, the midget-freak zeitgeist of Günter Grass's post World War II masterpiece *Tin Drum*:

*'Well, my Catholicism survived only in my nostrils.'*

In many ways I feel this childhood upbringing was responsible for establishing my dualistic tendencies towards spiritualism and scepticism. Call me cultproof. It's a collaboration I actually find rather agreeable like a lonely misanthrope or a bitter atheist. I endorse the mystery behind a book, hat, prayer, person or shoe choosing you, and not the other way around. I knock on wood if it's within arm's reach, but never use my skull as a substitute. I never put shoes on a bed. I also endow jewellery and sentimental keepsakes with good luck. And I believe in a trinity, especially when cooking to command the number of key ingredients — a pizza with three toppings is sacrosanct and should never be breached, and therefore three must be a magic number.

Meanwhile my *daveness* is always searching, eager for esoteric experiences. That's why along with being an uncommitted seeker I worship the occult mysticism of backpacking — and the ability to make my own luck. I summon chance with the roll of dice or flip of a coin. I inveigle serendipity with every random encounter. I am mesmerised by the orchestra of clairvoyant signs in nature while traversing barren mountains, penetrating dense green forest, crossing sinuous waterways and overlooking vast blue oceans and jagged panoramas. I have a personal aircraft takeoff ritual which I never fail to perform. It involves me drawing the sign of the cross against my lips and chest before whispering the Millennium Falcon battle cry:

*'Punch it Chewy!'*

If asked to encapsulate it, which it now seems fair that I do, my bespoken religion resembles a pilfered stash from the "free shelf" in a hostel kitchen where the half-empty packet of fusilli, random corner-cut spice sachets, tin of beans, bottled soy sauce or balsamic vinegar, vegetable bouillon, processed cheese slices and stale nub of a baguette represent the collection of superstitions, aphorisms and various religious dogma I've assembled like a bracelet of lucky charms.

I arrived in Cancún with my bracelet of lucky charms on a cheap junket airline from Germany. It was a Thursday and Thursday at the Hostel Ka'Bah was "BBQ Night". It was written on a white board so it was official too. Although it had a start time of 8 pm, a spread of cheap meat didn't appear on the hot plate until after 10.30 pm — mainly because the staff seemed very busy playing cards and drinking. And for all intents and purposes "BBQ Night" turned into a party night. So I was confused for a moment seeing "Party Night" advertised on the white board above the front patio bar the following afternoon. But it was Friday night in the Yucatán's capital of holiday decadence, so of course it was "Party Night".

I didn't know the Hostel Ka'Bah was a party hostel when I checked in. I was just looking for a cheap accommodation in a central location to catch up on some sleep after my flight. And when I lugged my backpack past the hostel, its outdoor seating, vacant and shaded from the afternoon heat seemed like a perfect alternative to relax away from the tourist hordes in Zona

Hotelara. As night took over the city backpackers gathered in a coven around the outdoor bar, mingling with talk of evening plans. Yail, who I keep pronouncing Gail until she is forced to spell it 'YAH-AYE-EYE-EL,' is provocative and flirtatious — just the way I like a girl. But I'd overheard she just returned to Cancún from Isla Mujeres to resume what she started with Scott, one of the itinerant staff who checked me in to the hostel.

Scott is native to Detroit and a former soldier in the airborne division — so it is no surprise to see him working out of a backpack at the hostel. Former military personnel are common to the theme of personal reinvention on the open road. Israel with its mandatory two years' service is famous for unshackling a legion of prodigal twenty-something soldiers every year onto the global backpacker circuit to a mixed reception. They shed the fatigues, adorn themselves in neo-hippie uniforms and scatter like dandelions from Dharamsala to Rurrenabaque — where they wrap themselves round bongs and campfires, growing dreadlocks, getting bitching tans, drumming drums and strumming guitars *(much like the rest of the backpacking community).*

Scott demonstrated a rather rigorous and militaristic work ethic not often exhibited in travelling staff. And evidently he embraced the complementary rule of playing hard after working hard. So after pashing the Israeli girl's face off earlier, and fuelled by the hostel's complimentary growlers of vodka and gin, Scott promptly passed out in a hammock.

I guess this is why Yail went in search of new entertainment and secrets, which to some is the same thing. She brought a vulpine acuity to the enterprise — methodically eliciting vulnerabilities in others without imparting anything of herself. I had experienced her type before — the type who travels the globe collecting confessions like souvenirs of experience. Maybe I was a curious target when Yail sashayed over to me — sat alone in the corner reading Russell Brand's *Book Wook II* with a six-pack of Modelo tinnies and chuckling quietly to myself.

'What makes you thing I'm running?' I ask Yail in response to her bold inquiry.

'Everyone who travels is running from something,' she says with a deep penetrating stare.

'Maybe when you're twenty-three-'

'I'm twenty-two-'

'I'm not running from anything?' I reply.

I didn't disagree with Yail. It's just that my 2011 trip to Central America set a precedent in my travels over the years. It was the first time ever I left without feeling I was in some way absconding to be somewhere else. I had a return ticket to Europe that was about to expire and I simply couldn't think of any reason to stay put. Bitten by desire or free of it, nothing quells the yen of independent travellers. However, before departing I did see my journey as an obversion of sorts, being rationalised and satisfied from the other end of a recondite spectrum that seeks fulfilment — like choosing to look up at the world from beneath the ocean rather than a more conventional perspective of looking down from a conquering height.

I suppose on a personal level my recent fascination in exploring my own path of self-realisation over years of travel is consigned to the older me — the one who carries more evidence of my mortality and is better at straddling what's come before me and what awaits me. I am not rare, or the only one in this situation. I hear other travellers often quip how they will travel their whole lives. But it seems to me what remains constant to both rewarding adventures and spiritual growth is the theme of pushing yourself beyond what is comfortable. A leap of faith or opening a new door is a persistent and figurative *(if not literal)* way to great insight, discovery and awakening. Zen practice typifies this purpose with the encircling tenet of Great Faith, Great Doubt and Great Determination. In other words:

*To live in great doubt we need great faith.*

The physical act of travel by its very nature awakens in all of us some form of spiritual journey. It binds scriptures and stories of vatic leaders like a gilded weave — and is a prevailing motif in homilies and fables built on a tradition of mendicant pilgrimages and gallant quests ending with great insight. I'm not suggesting backpackers are some displaced community of discalced bhikkus like David Carradine's Kane — aimlessly wandering the earth, following *the way* like some clichéd eighties television series. Admittedly, the iconic nature of independent travel today makes an easy target for this kind of parody. But in popular culture our exposure to dharma or *the way* is largely myth — based on B-grade martial arts movies where master and disciple spar kōan riddles interspersed with slow-motion sequences of *kata* performed atop perilous summits. So diluted teachings of the Buddha Way end up as memes, or regurgitated by celebrities endorsing a fashionably obscure sect of esoteric thought.

The broad themes get through — how we should all slow down, be present in the moment, bring clarity and peace of mind to each task in front of us and each embrace our own Beat Zen path. With this in mind, if the fundamental essence of Zen can be articulated as accepting one's ordinary life and recognising its extraordinary qualities through the discourse of everyday experiences, then for me Zen also consummately sums up the art of travel. Jack Kerouac, member of the ultimate band of Dharma Bums disregarded Zen as silly. Talking to Japhy *(Gary Snyder and 'number one Dharma Bum of them all')* Kerouac's alter ego elucidates:

> *'... my contention being that Zen Buddhism didn't concentrate on kindness so much as on confusing the intellect to make it perceive the illusion of all sources of things.'*

Yet, if Zen is the antidote to logic then for many people travel is the panacea to counteract the atrophy of sedentary living. With any journey a sense of change can be imperceptibly subtle and slow — and unless meditated upon, it can go unnoticed. So even though travellers regularly catapult themselves overseas without much care or thought, the original impetus doesn't stay the same — motivations mature the longer you're away. And the orbital shift in perspective from cumulative experiences is why backpackers choose protracted and circuitous overland adventures.

I tell Yail in the past my main means of evasion was to embark on an overseas odyssey. I also concede that escaping the claustro-phobic bullshit of my hometown was a primary component of my original need to put on a backpack and jump on a plane. I describe how I wanted to disappear, become nameless, shed the self I had contrived to survive the rigours of high school — and build myself up again without all the contaminated inculcations of 15 years of institutionalised learning.

'But I'm comfortable with who I am now,' adding 'I guess I'm travelling cos I can't think of any reason not to.'

I hear my mantra for the trip as I utter the words — less than 12 hours off a plane from Frankfurt it has found me. In the months that followed it literally became the mantra for the trip given the amount of times I repeated it to other backpackers in the discourse of daily introductions and conversation.

*'So what made you want to travel here?'*
*'I'm travelling because I can't think of any reason not to.'*

Yail laughs.

'What are you running away from then?'

'I saw you over there laughing at the book you were reading. I always think people who laugh while reading have the best sense of humour.'

'Thanks.'

Yail's evasive reply piques my curiosity but I can tell whatever she's hiding she's showing it off — and it's all too blatant and impenetrable to bother probing further. I see Scott's head roll off the side of the hammock and dangle at a painful angle.

'Is your boyfriend alright sleeping in that position?'

'He's fine.'

The nubile bodies painted around the courtyard sow an amorphous dissent of time since my previous trip ended in 2008. In some ways it feels like no time has passed, yet I also feel like it took forever to get here. I wonder if this is the fault of getting older, to view the last three years with a retrograde concussion. Or is it simply the prerogative of a mellowing soul to dismiss the senescent signs in my bones and my reflection? I don't feel any older so I'm happy to continue flirting with Yail. Her all-knowing eyes make me want to sleep with her as well, but I can't shake the image of Scott, literally! Because he's stuck motionless in the periphery of my vision still passed out in the hammock behind Yail — with his face now squashed against the mesh weave, like a dead cod caught in a net. I'm also old enough to know Yail's game and in spite of the hostel's wanton ways I respected the staff's strong affections and sense of care and protection for one another.

I noticed this early in the evening when Brendon stumbled into the Hostel Ka'Beh looking tequila-blancoed — a fragile disposition that wasn't helped by his ginger hair, soft cheese complexion, and an unnerving predilection to gape which bared the whites of his eyes, making him stand out like an unstable isotope. As Brendon headed inside to reception Salenna curtailed him with a scolding tongue.

'We need to have a chat.'

Salenna was the hostel matriarch — an American starlet tall and vertical from legs up to her 'fro with buxom curves and a heart warm as custard. Brendon nodded and followed Salenna to the corner where I had just sat down with my book and cheap beer.

'What happened to you – you've been gone for two days.'

'I-got m-m-ugged – and they t-ook my sshhoes... a-and then the police arrested me!'

I couldn't tell if Brendon's speech impediment was ingrained or not. His stutter could also be traced to the recent trauma of his incarceration and consumptive extravagances.

'Your shoes are here. You went out without them on.'

I looked down and saw that Brendon had indeed walked in off the streets in sports sockets. Brendon bowed his head solemnly and nodded some more like an authority of compliance.

'And we're fully booked tonight,' Salenna added. 'What are you going to do?'

'I just re-e-eally need a shower.'

Salenna's disciplined tone softened as she told Brendon to take a shower. She pointed to the row of hammocks, which based on "BBQ Night" regularly found a healthy occupancy each night by guests too shitfaced to find their bed. Salenna finally reassured Brendon they would work something out.

It turns out Brendon is also an obedient warrior of backpacking dissipation — prepared to step bluntly back into a path of ruin. He returns a few short hours later having overturned his pallid veil of detox. I doubt he even cleaned himself up. His candlelit face is dripping with sweat as he interrupts Yail and insists I taste the drink he has concocted.

'What is it?'

'It's – y-you know – ice...'

'And what else?'

'Ice – a-nd Ta-a-basco-'

'What else?'

Brendon shrugs.

'I'm good with beer thanks.'

Brendon turns to Yail who winces at the offer of the poisoned plastic chalice. Unfazed, Brendon lunges at nearby table of travellers to continue whatever mission he's on.

'I will be back. I want to talk about something to you,' Yail says and leaves to rejoin two more young female Israeli backpackers sitting at a communal bench in middle of the courtyard.

Following Brendon's disruption a fabric of discomfort slowly winds itself around me in the balmy evening. Despite the establishment's Bacchanalian thirst and profligate outlook, which in the past would have easily suited my sensibilities, I began to feel like it was the last place I wanted to be. Even though I'd just arrived at the gateway to my Central American adventure I was already reconsidering my plan, and wanted to get the fuck out of Cancún as soon as possible.

Yail didn't return to resume our promising conversion. I wasn't surprised. Despite her youthful age I had the impression she was accustomed to the art of subterfuge on the open road — and was adept at running away to maintain her carefree and unattached backpacking lifestyle. I too had my own travel-proven, pocket-sized arsenal of manoeuvres to stay unencumbered and sane on an extended trip. Some more practical than others such as my Emirates airline face mask and military grade ear plugs which would soon come in handy. I saw Brendon sprint off into the night, barefooted after scheming up a scheme with a pack of dudes wearing baseball caps and sports jerseys. I could already sense the indelible mark in the evening's steady descent into nocturnal debauchery. So I finished my last beer and headed to bed.

I woke early the next morning from a shallow sleep disjointed by tactless late-night revellers. I'd had enough of the Hostel Ka'Beh and was determined to get moving. I entered the bedsit kitchen to put the pot on for a brew. Scott was already up getting a chilled bottle of Appleton Special rum out of the freezer. He told me someone had left the gas on all night. And when he went to light a cigarette by the side door a fire ball ignited a fiery balloon that stopped millimetres from his eyebrows.

'How's your neck?'

'Fine, why?'

'Never mind.'

As I waited for the portable stove to heat the water I wandered outside. I could hear Salenna groaning in maudlin tones from the row of slumber-fermented hammocks. It turns out Salenna was no saint either. Ever since she called out to the Swede with the washboard body, 'Are we playing cards tonight?' I was certain she would bed him — and bed him she did. I knew this because the Swede and I shared the same dorm room, and the reason I knew we shared the same room was he occupied the bunk bed below me.

Behind a reflective windshield of retro eyewear I hear Salenna tell Scott how she had a nasty tumble in the early hours of the morning in Zona Hotelara. Luckily for her she had a ripped Swede to carry her back. But she cut her leg badly and bled all over his stonewashed denim jeans. She made an effort to wash them when they got back. Now in the sobering morning light she couldn't find a trace of them anywhere.

I gulped down a nasty cup of instant coffee and threw my *mochila* on my back. As I unlocked the heavy iron gates to the hostel I briefly thought about the Hostel Ka'beh crew. Context is important and I debated the likelihood of Yail, Scott, Brendon, Salenna and the Swede getting close to finding any true sense of happiness in Cancún — then I realised I didn't really give a shit. Trudging towards the downtown bus station in the buttery heat of the morning, the knowledge I'm leaving Cancún and the Hostel Ka'Beh behind alleviates the weight of my pack. I'm reacquainted with what makes backpacking so compelling — and only now realised how deeply I had missed this sensation of escape.

Whatever the individual urges are that persuade people to seek out places farthest from what's familiar to them, it is fair to say backpacking is a seductive endeavour. This is why independent travel stretches far beyond complimentary breakfast buffets, bottomless boats, open air tour buses, dining carts, border crossings to another *playa*, happy hours that last all night and make-it-happy menus, sunburns, shopping sprees, and the cheap shit we collect then vanquish to forgotten recesses soon after returning home because it suddenly feels tawdry and out of place in lives we left behind.

Overland journeys for me redeem the empowerment of freedom captured by youth on long summer school holidays — where from the outset of both journeys, of our burgeoning concept of who we think we are, and where we are going is continually challenged. With both adolescence and travel, time once again is integral — the indispensable pleasure of time to regularly reconsider what you only concluded 24 hours earlier to be an ultimate truth. Zen uses the term *shikantaza*, which literally means just to sit, and is the purest expression of Zen praxis because past and future lose focus as the body and mind become lost. Much like *vipassanā*, doing nothing and emptying your mind is a common and popular form in many styles of meditation. And what is travel if not unstructured meditation dedicated to filling time with nothing — to cultivate one's mind through a single deliberation summed up by the immortal words of the eponymous Clash song:

*'Should I stay or should I go?'*

When this is your own pressing dilemma each day it's not hard for your mind to be open to shit — like change, growth and creativity. However, thoughtful reflection requires a special kind of time, like the time that wanders — nomadic time. It is this freedom of time which makes travel and personal introspection such a unique and immaculate fit. Time allows travellers' quieter versions of themselves to find expression — to project themselves beyond the din of people who think they know you, and your predominant self, who is always greedy for more stage. Of course, the mode of travel defines the sort of inward journey. John Steinbeck alludes to this in *Travels with Charley*, his reflective travelogue around the USA when he writes:

*'The nature of the road describes the nature of travel.'*

To this I would add — and the nature of travel dictates the type of journey. With the megalithic rise of cheap airlines and connectivity it's become commonplace for people to drop in and out of almost any destination in the world. And now more than ever the array of affordable travel options spoils international travellers. But when you are transported between places at a cruising altitude of 38,000 feet and filter in and out of countries through neutral departure lounges, you are not exposed to aspects of change which come from within on overland trips. Self-seeking journeys require the time that is only found on marathon bus rides, multi-day train trips and high seas under full sail, drifting on rivers guiding you back to civilisation, hitchhiking across the rugged limbo between places, and between the footsteps that carry you across remote borders of ancient lands.

Don't get me wrong. There are just as many hedonistic and self-serving motives to backpacking. The overland travellers on the Hippie Trail in the sixties and seventies are often misrepresented as a spiritual soul-seeking movement. In reality they comprised a lot of culturally ignorant Westerners simply looking for the next high, which ended with the Cold War, Islamic Revolution and glam rock of the eighties. Not much of that has changed except for the places. And whether people truly change or not is debatable — I've seen the tussle in backpackers' eyes numerous times. But at least time lets travellers become acquainted with their other behind-the-scenes voices, letting them try each one on like masks, allowing them to flourish and find a voice on stage alongside the frontman of their personality.

# Chapter 4

# Los Amigos Theatre of Transformation

Travel and self-reinvention is a marriage as old as beyuls and earthly refuge — a natural consequence of jettisoning a pre-ordained life and immersing yourself in the unknown. Part of the lure comes from weighing anchor on social norms, shedding the ballast and residue of junk in your head and sailing clear of an orderly world. As Anaïs Nin famously wrote:

> 'We travel, some of us forever, to seek other states, other lives, other souls.'

However, travelling through Central America along the grand-daddies of all land bridges in 2011, I started to wonder if specific geography or regions amplified this kind of self-renewal. Was there something about isthmuses? Were they like ley lines — a thin joint of mystical energy offering enlightenment to backpackers as they gallivanted across the globe? Or was it just a fool's recipe — a cheap, compact mix of sand, sun, jungle and mountains to attract independent budget travellers?

I first encountered this phenomenon in 2007, midway through my previous trip with Maccas, my intermittent long-term travel buddy. Travelling from Thailand to Malaysia we hitchhiked down the Isthmus of Kra. We crossed the isthmus in less than a day but the journey which started in Bangkok spanned more than two weeks. It took us via Ko Tao, Penang and the Cameron Highlands to Kuala Lumpur where we planned to catch a cheap Air Asia flight to Cambodia. During this leg of the trip it revealed the most spectacular kaleidoscope of seers, sorcerers, activists, eco-vigilantes and backpacking messiahs I have ever seen in all my travels — all dressed in technicolor and each carrying their own personal offbeat religion.

Maybe back then I was desensitised to the carnivalisation of travel — the circus parade of felt hats, head bands, party pants, fire poi, devil sticks and obscure musical instruments. I'd been on the road for more than six months before arriving in the promised land of South East Asia. Maybe six months is all I need to get wrapped up in the myth of myself. But isn't that the tendency of humankind — to manifest ourselves in the sacred text of who we want or hope to be? Timothy K. Beal summarises this predisposition in *Roadside Religion*:

> *There is a deep desire within many of us to inhabit our sacred stories, to re-create sacred space and time in the here and now and to live into it with all our heart, mind, and strength. We want to make sacred space and time present. This desire to re-create the sacred — let's call it religious recreation — is a kind of nostalgia, homesickness (from ancient Greek* nostos, *"returning home," plus* agia, *"pain"), a longing to have our everyday lives set within the horizon of a sacred story. And in the process to re-recreate and reconsecrate ourselves and our contemporary world, in which it feels as though our sense of connection with the sacred is always being worn away by the pressures of everyday life.'*

Beal is referring to a recurring syndrome observed in the devout Christians he encountered on his reflective quest across the spiritual heartland of the USA. These people saw themselves in the role of Noah — believing the divine role of Protector and Saviour was bestowed upon them by the grace of God. But the process is not so different with travel — and it's easy for backpackers to believe the myth of themselves because it's continually being created.

Prior to our journey down the Isthmus of Kra, Maccas and I felt halfway transformed on our way through Chiang Mia to Pai in northern Thailand. We were in fisherman pants with forearms adorned in friendship bands and handcrafted jewellery around our necks. We each had collected a melangé of good luck trinkets and souvenirs and Maccas's hair had started to dread from a general lack of hygiene. But arriving in Pai for *Pai in the Sky*, a community-based reggae festival, we felt woefully inadequate in the bonhomie scene of idealistic and likeminded peregrinators. We quickly agreed upon a need to get hippified. What part of this compulsion was conformance is irrelevant — what mattered was Maccas needed a poncho and sombrero and I needed a hippie-wizard jacket.

Hippification is equivalent to becoming a feral nihilistic hipster. And the cardinal rule is harder than it sounds — to conceal a deep satisfaction of looking as absurdly outlandish as possible by draping yourself in a contrary and impervious cape of utter apathy. I admit I have only worn the hippie-wizard jacket once since that overland odyssey ended at the beginning of 2008. Still parading the liberty and dislocation I'd amassed after 18 months of travel I accompanied my sister to a local arts festival music gig outside the renowned Perth Concert Hall.

'You're wearing that?' my sister asks pulling a bushelled face of disapproval only sisters can pull.

'Yeah.'

'Euweh,' my sister moans with disgust that stops just short of protest.

When we arrived at the marquee venue erected outside the main entrance to the concert hall I head straight to the outdoor bar to order a drink.

'Wow, cool jacket,' the bartender says, 'where did you get it?'

'Thailand.'

'Awesome.'

'Thanks man – although I think my sister's embarrassed by it.'

'What do sisters know?'

'Exactly.'

I have witnessed backpackers administer all degrees of personal growth from a tot of rejuvenation to a sup of contemplation, onto a double-shot of self-scrutiny chased with a slug of disassociation, followed by a jug of probing reflection, another round of self-exploration, a nightcap of spiritual revelations then a toke or two from a break-of-dawn rebirth to attain a total sousing of personal transformation.

Strangers play their part as the ecclesial consorts for confession and moral guidance on the open road. Their impermanence is what qualifies them. Backpackers can get hooked on the provisional company of strangers because *(unlike old friends)* there's no background check — they didn't know you before you left so there's nothing to justify or defend when you choose to drift off the path of who you were. There is a seduction to the role of confidante — and dispensing a kerbside kind of absolution for minor infidelities and indiscretion *(in the name of self-freedoms)* to champion your evolving whims and attitudes. And while fugitive friendships embolden the liberation of a grand adventure, like any new company they can be both pretender and mentor — a troublemaking guru guiding and supporting you who's equally likely to lead you astray.

Unfurling notions of who you are *(from a symbolic to existential level)* is all part of the packaged bundle of backpacking. Questions gestate and aggregate over crests and swallows of the open road. There's no guarantee you'll find any answers while seeking harbour and solace in the unfamiliar. But you'll still return home, agitated by a potent mix of worldly experiences to help further challenge your ideas of *self* and where you belong.

Imitating accents typifies this nonphysical sense of change. I've heard Australian interlopers flaunt the most peculiar aberration of a British accent after only a few short months away. Others interject foreign phrases with a dubious "foreign" intonation when recounting tales of their recent travels. And they repeatedly transpose '*¿Cómo?*' and '*¿Qué?*' for 'What?' as if it's a mistake born of habit. It can all get a bit unbearable. Friends who have to cope with their mate sounding like they've been sired by the ancient Royal Monarchy can find it a bit offensive too — like they're having their faces rubbed in someone else's unforgettable journey. But most of the time it's unintentional — and the broad nasal accent of Australia soon resurfaces. Personally, I never felt there is anything pretentious about language acquisition. Mimicking accents *(like hippification)* to me simply illustrates a subconscious desire in many of us independent travellers to demonstrate change when returning home to a life perfectly preserved and sealed by inertia and ennui.

By sight alone the garb of long-term travellers conjure a gnostic sense of the old ways. On long overland journeys hippification signifies this spiritual initiation. And the longer backpackers' travel they tend to take on the hallmark appearance of a makeshift swami or true seeker. It's easy on the open road to look the part of a dirty pilgrim, live in the now, become ignorant of time and feel like you're seeking the *Way of the Universe*. Sitting on kerbsides and around fire pits with Thai-song, ukies, fire poi, beating tablas and bongs — there's a communal sense of invoking, or at the very least celebrating the rhythm and dance, and creative force to the subtle order behind all life. But the longer I travel the harder it is to see where the authenticity ends and perversity begins. My cynical half can't help note the discrepancies within the marauding leaderless cult — like children of Gaia toting hipster holsters and saddle pouches made of cowhide, the pseudo-spiritualists who just want to get laid, and the equanimous mantra-touting backpacker who won't let anything or anyone stand in his or her way of getting to their next destination.

I left the hippie-wizard jacket with my sister because I relocated from Perth to Melbourne for work. I still packed a fair wardrobe of brightly coloured rainforest linens and got an apartment in St Kilda. I revelled in the marginal shift from international budget backpacker threads to the outré street fashion of Melbourne's Bayside. I was comfortable strolling along Acland Street in my purple and blue harem pants, Nepalese prayer beads, white cotton shirt, and bumblebee Havaianas. While I looked the part of a dervish I bought the chattel that grounds you: a queen size futon, a modular couch, desk, Balinese coffee table and side table, antique gentleman's wardrobe, and kitchen effects only to find myself unemployed after five months. I sold everything and moved back to the UK where again unemployment tracked me down, and I found myself once more back in my hometown.

I felt like a crab, even though I was born a Virgo — scuttling sideways, on back and forth trajectory through life while everyone around me seemed to charge along an exigent path through life like Centaurs or Centurions. I felt like Phaedrus in Robert Pirsig's disjointed cult classic *Zen and the Art of Motorcycle Maintenance*:

*'To all appearance he was just drifting. In actuality he was just drifting. Drifting is what one does when looking at lateral truth.'*

I was determined to break the repetitious revolutions which perpetuated my itinerant life. So I sat down and penned *Loves, Kerbsides and Goodbyes*, which at the time distilled the previous decade of my life on the open road. After which I needed to exit, exhale, exalt in the cathartic weight of a backpack — to carry my own brand of personal sovereignty between places and imbibe a new scene.

I always feel an imperceptibility of time between trips. It's a passage I gauge from the tegument of independence and imperturbability which thickens the longer I travel — but then fades just as quickly like a holiday tan in the aftermath of a trip. So on arrival in Central America I wondered what happened to the backpacking fraternity in the three years that had passed from my last trip? The sense of disenfranchisement and reinvention was profound. Yet there seemed to be a veritable shift in its nature — was it me? And if not, what went wrong since I last felt a backpack on my shoulders?

Boarding the plane bound for Cancún I wanted to return to where I last felt the reassuring solitude on my previous trip. I don't know why I carried an expectation that Central America's developing status and improved regional stability would provide the remoteness and rewards between places I desired. Possibly because this was the backdrop to highly memorable and transformative journeys I'd previously undertaken — traversing Mongolia, China, Pakistan, Central Asia and through the Middle East back to Europe. I had not contemplated the region's ecliptical northern neighbour, and that spring break wasn't confined to within its borders. I was also unaware the level of NGOs and missionary activity in the region made you forget there was an Africa.

My *LP* Bible described where I was heading as 'unlike many cities in the world, Cancún just isn't afraid. It's unabashed and unapologetic, and in that its high-gloss charm.' With its 'drink-'till-you-puke specials,' my arrival in Cancún threw everything into doubt. But did this affect the temporal change I saw being defined by a new generation of iBackpackers? After two sleepless nights in the bawdy downtown hostel I tried to find my backpacking feet again in the ruins of Chichén Itzá and Tulum. I transited quickly through Belize to Flores in northern Guatemala — gateway to the superlative Tikal ruins and much further afield the remote ruins at El Mirador where my steadfast gaze was set on visiting.

Walking into the Los Amigos hostel on Flores Island was like entering the new modern class of hip cantina style eateries — where you are made to wait for ages and once seated made to feel inferior by all the clientele that look and behave as if they're infinitely cooler than you. If you like that scene you probably wouldn't have minded the Los Amigos. It wasn't that the vaudevillian costumes and characters of backpackers had necessarily changed — or the deep need to put themselves in the sacred text of their own lives. But what was once an eclectic chapter of the backpacking community, a distinction of bodhi-struck iconoclasts, off-road renegades and mavens of long-term travel, now appeared to be a mainstream movement. It was as if an entire new generation of maligned youth were engaged in a Kathputli theatre of backpacking to usurp their formative years of teenage persecution. The credentials were more like a to-do list:

i.    *Wear a silly hat.*

ii.   *Carry an acoustic instrument.*

iii.  *Introduce yourself as a citizen of the world.*

iv.   *Teach yourself to play a musical instrument (not necessarily the one you're carrying) in the middle of conversations.*

v.    *Regularly reference the time you've been away (without going home because that would be cheating) like it's a prison stamp of respect — even though it's kind of the complete opposite.*

vi.   *Become a malabarista, funambulist or some other species of circus performer.*

vii.  *Demonstrate your skills daily under the guise of training in the most public and inconvenient places around a hostel.*

viii. *Use the number of countries you've visited (like they're people you've slept with) as a qualification for anything.*

   *ix.*   *Engage in an extracurricular pre-industrial activity such as jewellery making, weaving and knitting.*

   *x.*   *Repeatedly express some vague plan to do volunteer work to set yourself apart from the ambitionless wandering wastrels.*

   *xi.*   *Seek out and attach yourself to a troubadour of like-minded folk which are one short of a Scooby Doo Gang and continue your adventures to the oblivion of everything around you.*

I wrote the above list sitting in Los Amigos's archetypal back-packer courtyard, which like many hostel amenities is designed for supreme chilling and utopian vagrancy. It was Dutch-owned after all and had a questionable reputation in the local community. But for the most part Los Amigos had the right recipe. The self-dubbed Flores Secret Garden was drenched in verdancy, tremulous candlelight, rustic wooden furniture, and a healthy supply of hammocks. And the requisite outdoor bar had happy hours of cocktail smoothies and a Western menu full of nutritious vegetarian options. What Los Amigos couldn't control was the hippie-fare marketplace of jewellery displays that made the entrance feel like the Court of Gentiles. Then there were the two dudes who duelled with traditional wooden flutes and maracas every night in the outside toilet, I guess because the acoustics make them sound better. Everyone was trying to be the cool kid in school — where eccentricity was the high currency being traded. But I wondered had they gone too far — was independent budget travel in jeopardy of becoming a self-parody, or was I late for the party and experiencing its decadent glow?

More damaging was this change came with a precocious mindset, brimming with callow pathos and effrontery. I felt continually harangued by a brood of posturing meliorists who blended equal parts sanctimony and ignorance in their singular mission to save every place they visited. They treated hearsay as a credible source, and scavenged opinions from Facebook posts,

Twitter handles, news links and overheard conversations, which they then repackaged and regurgitated as their own. Everyone seemed to be rant-fed experts on everything, able to deliver a saga on any subject at a moment's notice — and it endangered the egalitarian and broadminded spirit of travel community.

It could be said the tribe at the Los Amigos exemplified the dialectic to postmodernism, which simply saw a new pastiche of mannerisms define a new generation of backpacking hipster. But just as easily they could have embodied a post-postmodern vanity resulting from the instant and superficial participation in the new digital age *(otherwise known as pseudo-modernism)*. Don't get me wrong I quite enjoy a benighted dose of exuberance and am well up for a street jam. I rarely decline a carousing mission about a new town, or just about any revel and ruckus of nocturnal persuasion for that matter. But what I found so disturbing on arrival in Guatemala was the endemic shift of everyone justifying their uniqueness, and their presence in the country in exactly the same way. And like the punk movement, or any movement I suppose based on individuality, it's prone to failure due to our innate sense of conformity. As a result I feared this threatened to turn the backpacking scene into a sideshow.

My arrival at Los Amigos was also hard to digest because I couldn't work out what spawned my irritation. Was it my inability to relate to a new generation of iBackpackers taking the main stage of independent travel? Perhaps it was me — a premature symptom to a midlife crisis where I was struggling to legitimise my ageing stature while still waging a life on the open road. If so, the first sign would be considered rather obvious. It was when I got on a plane not necessarily with a desire to go somewhere specific, but rather without a reason not to go.

I can still recall when hostels, in particularly the HI Hostel Federation *(formerly known as the IYHF)* still implemented an age restriction and only admitted backpackers 26 years old and under. But young at heart is to feel forever young — right? In

fact in light of political correctness this was the essence of the
HI Federation's rebranding when age limits were deemed dis-
criminatory and finally lifted *(with the exception of Bavaria in
Germany)*. I still felt youthful. In fact I could still be downright
immature — so I gave my age no credence and gladly dismissed
it as a point of contention. Again I hear the sagacity of an elderly
John Steinbeck travelling along the blue highways of the USA:

> *'When the virus of restlessness begins to take possession of a
> wayward man, and the road away from Here seems broad
> and straight and sweet, the victim must first find in himself
> a good and sufficient reason for going. This to the practical
> bum is not difficult. He has a built-in garden of reasons to
> choose from.'*

I'm sure Mr Steinbeck would concur that no-reason-not-to-go
is a good enough reason to hit the open road again. But regardless
of my own self-doubt, I couldn't ignore the clowder of lounging
backpackers at the Los Amigos, or their phlegmatic reaction to
their surroundings. They didn't seem to care where they were
as long as it wasn't home, which had me confused about what
motivated the iBackpackers to be in the same foreign place as me.
So it became a bit of a game of "is it them or me" as I experienced rerun after rerun of the Los Amigos crow-stoned pageantry
in hostels all the way down the Central America Isthmus. What's
worse is I couldn't tell if my perturbation waxed and waned from
a place of envy or disapproval *(or worse still, both)*. But I quickly
grew to despise the bravado of postmortem discussions detailing
yesterday's antics — of misadventures, near scrapes and all-night
benders. From the litany of dumb crap such as jumping off high
cliffs, driving drunk, doing deals with dodgy drug dealers, shirking
travel insurance and smuggling weed across borders, I'd covered most of this ground in the past *(except for narcotrafficking
of course)*. Even so, I couldn't help view half the shit being spun

as puerile. I felt a dark desire to show up all these hippified kids weaving hemp jewellery like there's no future. The longer I travelled along the giant mandible between North and South America I started to feel like some antiquated innocent abroad, trying to protect the values of old skool travel. It was becoming ludicrous.

I appreciate every generation is born into the one that precedes it. I was born into the remnants of the Hippie Trail and the cultural ideal of the soulful traveller. For me travel is predominantly about a challenging overland journey because it promotes both an outward as well as an inward sense of exploration and discovery that only occurs with vast traces of time spent crossing foreign lands. With age I'm also able to recognise the legacy of the previous backpacking generation has enabled the more debatable sect of vacationing commonly known now as "drug tourism". This of course is something that has never changed much for the highly curious, hedonistic and spiritually minded fraternity of backpackers. So I couldn't help but wonder if this new hostelling scene I felt at odds with was a product of the modern age. Was Alan Kirby right? Had digitality and saturated online exposure to high speed cultural updates and downloads created a pack of narcissistic and anaesthetised arseholes? I was like Tom King, the weary ol' prize fighting lion in Jack London's *A Piece of Steak*:

> '... he knew youth now that youth was no longer his.'

Now I'm certain the issue was with me since I'm being the arsehole who's bemoaning technology and lamenting a time of yore. At least I was in good company. A compelling prerogative amongst many travel writers is to embark on a journey with a sense of suspicion or dread over their disconnection with a world they fear is fading away and becoming extinct. In William Least Heat-Moon's definitive cross-country memoir titled *Blue Highways: A Journey into America*, he addresses his own nostalgia for lost connection and a need for resurrection:

*'With a nearly desperate sense of isolation and growing suspicion that I lived in an alien land, I took to the open road in search of places where change did not mean ruin and where time and men and deeds connected.'*

The nostalgic era of travel I'm referring to no longer exists in the real world. It only remains on display in the sanctum of luxury travel — reserved for those who can afford executive airport lounges, first-class seating, upscale hotels and fine-dining restaurants. For the rest of us the cultural legacy lingers in memories, movies, gestures we make in jest and arthritic airline fleets with metal flip-lids on the armrest. But if you have a shit tonne of money you can revive these relics of tradition and service, and relive a bygone era of travel where flair, foot room, common courtesy and decency reigned. I have been fortunate enough to share this prestigious version of vacationing abroad with my parents. And I love it — and not just because they're the only people I know who can afford it and who are willing to pay for me as well.

I love the morning ritual at exclusive hotels and bed and breakfasts. The genteel exchange of pleasantries between immaculately dressed guests on their way to the lobby for the ballroom buffet breakfasts. And the endless banter with loquacious bed and breakfast owners that makes you wonder if lunchtime has passed by the time breakfast ends. I feel like I've gone back in time, or unwittingly stumbled onto the set of some costume drama where everyone is exaggerating antiquated customs — tipping their hats, begging their pardons and saying shite like 'Top of the morning.' I also love my Mum on holiday because she steps back into a youthful version of herself, epitomising a travelling class of yesteryear — cleaning the hotel room like it was her own before checking out, greeting guests and staff alike with unflappable cheer, and treating daily mishaps and bodily ailments with resilient vitality.

Travelling with my parents I feel these institutions are precious pieces in a museum preserving something intangible — a living history of mannerisms and etiquette that have otherwise been lost, eroded to the point of extinction by the modern world. They represent an outdated mode and style of travel where a refinery and comfort were essential because every trip was long and arduous. Epic journeys by sea and rail weren't an option reserved by rogue explorers and shoestring travellers — they were a necessity because there was no other affordable option. But it seems *(much like airlines and airports)* even these esteemed bastions of decorum are not impervious to the epidemic of time and social lethargy.

A year prior to my Central American trip I met my parents in England and travelled with them around Europe. And like my arrival at the Los Amigos, I was taken aback by the stolid shift in ambience at the historic hotels where we stayed. Even my Mum noticed. Her customary salutations were barely acknowledged, and the hoary guests who rode the lift to and from breakfast received her morning greeting with little more than a reticent nod. Who the fuck are these people, I wondered. The first couple of times she looked at me and scrunched up her face in mockery, and when they exited she poked out her tongue at them and smiled at me. But it was disappointing and the ultimate shame of it was the impersonal atmosphere affected her. After a while I noticed she stopped saying 'Good morning' and 'Hello' by way of passing other guests in the lift. Instead she kept quiet in the elevator when others got in and bowed her head as people tend to do in places of work.

Equally, it was demoralising to see how invisible everyone was to each other at Los Amigos and other hostels I stayed at travelling though Central America. Vacant stares and muted grunts greeted my cordial introduction to new faces in new hostels. Flyscreen doors recoiled in my face passing backpackers through doorways into dorm rooms and gringo haunts. And I rarely saw aid being offered to fledgling backpackers visibly struggling with luggage,

language difficulty or a booking crisis. I had to keep reminding myself that this is not how people should behave, especially
gentle folk of the open road — because like my Mum I found it
exhausting to maintain a spirited demeanour in the face of such
irreverence. And it wears thin when everyone talks at you and
no one listens.

I admit there is an inevitability to remove yourself emotion-
ally from the passing personalities and scenery on long trips. It's
what keeps a backpacker blissful and aloof, and is a captivating
motivation to travel — to remain drugged up on vagrancy and
immune to consequences. But then I considered maybe I was
being too harsh on everyone including myself. Perhaps being so
near the start of my trip I was not yet equipped with the levity or
glib apathy of long-term travellers to combat my rising intolerance
for hostel life — and the young crusading bodhisattvas and their
colourful mix of narcissistic tendencies. There is still no excuse
for discarding common courtesy or the little daily gestures of
decency that bind us. It is this degradation in the daily grind of
living toe-to-toe and on top of one another that makes us want
to run away to resort island beaches, fresh powdered mountain
tops, impenetrable jungle retreats, magical forest hideaways,
end-of-the-road river journeys and relaxing ocean cruises.

I don't know why all the iBacpackers chose Guatemala. Why
not Nicaragua where the missionaries gravitated to? I assumed it's
because every other Western kid chose Guatemala so they could
all party hard together while remonstrating over the evils of the
world with designs to save places that weren't theirs to save. They
were also all fluent in Spanish. So I had to continually endure a
spastic reaction of incredulity from every Spanish speaking gringo
with a *mochila*.

'I don't know how someone could travel without knowing
the local language.'

'If I only travelled to places where I knew the local language
I would never have left home,' I explain.

'That's different,' they say, implying a distinction which made Latin America sound overly familiar like it was their home away from home.

Language by its nature empowers. So it's understandable how some backpackers felt they communed with locals by right of their Spanish equivalency — and as such were more intimately connected to the prostrating toils of subsistence living. Maybe that's why they felt jilted at being included in the upper tier of dual pricing structures commonly implemented by locals to fleece tourists with inflated rates. Later on, staying in Xela I even got laughed at by a table full of language students when I pronounced *'calle'* (street) with a French inflection. And once again I wondered what the fuck is wrong with these people? Well it turns out they were foreigners who had already learnt to correctly attribute the 'yah' sound *(which yawed between our 'j' and 'y')* to the double consonant pairing of 'll' and enunciate 'street' correctly in Spanish by saying 'cay-yah'. Apparently this earned them the privilege to laugh at monolingual backpackers like me.

I wonder if a prototype language translator existed at the time would I have used it. It might have stopped me getting picked on, but wouldn't a Babel Fish gadget vanquish all the fun shit that comes along for the ride when you don't have clue what's being said? Despite being consistently five generations behind of every latest cycle of iWhatever I'm not ignorant to pros and cons of new technology. App stores and websites overflow with innovation which aid travellers — GPS trackers, itinerary planners, menu translators, currency convertors, online check-in, help forums and comparison sites. There was even a tranquil aesthetic to the iBackpackers curled over white-lit slates in the Flores Secret Garden at night — illuminated like recumbent outdoor ornaments. But will continuing technological advancements disturb the elementary joy of being lost and blissfully confused when exploring a new place — deciphering signs and maps, sleuthing for cheap accommodation, gesticulating wildly to make yourself understood when stuff doesn't go to plan, and randomly ordering off menus like you're in a kitchen casino, waiting in anticipation to see if your gamble paid off? And how will Couchsurfing and new apps promoting connectivity and promiscuity disturb old notions of serendipitous encounters on the open road?

Talking of Least Heat-Moon and the new digital world, a harder proposition will be resolving travellers' deeper compulsions for absolution and resurrection. I don't know how well acquainted the iBackpackers are with these more fallible considerations — nor should they be. But I wonder with so many of us *(now more than ever)* seeking lost connections and redemption by alienating ourselves, will mobile technology prove itself to be a help or hindrance? How will iBackpackers remove themselves from everything that is familiar and known and escape into the less familiar when the life they left behind is in tow via the smartphone in their pocket? And while it may provide a modern cradle of personal safety, will the ability to notify travellers of the latest security threat and terrorist attack abroad instil a newfound fear instead of fearlessness of the unknown? The answer of course is I have no idea. But I'm keen to find out. In *Neither Here Nor There: Travels in Europe* Bill Bryson expounds on the guileless delights of tenderfoot travelling:

> *'But that's the glory of foreign travel, as far as I am concerned. I don't want to know what people are talking about. I can't think of anything that excites a greater sense of childlike wonder than to be in a country where you are ignorant of almost everything. Suddenly you are five years old again. You can't read anything, you have only the most rudimentary sense of how things work, you can't even reliably cross a street without endangering your life. Your whole existence becomes a series of interesting guesses.'*

I felt the metamorphosis of backpackers at Los Amigos was absolute and equally unsettling as it was unbearable. And it seemed the kids at Los Amigos and those I continued to encounter backpacking through Central America were junkies badly hooked on the transitory nature of overland travel.

On my last night in Flores I sat by myself writing in my journal, wondering if it was possible to escape what you escaped to. Three gap year students walked past me in the garden and said hello. I invited them to join me and we shared a beer. I learnt Ashton, Caleb and Jackie were planning like me to head to Tikal. They also intended to camp onsite so without knowing more we booked the same bus and arranged to travel out there together the next day — because that's what backpackers do. All it took was a hospitable gesture by three Californians and my faith in the backpacking fraternity was partially restored. And while solitude has its own rewards, sharing experiences with strangers is how the sense of lost connections is mended, and new friends are made.

# CHAPTER 5

# CLIMAX OF EMPTINESS

I was still preoccupied exploring the spaces between places when I first met Katharina at the Linen House hostel in Belfast. It was the night before I boarded an early morning ferry to Stranraer on the coast of Scotland. I was immediately infatuated by her wide eyes, long bony body, creamy skin and rack of white teeth. Of course she had a boyfriend, which was a phenomenon of women I was most accustomed to at the time, and so nothing happened.

I stopped in Glasgow to visit my cousin. It was a brief layover as I was keen to return to Manchester and resume work to recover the savings I forfeited on my autumn sojourn around the Hibernian coast and countryside. However, as soon as I got back to work I found myself desperate to return to the west coast of Ireland — mooch around between the soft mist and bars of Galway, maybe get a job and live there for a while.

I'd barely lived a year in Manchester, arriving two months after Felix. He got a solid job working with his brother Charles on local television productions while I bounced from cafe to bar — always thinking of the next trip. Mindful of how this was a repeat of London, I started to consider my brevity of serious relationships could be connected to my reluctance to stay in a place any length of time. Regardless, my inveterate proclivity to swing from joint to joint convinced me Ireland was the answer. I needed literary inspiration. The sort of inspiration unleashed by the combative swaff of the Atlantic Ocean against the embattled shoreline — for me to imbibe its brackish wake as it carries across the ancient cadence of Connemara. So I made plans to head back to the west coast of Ireland in December.

Flying Ryan Air in to Shannon airport had its own zip lock bag of calculated motives stored in my overhead compartment. The airport was close enough to Galway. More importantly it serviced Limerick University where Katharina studied on exchange, and had admitted in a recent email she was no longer encumbered by a boyfriend. She said my arrival worked well with the exodus of students for Christmas holidays and welcomed me to stay with her on campus.

The flight was late. The final arrival time was inconvenient and I missed the last public bus. Given my shoestring aversion to taking taxis, ordinarily this would have sealed my fate at the airport for the evening. But Shannon airport in the dark of winter is in no way appealing. And destiny sometimes tempts us as much as we cajole it so I hailed a cab. Wrapped in a damp winter fog, the university campus of Limerick felt more Halloween than Yuletide. It was also abandoned apart from Katharina and the small order of international students who remained because of opposition or reluctance to pay high season airline tariffs.

The exiled group of exchange students held a party the following night where we hooked up effortlessly like young Europeans. In the kitchen while sitting on the corner of the sink and bench Katharina leant into me to rest in the vee of my legs. Then on the couch in the lounge room she sat on the floor by my feet, and like verdant creeper ensnared my legs in her long lithe arms while I'm persuaded into playing an Australian song on guitar.

I played Neil Finn's *You're Not the Girl You Think You Are* really badly, trusting Europeans should appreciate its dark layers of ambiguity *(and not really care Crowded House were Kiwis)*. In the final verse I finally found some composure so I repeated an improvised final bridge and refrain to end the performance with some confidence:

> *He won't deceive you or tell you the truth*
> *Woman, he'll be no trouble*
> *He won't write you letters*
> *full of excuses*
> *Come on, believe you have one in a million*
>
> *You're not the girl you think you are,*
> *believe you have won*
> *You're not the girl you think you are,*
> *believe you have won*
> *You're not the girl you think you are*

Back at Katharina's dormant student houseshare she confessed my arrival was "bad timing". So for some stupid reason I tell her I'm going to Galway anyway for a few days to scope out the likelihood of putting down a life there for a bit. When I get to Galway all I see is a city well staffed and prepared for the silly season. Katharina is caught between my heart and mind — something between lust and love which compels me to return to Limerick. I convince myself I've arrived in Galway too late in the year to make any inroads finding work and accommodation. After four nights I return to Limerick University.

Having recently terminated a three-year relationship Katharina treats me like an understudy. She knows what she wants and how to satisfy herself — so she always wants to be on top *(not that I mind)*. She goes slow like we're a well-rehearsed act with a history *(which we were with emails)* and forces me to pause a lot — like I'm trying to remember the next line. We make falafel and listen to REM. To this day whenever I hear *Nightswimming*

I am transported back to Katharina, and her student residence at Limerick University. The scene is a Christmas canvas in my memory — where I lie on her lap on the living room couch and through a dim veil of scented candles stare out through frosted glass into the embittered and hostile night:

*You, I thought I knew you*
*You, I cannot judge*
*You, I thought you knew me*
*This one laughing quietly underneath my breath*
*Nightswimming*

After three nights back with Katharina I confess while lying in bed I have to wear a grind guard in my sleep. I don't know why I elaborate and tell this to her in way too much detail. I think it was a pre-emptive manoeuvre. I knew removing it with an emphatic slurp from a web of sleepy drool insulted the chances of morning sex — so the truth seemed a better option. Katharina makes amenable 'mhmm' sounds. In the dark I imagine her nodding but I can't decide if she cares or is too bored to care.

'Cool, I will too then,' Katharina replies.

'You have a mouth splint?'

'Yah.'

'Why haven't you worn yours?'

'I suppose because I am lazy like you.'

We say goodnight and rattle the dark with the sound of us both juggling plastic guards round our mouths in an effort to fix them to our top palate. The psychosomatic duet from the brief clacker of plastic against enamel makes me once again think Katharina could be *it*. I fall asleep smiling, partly from fear of being out of my depth.

Katharina did complain in a way that made me sound like a loose impression of her ex — and that I was only affectionate once the sun went down. She was right though. We only fooled around after dark, like the night cast a lustful spell over our platonic daytime relationship. But I was trying desperately to remain aloof. We were cute together but I'm drunk on serendipity — and the open road is a high roller's table. Choosing each new destination feels like fishing from a fresh deck, behind which awaits a new hand of opportunities and encounters that in turn will invariably alter the next deal of choices of where to go further down the road. To stay put is to stand — risking my current contentment against the possibilities I'll miss out on by not moving on. As Johann Wolfgang Von Goethe astutely noted:

*'Travelling is like gambling: it is always connected with winning and losing, and generally where it is least expected we receive, more or less than what we hoped for.'*

Katharina invites me to the exchange students' orphan Christmas dinner and says she's happy for me to stay the week until Christmas. But I am so hungry for the next destination and new experiences I hadn't learnt yet to appreciate the pleasure that comes from exploring the limits of the place you're in.

I tell Katharina I want to revisit Dublin for a few days but will try and get back to Limerick for Christmas. I'm doing a standup job of ignoring my affections, which at the time are also torn by a Northern Irish species of Catherine. I worked bar with Catherine at the Cornerhouse back in Manchester and knew she was spending Christmas with her family in Omagh.

Catherine was all white skin with raven hair and azurite eyes. And I would later blame her winsome and mettlesome ways for instilling in me an enduring infatuation for the Northern Irish brogue. Back in Manchester she accessorised her university lifestyle with a boyfriend, a hobbit-sized, Harry Potter lookalike whom she met while studying. It didn't stop us mashing lips one night outside the Cornerhouse to a soundtrack of delinquent woops from passing scallies on Oxford Street.

'You are devilish – you know that.' Catherine said before jumping into the first of two Radio Taxis we'd ordered using taxi slips from work.

I'm low cost when it comes to compliments *(call it a Beat Zen cursling)* and could have survived for months on what Catherine said. This was handy since Catherine enacted monogamist rights in the sober light of days and weeks that followed. It's a female phenomenon that was already prominent in my playlist of travel phenomena – where their bodies held a baffling and ethical bureaucracy of physical boundaries and moral exceptions. I don't know why on the eve of leaving for Ireland she extended an invitation for me to stay with her during her visit home. But if the *Leaving Phenomenon* was showing a level of sophistication to complement my expanding maturity I didn't give a shit. I was just keen to spend time with Catherine away from her morals.

I emailed Catherine after leaving Limerick. I told her I was headed to Dublin and planned to travel north from there so hopefully I would pass through Omagh in the week between Christmas and New Year. When I got to Dublin I received an email from Catherine saying it would be unfair if I came to visit since her boyfriend Elliot always wanted to visit but hadn't yet. I rang her parents' house and her equally spirited sister answered. When I told her who was calling she told me not to call again and leave her sister alone. Since I was technically in another country I thought I was already rather proficient at this task.

Dublin loves Christmas the way a Wild West town enjoys a high noon shootout. When I arrived everything was already shut up and closed down for the festive holiday. To pass the days I schlepped through what felt like a nuclear fallout tracing grand circuits of the city. The dank fetid streets of Temple Bar echoed my unrequited affections. And my heart sank into currents of self-loathing and regret over leaving Katharina and Limerick. I guess the emotional discord was too much for my flesh and bones to defend against as I promptly contracted a monstrous strain of

Liffey influenza. By Christmas Eve I carried a slight fever while floundering along the abandoned streets of Dublin. Consoled by the abject misery that comes from gambling everything for nothing brought new meaning to the romanticism of missed chances.

I trudged along Grafton Street, through Temple Bar and over the Ha'Penny Bridge, then down Bachelor's Walk and back over the O'Connell Bridge — feeling the cobblestones sway under me in a reckless sea of nausea. I imaged myself in Dublin in a different time, with a different life. Maybe the antebellum of World War I and the Irish War of Independence, or the gritty arts scene of the 1980s — any historical context to sop the crucifix of wretchedness I was lumbering about, so as to not feel quite so pathetic.

Back in the Barnacles hostel common room loft I meet Jill, a Kiwi chef who has just finished her shift down the road at The Clarence, the boutique hotel owned by Bono and the Edge. She offers me half of her baked salmon and steamed vegetables. I feel like pooh and the farmhouse vegetable soup I ate earlier is a squid in my belly. But Jill says how it's a Christmas Eve tradition. Away from home it makes her feel Christmas is real here in the hostel so I accept her charitable gesture. Later, while watching the omnibus of Bond films in the common room a velvet warmth spreads like treacle around my body. I wonder if sharing Jill's sacramental meal has resurrected a dim inner glow that just might be my long lost Christmas spirit. Halfway through *For Your Eyes Only*, I discard such folly as delirium caused by the resurgent symptoms of my flu. And I retire early to battle a long night's sleep full of congestive fits and feverish Dickensian nightmares.

I wake early on Christmas Day and head to the communal kitchen. The dining area is deserted without any sign of the complimentary breakfast. On an easel and chalkboard I read an announcement stating the nugatory meal, consisting of a stale packaged croissant, single portion of jam and instant coffee has been cancelled. It wasn't because it was Christmas morning. Well it kind of was. It was to discipline the long stayers whose Christmas spirit was in such fine fettle at three o'clock in the morning they instigated a food fight in the kitchen then failed to clean up the mess. The message conceded *(I suppose out of respect to the propitiatory nature of the season)* if all the guests convene at 9.00 am to help clean up the hostel it would be reinstated. Good fucking luck, I thought as I gather my coat and scarf and head out into the icy chill to look vainly for an open cafe.

As I already mentioned I consider myself very much a thrift store pilgrim, where I savour the search along window displays with a vague sense of purpose more than the fleeting elation of stumbling on hidden treasure. I wonder if this is because finding what you're looking for forces you to move on — and what if you can't find anything else to move onto that satisfies you in the same way as before. It's an annoying habit of answers; they tend to generate more questions. Call me lazy but I guess that's why Zen enlightenment is so tough — to attain it you must realise there's nothing to attain. Approaching the final destination in a long trip mirrors this kind of paradox. Every travel writer, in their own unique way is compelled to address the reluctance to being found, and the welter of arriving at the end point of a journey. Part of me enjoys the thought that something predestined is controlling my life because while I have a penchant for concepts and formulating plans, I'm shit at implementation and easily discouraged — and there's a certain pleasure I find in taking myself out of the equation of life. It's the indemnity of surrender.

Movement inherently demands a degree of belief in something. It's actually way harder than people think — not believing in anything. Even a sarky pessimist or pleb standing in the mullock can have the hopeless conviction that it'll all be okay in the end. This is why backpackers who see travel as something more than a getaway, who identify themselves in the role feel safe just like people of any faith. Trails of adventure idolise new experiences and we become part-time seekers, accepting the eternal reassurance that comes from a pursuit without end. We tap into something endless because we build our deliverance on unsteady ground.

Talking of the delusions, desires and dislocation of backpackers, it's funny how these impulses which constitute a large part of any travel experience are the very things impeding a discriminating mind from attaining insight. Lao Tzu and the *Tao Te Ching* articulate this distinction with astounding ease:

*'Free from desire, you realise the mystery.*
*Caught in desire, you see only the manifestations.'*

The syncretism between Taoist and Mahayana Buddhism in forming Zen philosophy is profound. Both champion a sense of humility, inner peace and universal unity. It could be argued that Zen concentrates on the need to eliminate dualistic tendencies while Taoism embraces the interconnection of competing forces. Yin-Yang embodies the Taoist view of universal interdependence and sees Mother Earth as a complementary universal system of opposing forces and cycles. And with the help of oriental tattoos, cheap jewellery, Tai Chi and the eighties, the *taijitu* symbol found global popularity as an icon for peace and love.

The pristine vision and depth of humanity in which Taoism greets the imbalances of a mutable world makes it equally adept at chaperoning the buoyant ideals supporting a backpacker's journey. Heck, in the true spirit of Beat Zen I admit Zen fits because I liked the sound of the word — to be fair I don't think it matters what theosophical prescription is used to gaze upon the watery lip of the open road. Backpackers are pundits of going with the flow, which is the core principle of Tao. I personally think if it feels comfortable then wear it — rational or irrational, practical or abstract, sensible or fantastical. And under the pantheon of mystical thought it all fits because it's too easy to believe that you have stumbled onto an enlightened path when you're overlanding it, coulee to mesa, neck to navel across the planet, all the while lost in the moment. Backpacking induces a spiritual shift because at its essence the art of travel encourages a sense of letting go. The enchantment of travel is it continually puts you in the present allowing the vices of past and future to slacken — which is the core of *zazen* meditation practised to eventually achieve *Satori*. This is why Zen can be applied to almost any endeavour, whether it's an extreme pursuit, grafting out a craft, fishing an idle lake, dozing in afternoon light, shopping for the week, taking a morning jog, or simply chilling out holding a book in a sleepy grip:

> *'To learn the way of the Buddha is to learn about oneself. To learn about oneself is to forget oneself. To forget oneself is to be enlightened by everything in the world. To be enlightened by everything is to let fall one's own body and mind.' Eihei Dōgen Zenji*

The ultimate danger with backpackers is we all too often allow our vanities to promote a false sense of spiritual enlightenment. It's too easy to believe our own myth. It can be the simplest one — we are a nice person — because after all who wants to go through life thinking they're an arsehole the entire time. So we cease to analyse our actions and the impulses instructing them because we are nice, right? So how can anything we do *(or ignore)* harm those around us when we are being nice? In such cases travel like spiritual fever becomes a self-fulfilling prophecy. It's the same as Beal's "sacred stories". We place ourselves front and centre in a grandiose script dressed in a costume fitting the theme. And we play it out on a world stage where we are disciple, companion, lover, druid and champion commander. Thomas Wolfe romanticises this complex tapestry of the traveller's heart in his autographical novel *Look Homeward, Angel*:

> *'The old hunger for voyages fed at his heart. He thrilled to the glory of the secret life. The fear of the crowd, a distrust and hatred of group life, a horror of all bonds that tied him to the terrible family of the earth, called up again the vast*

*Utopia of his loneliness. To go alone, as he had gone, into strange cities; to meet strange people and to pass again before they could know him; to wander, like his own legend, across the earth — it seemed to him there could be no better thing than that.'*

Caught in a cold stew between Christmas and New Year's I was struggling to find anything romantic about Dublin. The malady of lost opportunities and winter's ill health ravaged my endearment for freestylin' it through life. New Year's Eve passed much like Christmas — feeling poorly and lonesome with a crucible of rank emotions writhing in my insides. I didn't necessarily miss Manchester — maybe because I hadn't put enough literal distance between northern England and myself. But as the new year plodded through January I thought more and more about Manchester — skylarking about in the impish gloom of the city with familiar friends. Whether I considered returning to Manchester a pyrrhic victory or glorious retreat didn't really matter — because three weeks later I made the choice to head back there.

Manchester fortified my emancipated lifestyle. I continued to return for short periods, solely for the purpose of working hospitality and retail to fund the next trip. But I was finding it harder to discern whether I was in control of my motives for travel and life. Had they started to take over and control me? I was conscious that friends around me were notching up definitive relationships, celebrating two, three, even four year anniversaries. Then they got married, bought houses and had kids, and most of these momentous highlights I missed because I was either too far away or too skint to travel back and share the occasions with them.

My Beat Zen lifestyle so far hinted at the profound existence of otherworldly forces. And I now appreciated my nomadic ways fostered a pattern of brief relationships — where commitment never came to the party because the conclusion was there from the beginning. Two years later in May 2003 I prepared to leave

Manchester yet again, this time for South America. As I said goodbye to the West Didsbury flat I shared with Felix it was fair to say I was *au fait* with the phenomenon of leaving. In retrospect it's hard to distinguish what persuasive elements of a backpacker's peripatetic lifestyle I was exploiting to maintain the guise of sovereignty in my life. No matter the cocktail of causes, leaving at regular intervals is integral to preserve the feeling of an uninhibited life. It is why upon returning from long overland trips travel junkies immediately declare their next marathon journey. It not only soothes the dysphoria of returning home and post-holiday blues, but gives a reason, an excuse to commit to nothing in the interim between trips.

Transitory romances and their consummate timing continued to grace me on departures. But as it became a customary tradition and as the novelty diminished I considered the phenomenon less and less. There was no fling before I embarked on an 18-month journey around the globe in 2006. On the trip I met Lisa in the wilds of Mongolia. When we said goodbye in April 2007 we had crossed Europe and Asia and were standing on the western shores of India. It was a relationship perforated by independent forays along an intertwining path that lasted eight months. To say I loved her is love that arrives late. But perhaps I needed to marry the open road with an undefined relationship to appreciate reward doesn't only exist in new experience. There is a different richness and return that comes from commitment. After all commitment, like mediation is an ideal dedicated to time — and in a relationship its dedication comes from love.

Don't get me wrong — if someone said I had to commit to living in one place the rest of my life I don't actually know if I could do it. But I also appreciate arriving in a new place eventually loses its lustre when you're romping around the planet indefinitely. Towns start to look the same, faces and languages become indistinguishable, one museum is like all the rest, one impressionistic artwork is the same as another impressionistic artwork, a bronze statue is a bronze statue, a church is a church, and a portal is a portal. So when does it get boring traversing the carnal quirks of each new body, until you've staked it out like pins on a global map?

It may sound contrary but I've never had a problem committing to one soul — one mind, one body, one taste, one scent and one love which shows in goosebumps and a lightness of touch. I'm not saying it's always easy to reconcile against a brand new flavour or pheromone that smacks you in the face — the heist of sensations and possibilities from catching a set of eyes that dare you without any guarantee. Whether a tenebrous gaze and coy smile is consummated or not it's what evolution equipped us to do. Considering commitment always makes me think of the understated elegance of John Cusack's portrayal in Nick Hornsby's *High Fidelity,* especially when Rob realises its importance:

> Rob: *I'm tired of the fantasy, because it doesn't really exist. And there are never really any surprises, and it never really...*
> Laura: *Delivers?*
> Rob: *Delivers. Right. And I'm tired of it. And I'm tired of everything else for that matter. But I don't ever seem to get tired of you, so...*

Commitment is a love which supersedes the one that came with her bitchin' ayurvedic body and winsome face. It's a love of moments. It levitates the minutiae, which ordinarily falls discarded between the gaps in the day. And it emboldens our desire to be around one another all day, every day, even when we're both doing nothing in particular. To spend an hour debating where to go for coffee, sit outside or on an upstairs porch, watch her hair shine like strings of molasses and wild honey in the daylight, chase down the Diggity Doughnuts truck, get afternoon margaritas with free chips 'n' salsa, walk along the beach, happy hour by the water, taste the salty sweetness of her kiss and see her green eyes reflect the wash of the sweetgrass caught in the autumnal high tide, sushi for dinner, shower sex and a late-night movie on her Macbook while laying back in the same lumpy bed. Commitment forms rituals and discourses inexplicable to everyone close to you including yourself because meaning is no longer held by words. It's the performance which massages the empty spaces between poignant moments.

*'Look at me – I'm Dave and all I want is Vegemite, and a Fosters-'*
*'We don't drink Fosters in Australia.'*
*'What's that other one…. E-something?'*
*'VB'*
*'Yeah VB – and I spend all my time putting words into sentences, and itching my beard and going mmmm, and staying up on my couch watching movies and getting shitfaced.'*
*'You are fucking mental.'*
*'That's so mean. You can't say that.'*
*'Yes I can.'*
*'I'm not mental.'*
*'Yes you are.*
*'You're way more mental.'*
*'No way. You're way more mental.'*
*'You are.'*
*'You are so cute.'*
*'You're way cuter than me.'*
*'No way.'*
*'Yes way.'*
*'Wanna do it?'*
*'Maybe later. I'm still sore.'*
*'Is it my fault?'*
*'Kind of.'*
*'Want me to kiss it better?'*
*'Huh? Oh gross.'*

Commitment offers familiarity which is in no way boring because it lets all these little moments of kindness and selfless gestures shine. The snacks she brings home for you after shopping; the earnest consultations over what vegan cookies to bake because she wants you to enjoy them just as much as her; the hungry embraces; the tireless swarm of baby kisses on your sleepy face; the neck massages when you've got a headache; a spontaneous decision to come find you; apologies she doesn't owe but gives to you anyway; and the beer she picks up at a gas station on the way to Edisto because you look sad. Rather than running away to somewhere new I want to wake where I did yesterday morning — next to her in her downtown Charleston flat so we can create the day together. In time idle repetition will settle in the grooves, but unlike travel I won't tire of this routine.

# CHAPTER 6

# DARWIN SYNDROME

The risk of growing more and more detached on longer journeys is difficult to monitor. While losing affinity for a regular life you conform to another — growing increasingly ingratiated to the roving fraternity of budget backpackers and terminal drifters. It's common to think one realm is more righteous than the other. The tyro traveller is automatically converted by a rootless life with a backpack because it defiles the normalcy that was left behind. And the intransigent overlander will prize the fleeting gratification of visiting new places and meeting new people over the rewards that come from committing to one place *(and contributing to something greater than one's self)*. Rory MacLean's notable tale of Rama Tiwari in his travelogue *Magic Bus: On the Hippie Trail from Istanbul to India* surmises this fundamental flaw of independent travellers on the Hippie Trail in the sixties and seventies:

> *'They imagined peace of mind was not with their families or in their home countries. They didn't see we can only live in happiness if we conquer the restless dream that paradise is in a world other than our own.'*

In February 2007 I felt this confusion when I arrived in Darwin with Maccas after almost a year backpacking. Prior to returning to Australia we were in Cambodia. We loped around Siem Reap, Phnom Penh and Sihanoukville then hitchhiked back to Bangkok. We'd been in South East Asia for two and half months. I was looking for a change of scenery and Maccas was counting down the final days of a gap year abroad. So we booked a Tiger Airways flight to Darwin with a 10-hour layover in Singapore. We touched down after 2 am and for the second night in a row we slept what was left of it at the airport — laid out on stiff blue carpet in the arrivals hall with duty free Johnnie Walker which we drank out of disposable coffee cups I pilfered from the closed cafe. In the morning we caught a taxi and checked into the Melaleuca on Mitchell. There amidst transient carpools of Europeans travelling between Broome and Katherine we encountered a crew of four young Aussie labourers permanently living at the hostel.

It's hard to say how much their casual racism affronted me. This was my homeland — and it was such a cliché. I often joked with other expats and foreigners who spent time in Australia about our classic breed of moderate rednecks. But I'd been back for less than 24 hours. My personal beliefs were in reflux, struggling to acclimatise to a bigoted landscape that was so well preserved in contemporary rural Australia. I guess I was mostly disheartened. Discovering this malignant legacy of Australian culture so quickly on arrival was like running into a turn of bad luck. And it threatened to sully the fondness of recent memories travelling with so many open-minded and free-thinking individuals. It also pissed me off this local crew permanently lived at the hostel, making them an unavoidable scourge of my return home — fuelling my contempt, along with an insatiable desire to get back on a plane and fuck off out of Australia again.

Don't get me wrong. I don't have an issue with hostels accommodating long stayers *per se* — as long as they're not fascists.

Living out of hostels negates the complications of renting rooms through private landlords and real estate agents. It's an ideal fit for people on working holidays and how many itinerant workers get by. Through my own struggles from twice relocating to Ireland I observed a predominantly Aussie IT workforce living in hostels around Temple Bar. Due to the contrary dynamic of short stay travellers, long stayers were segregated where possible and lived in six to eight bed dorms.

At the Abbey Court hostel on Bachelors Walk I was made to spend a couple of nights in a long stayers section. The frowsty dorm room looked and smelled like a behemoth student house had been condensed into a solitary room by a darkness of alchemy. When I asked how they could live like that for so long most of them shrugged indolently as if they had become institutionalised, and no longer remembered the veritable elation of walking into your own pad with your own shit exactly how you left it when you went out earlier in the day. Some mentioned the housing shortages in central Dublin, which I was intimately aware of.

I'd already visited a handful of old Georgian apartments with a cohort of Italians, eager to bust out of the hostel. These commodious single bedroom flats that came with untenable rental fees were the only option in central Dublin. It was a simple matter of arithmetic and imposition. We would divide the monthly rent six ways. Fuck privacy, sleeping head to toe — just as Aussies did in London, the British did in Bondi, and all the youth all over the world did while struggling to find their way in exorbitant super cities full of promise and ruin. But every flat we saw was essentially a large bedsit. The bedroom, awarded to the one of us who paid a proportionately higher amount of rent, was a wardrobe with a locking door. And the bathroom was a dank pisshole with a curtain and showerhead. Pragmatically, it would never work and had every potential to be infinitely more disagreeable and objectionable than the 12-bed dorm I was currently sleeping in.

Back at the hostel we mulled about the kitchen in a dispirited funk of ennui. Flavio ate carbonara from a huge pot with ruttish energy and badgered me, like he always did whenever he made food, 'to please him,' and try some. I had known Flavio for about two weeks and was the closest to him out of the Italian contingent. He had been in Dublin five weeks and was still without employment or permanent accommodation. He was also addicted to Spar's apple flapjacks, which he said he couldn't stop eating because he was 'nervous' all the time. The stress of the situation was clearly getting to Flavio, who like the majority of young Europeans came to Dublin to improve their English. I'm not sure why they chose Ireland over the UK but as a Frenchman put it:

'A lot of my friends who went to London had a very difficult time.'

Flavio and the Italians had not seen the gold rush opportunities the previous year when I suffered an ague of Cathakarinas. Across Dublin shop fronts protested the economic boom with job posters desperately seeking staff. This is what misled me to cross the Irish Sea a year later and be greeted by a mini recession. The financial contraction after four years of expansion aided by the EU spooked jobs into hiding. And word on the street was employers were prioritising Irish citizens for vacancies above foreigners. The racial unpleasantness in Ireland reminded me of Australia — twinned cultures renowned for their infectious hospitality, glib humour, free-range blarney and love of all things barley and rye. But scratch the surface and prejudice menstruates like crude oil from a boggy swamp.

'The only thing close to happiness is misery,' Flavio announces in his heavy Roman accent between mouthfuls of pasta. His English was poor and it sounded like he was quoting a poignant Italian proverb that had been lost in translation. Accidental or not, in that in the moment I knew precisely what he meant.

Frissi, a skittish Italian elf with a silicon shoal of Rapunzel hair bounces in and raps at Flavio in a staccato verse of Italian.

I'm not sure what is said. I imagine Frissi is chastising Flavio for his glum demeanour because he huffs in response like a tired elephant and resumes eating.

We continue to scour property listings for accommodation. We combine it with our daily search for employment — an oppressive ordeal that has us joking and glamorising the situation like we're jolly caricatures in the Great Depression. Each morning after breakfast Flavio and I left the hostel together as if we were heading to work, but we'd soon peel off to navigate different beats — in an attempt to stave off the monotony of routine failure. The most economical circuits which passed high concentration areas of shops and hotels were in Temple Bar and around Grafton Street, Dawson Street and St Georges Street. If I could be arsed I'd circle Merrion Square before heading back across the north side of the Liffey and continue down Henry St, passing the Ilac and Jervis centres and back along Bachelor's Walk to the hostel. Sometimes I stopped to watch the Liffey's formidable march out to sea. I respected its intractable abidance and tried to imagine myself as an immaterial force of the natural world — see myself as a Pavlovian impulse, an infinitesimal component contributing mindlessly to the complex and infinite bravura of existence as we know it. Then my stomach would growl with hunger. I'd think of the soup and bread I had in the hostel and would start compiling a shopping list in my head for an afternoon trip to Dunnes.

It was round midday by the time most of us got back to the hostel — just in time to pick up a fresh warm copy of the *Evening Herald*. If one waited until evening there was always a copious sea of discarded copies covering the surfaces of the hostel. But by midafternoon the *Evening Herald's* worth was used up and wrung dry as everyone in a similar situation shared the same instinct — and pushed to get an advantage by frantically ringing up fresh job listings, leaving names and numbers like we were commodities then make appointments that evening to see overpriced apartments.

I used to think Antipodeans by default would be the brethren I'd want beside me in a fix — in the trenches, deep in the shit. Now I don't hesitate to include Italians as well. Australians' lackadaisical nature and impertinence in the face of adversity is a perfect fit for a crisis. But while we gladly chide our Imperial cousins for being a bunch of whingeing Poms, we seem blind to the prevalent behaviour in our own culture — which is somewhat forgivable since we do it with way more laconic and colonial charm. But man, Australians can whine. Aussies in Brittan whine about how shite everything is all the time: the weather, the coffee, the beer, the weather, the whingeing Poms, the beer and the weather. Even the summer season back in my hometown brings a ludicrous discourse when a reprieve of mild weather gives cause for locals to complain that it isn't like "real summer". Then when real summer returns with a +40C fuck you heat wave they complain it's too fucking hot. But to be fair I think it's the same everywhere — where entropy and dried-up desires breed pettiness.

By contrast, the Italians' rational veracity to see something neither worse nor better than what it actually was — to treat a shit situation as simply that brought a refreshing repose in our current circumstance. Without the diabolical overture I was reminded of the irrefutable logic of the fiendish old Italian man in Joseph Heller's definitive World War II satire *Catch 22*.

After a week it was evident the properties we had viewed were all rejects of Dublin's housing crisis — listings that remained available because no sane person would agree to the flamboyant rates that offered so little value. While the Italians continued to retrace familiar steps around the centre of Dublin I set my gaze to the suburbs and persevered on my own. After another few days I found the ideal place down in Rathmines.

Dominick answered the door and walked me inside. After a brief tour he explained the other housemates weren't home but saw no issue with why I couldn't take the room. Dominick's slothful post-student indifference seemed like an easy fit. But after careful calculations I realised I couldn't afford the rent — hell, I couldn't afford to live anywhere in Dublin. After subtracting Dublin's usurious living costs and rent from the pittance of a weekly income I'd receive from my new job at Thunderoad Cafe I didn't come up in black. I didn't even come up evens or reach a figure close to being supportable.

From my time in Ireland and later when I relocated to St Kilda in Melbourne I appreciated how the path of least resistance entrenched long stayers in hostels. However, I could never tolerate living in a new city, with all it had to offer without puncturing the bubble of hostel living. In Dublin I wasn't like the Croatian, Czech, French, Italian, Polish, Romanian, and other European travellers all eager to improve their English proficiency. English was my first and only language. I may have been just as imprudent as a student, but I didn't have to live the student lifestyle in a densely populated and inflated capital city. I didn't need graveyard shifts to fit a study schedule, or compromise on dilapidated housing simply because it was cheap. I started to reconsider because I was free to. I had dual citizenship and a useless arts degree — enrolling in further tertiary study like so many of my European friends seemed pointless. I could escape this disconsolation and toil. Put plainly I started to reconsider Manchester, yet again.

Five years on I suppose it's fitting on some level that I'm at a rooftop bar in Darwin, beside a boisterous gang of Aussie longstayers. Darwin is a regional pearl in the oyster of what's ocker and true blue so I really shouldn't be shocked by their incessant rhetoric about anything that isn't fair dinkum and "Tip Top" Australian. For those unacquainted with trademark wife-beater-and-stubbies racism, it usually involves beguiling inconsistencies about who is a "Real Australian" interspersed with the quintessential Australian catchphrase omitted from tourist campaigns:

*'Give me a break. I'm not a racist but...'*

Typically, ethnically challenged people are also really hard to ignore because they're fucking loud. Deaf to innuendo, I ask them quite plainly why they didn't leave the hostel.

'Why would we?'

'Because you live here.'

'Here there's a bar, a pool-'

'Different international chicks every week?'

'Wouldn't you want to have a place to call your own – it's sort of the point really of working.'

'Cost the same-'

'Makes no sense.'

They baulk when Maccas and I say we're off to get dinner and a side of respite at a nearby Vietnamese takeaway. How sad I think that their world is reduced to guttural syllables of division: *gook, chink, wop, wog, boong and dago*. Food gives little reprieve so Maccas and I abandon the scene entirely and take our guitar out on to the streets to busk. But where every concrete kerb and dusty roadside from Mongolia to Malaysia offered a venerated platform for performance; the public bench up the road from the hostel is a pillory that derides us gonzo outlaws. Caught between the familiar and unfamiliar I'm stricken by an isotope of *depaysement* I like to call *Darwin Syndrome*, the unsettling displacement from being back home in Australia. Typically associated with the culture shock of being in an unfamiliar or foreign place, *Darwin Syndrome* is a disorientating embellishment because it's the reverse of what I expected — feeling disappointed and dejected for being out of place and unwelcome in my home country.

I wonder if Tiger Airways flew through a wormhole from Singapore to Darwin. Or was Darwin simply a geographical oddity that is 40 years behind current thought? I take my mind off it all and play old classics. The White Stripes' *Same Boy You've Always Known, I Never Picked Cotton* by the Man in Black, BJM's *Ballard of Jim Jones* and *Babe (Love of My Life), Hold On* by Tom Waits and The Lemonheads' *Being Round*. The rancour of passing locals is unnerving — leery glances and intimidating stares beneath brims of furrowed sunburn. I can tell Maccas also senses the raw public animosity.

'Oi, think we should move?'

'Fuck yeah.'

'Coles?'

'Why not.'

We relocate down the road to the stairwell of a multistory carpark adjoining the Coles supermarket. I channel my aggravation into a rendition of Cat Stevens's *Where do the Children Play*. I then play the *Cool Hand Luke Song*, trying to conjure Paul Newman's chakra-melting moment of atonement when he sings the song — the executable realisation you having nothing to lose when you have less than nothing. A security officer approaches.

'I'm going to have to ask you boys to move on.'

'Are you Coles security?' Maccas inquires.

'Yes.'

'Does your jurisdiction include the staircase?' I ask.

'No.'

We weren't being dicks on purpose. If anything we were wallowing in the comedown of being lost — where I think we were both trying to recapture the high of recent memories. The latent warmth of which was suddenly imperilled from the abrasive hospitality and melancholic grip of being home.

The private security guard points to a cleft between flagstones. He draws an unofficial demarcation in pavement, ceding the concrete steps from the penumbra of his control. But I guess due process and all at that in country regions is more of a guideline than a strict code of conduct — because despite making a point of pointing out he has no authority over our peaceful protest he then adds,

'I'm still going to have to get you boys to vacate.'

It is said in a very agreeable yet persuasive manner. And I imagine as with any other issues of noncompliance in the guard's life, it involves a brief phone call to his brothers or cousins down at the local cop shop. We give up and decide instead to head to the Victoria. The notorious downtown pub-cum-club is an easy choice because two pretty young reps from the Victoria gave us VIP stickers while we were busking. Not knowing what VIP stood for in Australia's backcountry seems like a fun way to suppress our discontent with a few stiff drinks.

I'm refused entry because I'm toting a guitar and Maccas is refused entry because he has a towel. I actually don't know why he had the towel, but we used it as a collection mat for busking which amounted to zilch.

'But we're VIPs,' I say earnestly and point the pink sticker on my t-shirt.

The doorman remains uninterested, which doesn't seem much effort for him.

'Isn't there a cloak room we can use?'

'You can put the guitar in a locker, but not the towel.'

'Perfect!'

Sharing a fatalistic outlook, it's easy to cast aside the absurdity of Darwin's nightlife and return to the hostel bar. Thankfully we meet Keepo that evening back poolside at the rooftop bar. Keepo is on old blowsy British expat with a dungeon of teeth. He gives an ambiguous account of how he 'worked through' a Kiwi passport before getting Australian citizenship. He says he came to Darwin for work. He's certified in demolitions, as well as being a truck driver. He's staying in the hotel-styled addition to the Melaleuca because he just got back from the Philippines *(which for guys like Keepo is as explicit as being spotted exiting a brothel)*.

Keepo reminds me of an illywhacker from a bygone era, and like his scurvied teeth he's uncompromisingly real. He gives us lurid Velcro stubby holders of titty bars he visited in the Philippines and ersatz Harley Davison souvenirs he intends to resell in Australia. Over the next few days we regularly run into him around town — always perched on the sidewalk talking to some pretty unassuming Pilipino bank teller or Vietnamese supermarket worker.

The next day when we see each other on the street Keepo invites us up to his hotel room to split a handle of duty free JD. I'm curious about an expat's view on racial discrimination in the Northern Territory and mention our resident racist at the hostel by way of example.

'Them there are a pack of pissants,' Keepo exclaims while pointing vaguely out the window.

He retells the story of a Dutch backpacker he met last time he stayed at the Melaleuca on Mitchell. The same group of long stayers ferried the Dutchman out of town to score weed off a local dealer. He was on a working holiday visa and stressed he couldn't have any trouble since he'd immigrated with a history of petty adolescent crimes. There was some tacit druggy-drug repayment in kind for the ride which Keepo didn't have the particulars. And of course it all went tits up — well, not for the four Aussie boys. They returned to the hostel an hour later hooting and carrying on with a free bag of weed courtesy of the foreigner who jumped out of the moving vehicle on the way back to town. The Dutchman turned up at the hostel early the next evening — alive but severely dehydrated and badly cut up after traipsing across the outskirts of the Never Never to get back to town.

According to Keepo he was still stewing about the fiasco, claiming he was sold out and everyone was in cahoots. In his version of events they were tailed from the moment they left the dealer's outback hideaway — a glowering set of headlights in the void, trailing them at a sinister and steady legal speed limit. It was more than 30 kilometres back to Darwin and in a packed cab after a dope deal tensions quickly turned to paranoia *(which is not uncommon when illicit drugs are involved)*. Apparently the Dutchman kept insisting on being let out but the driver refused. Keepo said he even did a pretty good job on the accent while telling the story.

'*Nauh wayyy mayyyte-*'

'We'd look guilty as sin if we dropped you off in the middle of woop woop.'

'But I can't be here-'

'Don't sweat it o'right.'

'I told you this! I cannot be involved with the police.'

'Who said anything about the cops mate?'

'Oi, are the pigs tailing us?'

'Who the fuck else is following us out here in bum fuck nowhere.'

'Heard Jason got fuckin' ratted out last week.'

'Shut the fuck up Gaz.'

This was the point the Dutchman decided he'd take his chances with the black abyss of the Australian outback. So he flung himself out the ute and into the night's embrace — to kiss the speeding dirt and gravel with a flying cartwheel. Keepo chuckles as he gets up and sloshes a skinful of whiskey into the two water beakers and wine glass we're drinking from.

'He kept saying, "I could have died, ya know" and he really could have – once when he leapt out the car, and twice getting back here on foot.'

Keepo's natural sympathy for an outlander illustrates the rich layers of prejudice when he returns to the subject of racial profiling in the Top End.

'Problem here is there's good ones and bad ones. Most of us lived here a bit know the difference. The lazy abos are easy to spot – always drunk-n-stealing and getting in fights. But they give the good ones who just wanna work a bad name.'

Keepo drinks quickly and keeps talking about going to the casino, which to me sounded like 'casino then brothel'. He goes to the toilet then we hear the shower running. Behind the bathroom door Keepo's grumbling like an uncorked sailor who's talking to the moon. It starts looking like Keepo isn't going anywhere. We say goodbye, telling him we're going to watch the cricket live at the local bar near to the hostel, if he fancies it later.

At the bar we're refused service for looking like we've had one too many sherbets. We're instructed to drink a supervised glass of water each before they will serve us our pints. Maccas is flummoxed and starts to object. He's a cricket fanatic and since Bangkok he'd banged on about watching the latest test match. I suspect little thoughts like these were deferring the onslaught of reality he put on hold when he left home year ago. I hold Maccas back, telling him complaining will only make it worse. I knew from time across the other side of the bar that debating matters of insobriety with the barkeep *(in control of dispensing it)* never in the recent history of the world facilitated a drink. His chagrin is forgivable given he has a riot of JD in his gut, and up until now we'd drunk ourselves to ruin on beaches, buses, train carriages, at airports, hostels, hotels, tree tops, tea houses, kerbsides, karaoke bars, yurts, rum joints, beer dens, by campfires and all the other places in between. And common to all these establishments was no one gave a fuck how much you consumed. You could happily pass out at a bar in northern Thailand as long as you woke up intermittently to order another round. This is also possibly the reason we appear more rye-toed than we feel. We oblige by sipping our water before getting in a pint but the mood is gone — thoroughly shat on by all these First World rules and regulations.

I later wondered if the open road and nine months of travel predisposed me to don what I call the "Expat Cap" — a figurative state of Stowian homesickness, inciting a dystopic vision and denunciation of your native country. It's a cap that I now wore with gusto, disavowing everything about the place I came from. It's not so far removed from travellers who dismiss the company of their countrymen for fear it will somehow stifle their quest to have a *real* experience. The ultimate extension of which is the maverick anthropologist who believes only profound understanding and authentic discovery can come from total immersion in a local culture. All of which again implies a sense of travelling the furthest from where you were and who you were when you started your journey to attain a truth of sorts.

The game of backpackers rejecting the tourist scene is an old one — an allergic reaction to what's familiar. Usually, it's in favour of finding a more faraway and honest experience in the company of locals. *Paris Syndrome* characterises the extreme shock that afflicts some tourists visiting a foreign city. Notably affecting Japanese tourists in the French capital, it exhibits a melangé of psychosomatic and delusional symptoms including feelings of anxiety, depersonalisation and persecution. Under a curtain of estrangement, it's hard to discern what part of my reverse culture shock, or *Darwin Syndrome* was exacerbated by personal circumstance, the acrimonious welcome, or the racist young fucktards at the hostel. It was with a wry turn of humour I at least conceded the Northern Territory's renowned tourism slogan was indeed correct:

*You never never know if you never never go!*

Sated in the disenchantment of being home I went off and bought a didgeridoo to cheer myself up. But time in Darwin was prison time and it intensified a feeling of being stranded. Although this emotional clinch tirelessly propelled me overland, I now felt trapped and unable to escape because of the expectations from family and hometown friends awaiting my return. Back at the Melaleuca on Mitchell I meet up with Maccas and Keepo at the rooftop bar. Keepo tries to apologise for the other day like he let the sports team down but I don't let him.

'Some days we fly and some days we swim Keepo.'

'That's true that is.'

Maccas and I had grand intentions of resuming our adventures, hitching down through the mighty red centre of the country and heading to the east coast. But feeling like pariahs in our homeland *(derived in part from the extended period we were both away)* had become so acute Maccas and I disbanded our fellowship on separate flights to our respective families' homes in Sydney and Perth.

Culturally, it's easy to reduce our desire and derision to colours and odd shapes when looking at a map of where to go next — whether it's the blue civility of Europe, the orange spiritualism of the East, or the vermillion of autocratic republics and aggressive super-powered nations. To a wayfarer it's a game of Jungian symbols where countries take on identities that represent or share an affinity with what we're seeking to revisit or explore next. Invert the process and this is how a lot of travellers view their home country when returning after a long trip. And because it is their home they treat it like their own house. In the same oblivious fashion newly returned travellers can make an indulgent mess of heartfelt reunions by smothering small talk with a new found social awareness and political activism — filling conversation with thick, awkward indignation over the nation's current socio-political agenda. But it's hard returning home without flaunting a new found humanistic awareness to prove how we have changed.

Many long-term travellers eventually succumb to the parabolic route of the hero's journey — and we return home to find what we were looking for in life or love and settle down in the exact spot we left from *(or at the very least to recuperate in the loving cradle of friends and family before absconding again)*. It falls into the old adage that we ultimately see what we want to see when we're ready to see it. Or, in the words of T.S. Eliot from *Little Gidding*:

*We shall not cease from exploration*
*And the end of all our exploring*
*Will be to arrive where we started*
*And know the place for the first time.*

Instead of stumbling on some homecoming tree root of remarkable discovery, I like to think the power of returning home gives perspective to make us realise we already have all that we wanted all along. Whether it's hardwired to our DNA to be continually unsatisfied and searching for grass that is greener, only the few, true errant adventurers and expatriates with stubborn palates, opinions and wallets to remain abroad succeed in doing so. Thomas Wolfe understood the expatriate's disillusionment of where they came from better than most. He saw home as an apparition — and like a trick once you turn your back on it the magic disappears. So when you do leave home to go see the world it doesn't remain. Like Christmas and past lovers it sticks to you, but as a nostalgic figment in your memories. Back in my hometown a solitary insight did take hold, but I must admit pragmatism ruled any deeper yearnings. It was the realisation I'd spent the good part of a year overlanding it halfway round the globe and I'd only used half my savings — time to go!

# CHAPTER 7

# OPERATION EL MIRADOR

When I arrived in the Yucatan in 2011 recollections of my time in South East Asia and the Sub Continent surfaced at the Weary Traveller hostel bar in Tulum. Long scabrous beer benches full of beach-crusted backpackers and a casino of drinking games, easy and sultry predawn hookups, breakfast pancakes and do-it-all-over-again effrontery, which reinstated the dull intolerant throb of already feeling beached out. I was in a hurry to return mentally to where I was on my previous odyssey three years before. So I transited quickly through Belize *(avoiding the subsequent discalced beachside reproductions on Caye Caulker)* and crossed into northern Guatemala. I headed in the direction of Santa Elena and Flores Island, the deferential gateway to the unprecedented Mayan ruins at Tikal. But I had been reading my *LP* Bible prior to arrival and already set in motion a wilful desire to travel unassisted to El Mirador, one of the most venerated and remote Mayan ruins.

El Mirador is buried under a sea of jungle mere kilometres from the Mexican border and boasts one of the biggest pyramids in the world called El Tigre. This was a titillating motivation in itself since atop El Tigre on a clear day you could apparently see across a vast green carpet canopy to the elevated temples of Tikal over 60 kilometres away. I felt tackling such an arduous journey so early in my trip was necessary to re-animate the backpacker within me which had withered into a goading presence in the back of my mind since the end of my previous trip.

In the realm of global budget backpacking travellers are impelled by a persuasive array of impulses. However, it would be wrong to say travelling is an exclusive sport for the shiftless youth and nugatory offspring of the wealthy. Travelling exists on many planes to satisfy the carefree, the mercurial, the lackadaisical, the disillusioned, and the unfulfilled. And most backpackers fit into multiple categories. A yoga addict will enter a Kerala ashram for a two-week spiritual retreat then skid back to Goa for a German-inspired acid and ketomine-fuelled trance rave. And that's how many of us journey through life, vacillating from hedonism to temperance like a complacent epicurean.

Aside from the youthful prerogative to get the fuck out of home, I've noticed over time an increasing proportion of Beat Zen vagabonds ageing along the open road like me. And it's fair to say the diaspora of shoestring travel hides a midlife crisis well. Backpacking is an indigent existence, so it's easy to trade the sports car for kite surfing in Brazil, a Caribbean cruise for diving off Utila and Roatán islands in Honduras, or foregoing a guided ascent of Mount Kilimanjaro for free wheelin' it down Death Road *(North Yungas Road)* just outside of La Paz in Bolivia.

Today gap year travellers are one of many groups competing for the glory of open-ended journey. Travellers are recently divorced, or been through an ugly breakup. Others have simply had enough of life and are looking to get away. The added appeal of an overland venture is it puts you out of range of instant updates and pushbutton notifications *(or lack thereof)*. It unplugs you from the masochistic preoccupation of tracking and following how super-awesome, well adjusted and successful everyone around you *(including your ex)* appears to be. Backpacking alleviates the superficial need to prove you're happy with your cosmetic and consumptive life. And it frees you from the internment of all the other little distractions which inhibit happiness — because while following *Project Happiness, One Green Planet, Ram Dass, Osho, LifeHacks, Humans of Wherever, Yogatopia,* and *Survivalist Rising* helps us appreciate life and shit, it's easy to get stuck comparing yourself to every internet stranger which highlights all the hard-to-pinpoint stuff you wish you had but don't.

Many travellers also use global adventure as a form of therapeutic dialysis — to search for a solution or some sort of inspiration while on hiatus from life or a career. Then there are also those of us looking for a complete holistic makeover. Some are running away from something in the past much darker and traumatic. Finally, there are the ones who have forgotten their way home, or discarded it completely in dedication to a wending way of life.

Despite backgrounds or budgets backpackers commonly gravitate to regions without the wealth and comfort we are born into and have come to expect. It comes with the territory of being on a journey. My first trip to Morocco and Egypt in 2001 changed me. Sure I was used to the plight of Africa — aid agencies campaigning to help poverty, sponsored events such as running a marathon or shaving your head, benefit rock concerts, along with unimaginable images of suffering broadcast on the nightly news. Hell, I once gave a public speech in high school on Chad — I didn't even know where Chad was, except that it was in Africa and was starving but wasn't hogging the limelight like Ethiopia.

In Marrakesh I waded through the photo album of a newcomer — young entrepreneurs setting up office on sidewalks, old Berbers occupying backstreet hovels, a sleuth of shoeshiners pestering me to polish my Gortex boots, the prolix purveyors thrusting dried apricots and dates into my hand, an ambush of grubby streets kids hawking damaged old trinkets and candy regifted from the garbage, musicians with imprisoned mascots and all the other antiquated scenarios of peddlers and charmers that don't fit the modern world *(which is why I'm there)*. It's not the sights alone that get to me. It's the milieu of sights, sounds and smells roiling through the souqs with a suffocation of people — barbequed *broquettes* and rotting trash, spices and manure, mint tea, fruit flavoured vapour of smoking shishas, dust and grime, and everywhere people — people with nothing — holding onto, salvaging, panel beating and bartering with junk, harassing me with it like it's worth something and I must buy it. I escape the ancient medina quarter by crossing the Djemaa el-Fna and head out towards Guilez, the "new town" of Marrakesh. Walking along a deserted four-lane avenue I feel myself able to breathe again — long slow breaths in the scorching midday heat. But less than a mile later I stop and question where I'm walking to. Like a child I'm already bored and miss the mayhem.

I experienced the same emotional hurdles in the crowded markets of Cairo and again in South America. I thought these experiences would equip me to face the deprivation in China, India and Nepal where so many live, eat, defecate and die in the street like dogs — but it didn't. You do get used to it, very slowly. And this is partly because it's not always easy to validate your presence in poverty stricken areas. I guess this is why all backpackers on some level indulge in the image of a pauper abroad. Many of us take on the mantle of a frugal student because it's easy. The act of verisimilitude in some ways is a necessary mechanism to mollify what Paul Theroux rather harshly depicts at the start of *Ghost Train to the Eastern Star*:

> *'Travel is not merely the business of being bone-idle, but also an elaborate bumming evasion, allowing us to call attention to ourselves with our conspicuous absence while we intrude upon other people's privacy — being actively offensive as fugitive freeloaders.'*

Although there is truth to our shoestring lifestyle, the diametric reality is that ours comes with the ultimate freedom of choice — living an impoverished existence to extend an overseas trip for as long as possible. This is why Nansen Fugan, an eighth century Zen Buddhist master said to experience *Daikensho* one must be ready to give up everything. This is a common theme reiterated in many spiritual teachings. And it's because charity, despite being a fundamental starting point on the path to unitive consciousness is a tricky son of a bitch to get a handle of. It's a bit like letting go — you do it at the start because it feels good, but at some point you're supposed to appreciate all the inconsequential crap surrounding you — and realise it's the right thing to do. In other words, fake it 'til you make it. Passing through the samsara of destitute townships and indigenous communities many backpackers entertain the notion they are counterparts from opposite ends of an exiguous spectrum — another myth we convince ourselves of to develop a communion with locals. But in reality there is very little shared history or life experience.

Watching the totem cavalcade of tour groups pass by in Central America makes this division devastatingly clear — ambitious tourists and travellers lead the charge, trotting by on old nags followed by light-footed guides leading pack mules carrying water, camping equipment, and a guarantee of three meals a day. It's not without reason. A fractious past and history of banditry, grievous assaults, rape and fatalities of a number of tourists had established a unilateral acceptance of tour services in the region. I guess the positive outcome was it stimulated the local job market, but in a fairly corrupt and unregulated system, how much it benefited locals was a private affair.

A myriad of tour and hiking operations littered gringo capitals as a result. All of them basically offered the same shit for slightly different prices. But in the past year I'd read the Guatemalan Government ratified law enforcement and punishment to improve tourist safety. The reduction in tourist-related incidents suggested it was starting to work. However, no one seemed to be second guessing anything except me. I had good reason to. From years of experience my *mochila* was streamlined, predatory, operating on pure faculty and bare essentials: one-and-a-half person tent, spring season sleeping bag, first aid kit, collapsible stove, single person pots and pan set, fishing tackle, mosquito net, and an equation of layer clothing which enabled me to yaw from freezing point to tropical sweat. I also really *really* fucking hated travelling in tour groups. And while the paraphernalia of independence accrued a heavy weight, it was a joyful weight of freedom. This is how I found my unique travel mantra which I repeated over and over on arduous long hikes when the weight on my back grew into an atlas and the straps sank into my shoulders like blunt blades:

*'The weight on my back reminds me that I'm free.'*

I arrived into the broiling tumult of Santa Elena's Terminal Nuevo de Autobus on the southern purlieu of the city. At the time the region was still reeling from the recent discovery of at least 27 decapitated farmers. Everyone blamed the Zetas, the notorious Mexican drug cartel. They appeared daily on the front pages of newspapers for their violent and savage campaign to gain criminal supremacy in the region. But there was no evidence of fear or uncertainty on the streets — I guess because it was a reality that locals were used to.

Cultivating my combustible and doughty backpacking spirit I rebuff the strident tuk-tuk drivers. I scoff when they claim it's over four kilometres to Flores Island. It was no secret that's where I intended to stay. The colonial protuberance gloriously preserved on Lago Petén Itzá is where every gringo arriving in Santa Elena stayed. With cool contempt I treat their assertions as gross exaggerations and let my shoestring belligerence bristle and expand in the clamour and midmorning heat.

I pass backpacking malabaristas spruiking amidst gridlocked traffic. Again Theroux comes to mind as I wonder if these young travellers feel compelled to juggle before stationary vehicles full of sweating bodies stuck in traffic out of some desire to ingratiate themselves — to feel a deeper connection to the entropic surroundings of northern Guatemala. On some subconscious level did they feel, like Theroux suggested, a sense of intrusion? Was their performance a way of payment in the form of entertainment for being a guest in a foreign land? Faced with pure idleness, some sort of justification made some sense. After all, every journey needs a purpose. Then again they may have just been hawking for a daily food and drink allowance. I continue to push through the street congestion in the febrile apex of the dry season. I feel my travelling self being re-established under the onerous weight of my pack and growing discomfort. I imagine alchemy transmuting my aching shoulders into anvils. An hour later I reach the connector linking Flores to Santa Elena and happily concede with a tired swallow, 'Fuck, the tuk-tuk drivers were right.'

Settling into my stay on Flores Island I feel a composite of my backpacking self *(which I'm desperate to resurrect from my last overseas odyssey)* stymie in the gringo environment. The hostel atmosphere bolsters my eagerness to get off the guidebook trail and independently hike over 120 kilometres to El Mirador and back. I would be lying if I did not admit I obtained a perverse degree of pleasure doing that which was challenging — and to which others reluctantly refused and therefore admonished as foolhardy, or impossible. But my primary motivation for independent adventures is the deep sense of solitary satisfaction I derive from the experience. I had already tried to explain to a few backpackers in Valladolid and Tulum, and did so again in Flores. And the fatalistic response of 'it can't be done' swiftly transplants me back into my resolute travelling boots.

I had already challenged the backpacking establishment and their conventional methods of travel many times. And I was used to the scepticism of other travellers when hearing about something they hadn't done, or wanted to do but had convinced themselves against. However, in Flores preparing to hike to El Mirador, I acknowledged in spite of my confidence and experience the fundamental consideration of having to carry my entire water supply for four or more days made me contemplate company. Based on tour group itineraries it was a four to five day round trip through dense lowland jungle, which in the height of the dry season was without a solitary natural or replenishable water source. One or two other people brought safety, comfort and confidence sharing the load of supplies. It also enriched the experience through camaraderie and shared moments — and when considering the added peril of getting utterly lost in an immense basin of jungle akin to an ocean, *(which is rumoured to also contain murderous drug traffickers and pothunters)* forming an intrepid party of inquisitors made sense.

So in Flores I ask around the hostel for other backpackers considering the hike to El Mirador. Eyes indolently roll back into matted heads. Perhaps they've got more pertinent issues — calculating whether it's worth braving the torpid heat to saunter up to the taco stand by the mirador at the top of the hill, or pay five times more at Los Amigos for the vegetarian lasagne. They could also be debating when they should order their first drink, deliberating over mojito versus daiquiri *(and if it was to be a daiquiri, strawberry or mango?)* Typical answers delivered:

- *'I was thinking about it but couldn't find enough people to make the tour cheap enough so I just went to Tikal instead.'*
- *'I just met a couple of guys who came back from the tour and said it wasn't all that so I'm gonna go to Tikal instead.'*
- *'Are you crazy?'*

Listless bemusement, rather than reproach from backpackers lounging like iguanas about the hostel's garden restaurant bar wasn't an unwelcome change. I turn to the internet and scour it like a hacker in the movies. To my surprise the condemnation absent from the hostel crowd was certainly compensated for on backpacker forums. Responses to queries about independent treks to El Mirador on LP's Thorntree listed a portent of dangers, which steadily grew more and more ludicrous:

- *'The Petén area is full of clandestine air strips that the drug cartels use for landing their small planes from Colombia. Illegal logging is another activity where forest rangers have been killed by the people that cut fine woods for export. And not to mention archaeological sites predators.' Delmonte 27/02/2011*
- *'There are lots of places to trek in Guatemala that can be done more sensibly without a guide and aren't incredibly hot, malarious and home to rabid foxes.' Hopefullist 10/02/2011*
- *'Chuck in crocs, narcotraficantes and loggers and tomb robbers armed to the teeth as well!' Stewpot 10/02/2011*
- *I'm sure you don't want to take a chance paying a much higher price with your own lives...' Delmonte 27/02/2011*

Needless to say I got the point. My research did reveal more pertinent and obvious perils of getting lost on the multitude of unmarked trails, along with the primary concern of water *(which could debatably be purchased from guards along the way)*. Further cyberspace investigation produced some useful directions and information. It was also suggested that threats and fear over an independent undertaking was mostly hearsay fuelled by locals protecting their trade. This made sense. It was a common ploy I'd encountered countless times in poor rural areas whetted by a moderate influx of tourist dollars. I'd been duped a number of times from a range of tactics designed to muster tourists onto fare paying packages — from enterprising bluster aimed to bamboozle tourists all the way to underhanded manoeuvring with local enforcement prohibiting independent endeavours. Usually, it took to the stage as some bogus new law preventing travellers hiking without a guide after an unnamed backpacker got lost and died, or a fallacious fee introduced to protect the environment for the ecological footprint caused by increased tourism. I didn't blame them. But I didn't support it. For the most part it's because I trekked to be alone. The suggestion that concern over tourist safety was the work of rumourmongers only stiffened my resolve to gather supplies and depart in two day's time.

As is often the way with solo expeditions, the first and most frustrating obstacle is always the fundamental task of getting there. Warnings on internet forums and blogs about the difficulty in finding the departure point for the mythical bus to Carmelita, the gateway town three to four hours north of Flores proved correct.

To see each destination possessing its own individual personality, one only has to reflect on the infinite and subtle variances exhibited by every city's unique and utterly baffling transport network. Radiant frustrations materialise trying to decipher the ticketing system; decrypt the arterial schematics on brightly painted placards; orientate yourself with multiple terminals and commuter hubs; memorise the clandestine stops marked by a random street sign or shop front; and finally decide whether to validate now or at the end of the journey.

In Flores, the principal dilemma was confirming where the service to Carmelita left from. Did it depart from Santa Elena's southern Terminal Nuevo de Autobus where I arrived, or the chaotic market terminal which was devoted to more regional destinations? Additionally, there was the less likely option of one of numerous unspecified patches of kerbsides in the city where I noticed transport routinely stopped. The *mercado* transport hub was conspicuously omitted by the *LP*. However, calling it a terminal spuriously labels what was essentially a pandemonic slab of asphalt in the centre of the market. Its location was much closer and more convenient than the main terminal. To add to the confusion, departures from the main terminal often made a second stop at the *mercado* anyway.

I noticed this the following day as I bought food supplies in Santa Elena. The market district corralled chicken buses along a slow, painful incommodious route to its centre followed by a long, elaborate sequence of manoeuvres to park up while vendors and stalls shuffled around the movement like flies. Passengers who already boarded at the main terminal then had to endure a lengthy pause for loud, incomprehensible badinage with portraits of families carrying households of luggage. Operators were only satisfied enough to leave when a bus was brimful with people and chattels. And only then did transport depart by winding a tortuous path out the other side of the market. I asked around the turbulent *mercado* so I could leave the hostel the next the morning confident I was heading to the right place.

'¿Dónde está autobús para Camelita aquí?

The stupefied looks were probably a reaction to my Spanish rather than the existence of public transport to Camelita. But everyone seemed so confounded by my inquiry a less intrepid person would doubt whether Carmelita even existed. Upon reaching an impasse a few of the more exuberant and urgent drivers must have concluded I was at least heading their way and tried to bully me onto their crowded vehicle. Staff at Los Amigos deigned a look of confusion too. But I suspected their lazy shrugs were an extortive practice to capitalise on the commission of selling tours out of the hostel. What was certain by way of consistency from my research was a bus departed daily at 5 am and 1 pm. The suggestion to take the afternoon service, spend the night in Carmelita and get an early start the following day was sound advice. But from experience I felt confident a predawn departure and midmorning arrival in Carmelita would not greatly affect the approximate 25 kilometres first day trek to El Tintal. I also concluded given so many regional services left from the *mercado*, it offered the highest degree of success catching a ride to

Carmelita. So I was determined to wake the following morning at four, store my surplus gear in a locker and walk to the terminal for the morning service.

Marching through the quiet chill of predawn there's an unsettling stillness and desolation compared with the daytime bedlam of Santa Elena. By the time I approach the deserted south entrance to the markets I'm already consigned to failure. It's ten minutes to five and I still haven't spotted another soul, not even a dog. I instinctively know I'm wrong about the market. Time's running out. I draw on instinct. I abandoned the mission to the market without really knowing what to do next.

A lone taxi driving past halts. After an urgent broken conversation in Spanish he assures me the Carmelita service does leave at 5 am but from the main northern terminal. To find the first and only local Guatemalan who recognises the pueblo Carmelita, as well as the existence of a chicken bus at 4.55 am on empty streets tempers disbelief. I'm half sure he's lying simply to get a fare. But fate is a vixen, a siren, a star and a trickster. I have no recourse so I get in — and of course it's when I'm at my most desperate and wary *(from a history of touts, beggars, thieves and iniquitous company)* that I taste the rich bitter compunction of an honest cab driver. He spins around and heads back to the main street. He rockets up the same road that took me an hour to walk in less than four minutes. He recklessly steers the taxi through open departure gates and into a dark vacant terminal. He pulls up in the far corner beside a bus. A splattering of sleepy-eyed locals wait patiently while a man and boy strap produce down onto the roof.

'Carmelita?'

'Si.'

'¿A qué hora sale?'

'Ahora – vamos!'

Many destinations that deviate off the Pan American in Central America share a common theme: distances are relatively small, roads are appalling and travel time is agonisingly long. The pleasant consequence is if you are lucky enough to see out a window that isn't encrusted in dust and grime, or obstructed by general crap, time is at your disposal to imbibe the pristine surrounding. The bus ride to Carmelita gave me time to consider my primary concern — and it wasn't whether I felt like breakfast, where to go to next, what inappropriate hour would beer o'clock strike today, or mull over the inflated price of a packaged tour. It was as basic and fundamental as it gets — water!

Hiking solo, as I was inclined to do — to rely on myself and the supplies I carried is for me one of the most gratifying endeavours of travel. The art of walking between places also amplifies the spiritual shift brought about by travel. In Zen praxis *zazen* mediation also incorporates *kinhin,* a controlled method of walking and breathing to sustain a meditative state by reviving tired legs and avoiding sleepiness. It is pivotal in strengthening one's *samadhi* to bring about higher consciousness through non-dualistic awareness. Dōgen, the thirteenth century Zen master and founder of the Sōtō school of Zen Buddhism in Japan was one of the greatest advocates of *zazen*. He believed its method laid the foundation towards enlightenment, and if properly experienced could constitute enlightenment itself.

For me, trekking embraces the essence of this practice. It's not unlike the hypnotic rhythm which resonates through all modes of transport between places — whether it is by foot, horseback, highway, railway, sea or sky. In this time and space between destinations I find the quiet reverie of movement gives way to a state of deeper contemplation — using form to perceive formlessness. But all the jouncing over ungraded track now agitates me. And the tantalising apprehension of the hike swells with the rising heat the day. From experience I'm confident of my outdoor abilities and self-sufficiency in the wild. But it's only when preparing for the trip that I realised I always trekked by a water source — whether it was hiking up a glacial torrent, crossing a lowland delta or following a river's downstream flow. The reason was simple — why wouldn't I?

A natural water source on any flurry into the wilds is life affirming. The soughing flow of a mountain river to me is more than just a tranquil soundtrack to a rigorous uphill hike. It's the kitchen sink, fridge, bathtub and night-time lullaby of the outdoors, which makes a trek infinitely more enjoyable. Pitching a tent by a gurgling stream, dipping my pot in the flow to put pasta on the boil for dinner, and chilling a longneck under the anchor of a rock in the gelid water is a prize I'd thank the many gods for. Don't get me wrong, water is always a constant consideration. But it was always a mild concern involving the weight of discomfort — calculating how much to replenish each time you encountered a river or circumvented an alpine lake that would carry you to the next convergence.

I had never seriously deliberated my daily water consumption before now. From my internet research I noted it was possible to procure or buy water at El Tintal, the halfway point and again at El Mirador. But critics retorted, 'What happens if you can't?' Tantamount to independent travel is self-reliance so I bet on nothing and resolved to carry my entire water supply for a round trip of over 120 kilometres — but was it enough? In Flores I settled on a daily ration of two litres, which I based on vague recollections that each time I bought a 1.5 litre water bottle it tended to last approximately a day. So I increased the quota by a half-litre to compensate for heat and exertion. I also factored in the five-day tour itinerary promoted by the hostel and every tour agency in Flores was in reality three to four days of trekking. This is because despite elaborate itineraries full of fanciful descriptions, the first and last day of any tour sold anywhere in the world is devoted to the laborious task of picking up all the participants at various hostels and hotels scattered around town and transporting them to the starting point of the tour, then completing this process in reverse at the end of the tour. So I adjusted the last day's allotment of water to one litre. I also rationalised if I imitated the tour itinerary and spent an entire day and night leisurely exploring the El Mirador site I may not consume my daily two litre limit, which gave me a half-litre leeway. Again, the same question keeps soldiering through my head as we encroach deeper into verdant oblivion — is it enough?

We stop at a crested gas station for petrol and breakfast. I buy a Coke and another half-litre of water to subdue the growing conviction my water bladder and five 1.5 litre water bottles are woefully inadequate. When we resume I fall in rhythm with the tired whine of the bus and sticky crunch of gears. It's hard not to put the nine litres of water in my pack and half-litre for the ride on fragile scales balancing life and death. I quell my doubts by listening to the grind of the engine as it fights its way up steep ravines of dense jungle. Winding down the other side it purrs relief then rollicks across umbered streams to dump its momentum at the heel of the next uphill climb. I remind myself that the trail to El Mirador is ostensibly a mule track. In the heart of the dry season it would be impossible to lose, especially with an established trail of mule shit. And even if I did get lost or ran out of water it was a one-way route, not a loop *(which was my preference)*. This meant I could more accurately judge and control my water intake and at the first sign of trouble I could simply turn around and head back. The trick and ultimate danger *(as always)* is realising this as it happens — being too brave, stupid or optimistic to see when shit's going south is often the basis for fatal fuckups.

Restlessness finds harbour as I contemplate the other major difficulty reported on internet forums discussing independent treks to El Mirador — finding the trailhead. I had been there so many times before. Ascertaining unmarked trailheads is a crux of independent hiking so obvious, it's easily overlooked when planning a trek. Unless you're a local with intimate knowledge of an area, even the most detailed directions and intricate map can still have you staring blankly at an undisturbed section of undergrowth like it's the sea yonder — with an annoying pointy voice in your head saying, 'Can't you see it? The trail's right there!'

The crowded bus eventually starts to lighten as we approach Carmelita. It's later than I hoped or expected we would arrive. The heat of the day has already stolen comfort. As it escalates and expands in the air with an insurgent tropical density, a bristled sense of urgency takes over. I'm anxious to arrive. I need to find the trailhead before the true perihelial heat of the day besets the jungle and hampers my plan — to embark on the most audacious trek of my life.

# Chapter 8

# Waterlust

The bus coasts into the dry expanse of Carmelita. The indelible sensation I've arrived at an immovable frontier rises up to welcome me. The feeling alone is worth the ride and once again consolidates the surety of being exactly where I wanted to be — at the end of the road. Like in Murghab, Lhasa, Tosontsengel and before that in Tariat, Uyuni, Tupiza, Coca, all the way back to passing through Meekathara and Wiluna on road trips as a kid, the trepidation of launching myself into the unknown is arresting. It's what repeatedly draws backpackers down a gangway. Having quit jobs and farewelled friends, we glow in newfound sovereignty as we inch towards an aircraft that's taking us to place we've never been. This is why I've always been drawn to the end of the road — the palpable mix of apprehension and awe which aligns like a cosmic event.

Unlike the visible sufferance that commonly inflicts remote townships, Carmelita appears sedate and humble in light of its obscure isolation. Small packs of dogs trot mindfully between the organised sprawl of wooden huts. Kids knock about with a ball in the dust or play some other recycled game that doesn't require batteries or something out of a box. Occasionally adults idly drift by on rickety bicycles.

I spot the soccer pitch on the left side of the window as we pass through the fringe of the town. It marks the trail to El Mirador and gives me confidence. But when I alight and quickly organise my pack and water bottles and swing my rucksack onto my back, its weight seems to have doubled in the heat. I already feel tired. This isn't helped by the indolent sense of accomplishment of getting here, which was the major hurdle to the hike I haven't even commenced yet.

A couple of young boys approach.

'¿Guía, guía?'

'No, solo,' I reply to blank faces broken by quizzical stares.

'¿Mula?'

'No gracias-'

'¿Guía?'

'No, yo solo. Gracias,' I reiterate with walking fingers to show my insistence on hiking alone.

I'm in a rush, not just because it already feels like the furnace of midday is upon me. I was trying to evade any connivance of deception and fraud which gathers around gringos in forsaken gateways.

'El Mirador?' I inquire. The driver and a couple of indifferent locals point in the direction of the soccer pitch. Although the location of the trailhead was never clarified from my internet research, it's infinitely more reassuring and helpful to see a big blue sign as I approach the soccer pitch which read:

Ruta Turistica

Carmelita – EL Mirador

Sendero

I turn north and head into the unknown, mindful an additional sharp turn onto the trail is reputedly not far away and easy to miss. In the near distance I see two backpackers appear out of the jungle. I take sight of the travellers as another positive omen. And a headful of discouraging internet posts disperse to lighten my load — also because it is soon revealed the backpackers have exited right by another big fuck off blue sign to mark the trail:

BIENVENIDOS
Ruta Turistica
Carmelita – EL Mirador

Replete in exhaustion and soaked in sweat, the hikers do not seem to care or notice I'm alone. They are accompanied by a complacent guide, knackered mule, and breathlessly inform how the day's trek to El Tintal is relatively easy — indicating the gnarled and unserviced 4WD track we are on continued almost all the way to the camp. This is a phenomenon of solo travel I have always valued — putting faith in the arms of serendipity, and allowing them to open wide to welcome chance encounters and impromptu invitations.

My initial optimism quickly withers as the sun assaults the sky and soars to its baleful apex. From experience and stubbornness I always pushed myself hard on the first day of a hike — to break my body and mind into the rigours of the endeavour. I religiously walked the first two hours of the day nonstop. After that I took short incremental stops on the hour, and only took a substantial break for lunch or triumphant reward after an accomplishment like summiting a peak or traversing a high pass. The first time I look at my travel clock after leaving Carmelita I'm exhausted, burning with thirst and have to stop. Only 45 minutes have passed. The two backpackers I encountered earlier remarked this initial stretch of the hike was particularly demanding because the 4WD track was too wide to provide any real shade cover.

I have always despised treks that were effectively off-road trails. Now I despised 4WD tracks imitating hiking trails even more. I hiked to immure myself in nature — to amble along intimate narrow trails through thick wooded forests, sumptuous glades, bulbous pastured valleys sculpted by prehistoric glaciers, and to ascend serrated mountain tops of captivating panoramas. As I drop my pack and collapse onto a nearby tree stump it feels like the dense dry jungle is deliberately guarding the conciliatory wind from me.

When the breeze is too feeble to stay above the tree tops it descends down across the dry track and licks my face. The sweet relief is glorious, but all too brief and intermittent to ameliorate my condition. I suck on the snorkel of my water bladder with impunity. I try to curb my intake. But thinking about only serves to tease my thirst along. The further I trudge onward an increased sense of entrapment and alarm grows, as if I'm being sucked into a carnivorous and infinite wrack of green, which is slowly drawing the life out me.

I clock watch obsessively — five minutes feels like fifteen minutes and fifteen minutes feels like an hour. Half an hour elapses before I have to stop again. I realise the rules in the jungle of northern Guatemala are different and despite my comprehensive experience I have to adapt if I am going to accomplish the most fundamental objective of survival, let alone the moderate achievement of completing the hike to El Mirador and return safely to Carmelita. As I fight to find a rhythm, out of forethought I jot down prominent landmarks in a notepad and their approximate distance from Carmelita.

I find solace in the tangible display of my experience and sureness in the path ahead. After all I was walking along a big-ass 4WD track. I recall how many sceptics on travel forums warned independent hopefuls that the intricate network of unmarked trails increased the likelihood of getting fatally lost. It's clear to me the braided tracks are a signature of mules and goats and other ungulates and the remnant tracks will eventually converge at some point. It restores me somewhat to recognise the unique set of skills I'd accumulated from a multitude of past treks — expertise I took for granted in everyday life but had been tried and tested and assimilated over time so that they were now instinctive. They were part of me. And I drew upon them involuntarily like walking and breathing.

In contrast it's funny how things seem so logical and minor until you care to think of them. Then such presumptions become so blatantly obvious and flawed the absurdity drowns you. This feeling besieges me approximately 16 kilometres from Carmelita when, for the first time I consider what is El Tintal. I have absolutely no idea what I'm rambling head over foot towards for the first night camp. The thought surfaces as I blindly stumble into a rather modest yet desolate clearing. It contains a thatched structure, possibly to pen poultry, or other farm animals, and a small, sturdy bivouac roofed with sheets of industrial black plastic. Was this El Tintal?

By now I had been walking solidly for four hours. If I maintained an average walking pace I was still approximately 10 kilometres from El Tintal, which would take an additional two to three hours. But I was also mindful the posted mileage of treks could be less than precise. Sometimes they were an estimate at best. And the suggested timings were highly subjective — guidelines to accommodate the most unfit and infirm tourist. The derelict camp and its crude conditions certainly didn't correlate with elite groups of backpackers shelling out in excess of $160 per person for a tour. Of course in hindsight I realise it would have been much more fucking prudent to find out precisely what El Tintal was before embarking on the hike to El Mirador. And it's stupefying to consider my feeble conclusion was based on the shared determiner *el* and I had simply decided El Tintal must be some diminutive archaeological site to the hike's namesake El Mirador.

For the first time I feel utterly lost. But I'm also way beyond caring — my demand for water is viral. I can't stop myself from consuming the vital supply, or calm my galumphing heart. It does little to appease my thick, sick white tongue, or curb the pustular spittle forming at the corners of my mouth. I drop my pack and spread my ground sheet. I roll impotently onto my back and rip off my shoes and socks to a flutter of sweet relief.

I then peel off my top and cargo pants and collapse in the cool shade. With nothing but $H_2O$ on my mind I feel my wealth of skin continue to seep salty pools of water. They gather in the minute ravines of the ground sheet as I desperately will myself into a restorative peaceful state of rest. And yes — I do suck up the salty pools of my own sweat because Bear Grylls's voice in my head won't shut up about it.

From internet research El Tintal was considered the second notable spot on the trek for losing the trail and getting lost. Before falling into a light siesta I notice a prominent fork in the trail ahead. I see it leads to a set of wooden stairs which traverses a rocky buttress to the left of the camp. From information I had read I'm compelled to continue straight on the modest trail that seems to disappear into the jungle palisade at the far edge of the camp. But *straight* in the middle of the jungle is as flexible as a person's will and their words — and can bend from literal to figurative like semiotic saplings. With my eyes still closed I recall Robert Frost's immortal poem *The Road Not Taken*, and the famous final lines:

> *Two roads diverged in a wood, and I,*
> *I took the one less travelled by,*
> *And that has made all the difference.*

No shit Bob, I thought. But in the jungles of northern Guatemala one should never *ever* take the less travelled path. As a result I struggle to reconcile why anyone would fashion steps into a jungle hillock in one of the remotest parts of Guatemala near the Mexican border if it wasn't in aid of the *primero* tourist attraction?

Lying in a sweaty stencil with the thinnest breath of wind brushing over me, my sudden quandary of which way to go ferments into a fizzy bottle of half-waking nightmares. At this exact moment destiny called Carlos barrels through the centre of the clearing on a *bicicleta*. Shocked by my presence he lets out an audible yelp before braking hard and turning to greet me. He confirms I need to continue straight through the camp, saying I should arrive at El Tintal after approximately 20 minutes. With flamboyant gestures Carlos explains he is riding back to Carmelita but his amigo is still stationed at El Tintal.

My obstinance holds firm. But every step carrying me further into the dense jungle reactor of sodden heat weakens my legs, slows my pace, sinks my pack's strap deeper into my shoulders, cuts into my hips and corrupts my will. My extended rest does nothing to succour my chronic thirst. And every guilty sip seems to trickle ineffectively, helplessly through me as I'm forced to stop and piddle it out at regular intervals. I replenished my water bladder with one bottle of water after Carlos left, and by sight and touch I know it's already been drained a substantial amount. I'm too fatigued to calculate precisely but by day's end I know this will put me well in excess of my estimated daily quota. Instinctively I know I've fucked up and not correctly accounted for my consumption against the exertion and perspiration in the voracious climate. Goading me along is my despair over not knowing if I can buy water at El Tintal. The long agonising day has branded me with the harsh reality that if I can't obtain more water at El Tintal or El Mirador I'm screwed. And if I didn't get water at El Tintal would I gamble running out completely in the hope I could buy it at El Mirador?

By now I have the cursed skin of a wretched amphibian and I can't help irrigate the irrepressible fear that everything here is against me. My backpack harness presses against my back like a wet towel. My t-shirt is sodden and saline streaks mark my belly like bengal stripes from when I've wiped my brow. And my broad brimmed hat is a damp sock on my head. I imagine I have stumbled into a knight's realm. I'm on a quest through an unknown forest. Unbeknownst to lone souls like me who deign to take a shortcut the forest is bewitched. It is a living, breathing entity that divines the purity of those who pass and reacts accordingly

— to offer safety and nourishment, or impose a grizzly fate. I question whether I have damned myself for allowing vanity and competitiveness to overwhelm my naive thrill of the journey. Was I being punished for letting egocentric desires commandeer my epicentric focus? I think of Robert Pirsig's astute comparison of the *ego-climber* and *selfless climber* in *Zen and the Art of Motorcycle Maintenance*:

> 'To the untrained eye ego-climbing and selfless climbing may appear identical. Both kinds of climbers place one foot in front of the other. Both breathe in and out at the same rate. Both stop when tired. Both go forward when rested. But what a difference! The ego-climber is like an instrument that's out of adjustment ... He's here but he's not here. He rejects the here, is unhappy with it, wants to be farther up the trail but when he gets there will be just as unhappy because then it will be "here." What he's looking for and what he wants, is all around him, but he doesn't want that because it is all around him. Every step's an effort, both physically and spiritually, because he imagines his goal to be external and distant.'

I play the game of willing El Tintal into existence beyond every kink and rise in the trail which attenuates my view of the jungle to a few feet, and solidifies a claustrophobic sense of dread. I cast my mind back to laborious hikes through Peru, Pakistan, Kyrgyzstan and Tajikistan which were now gilded in a magical memory palace — traversing frigid fordable streams, springtime arroyos gushing with freshly melted ice, unstable eskers and wide black glaciers of solid ice. Scrambling up higher and higher, feeling the air thin and cool in the reservoir of my lungs with each guttural breath, I navigate a loose path through cairns and faint markers. Periodically feeling utterly lost, my spirit stays firm. I'm encased in the affirmation you can't get lost climbing a mountain when there's only one direction — UP! I pass through the lasting embrace of a lightly shaded high valley and march up the desolate permafrost of a sun-dipped mountain summit. I feel here and everywhere all at once — the burning apostasy of physically drawing myself closer to some kind of halidom reserved for the gods. Beyond cultural and generational shifts I ponder whether there is something knitted to the nature of all artful travellers like Kerouac. Are we all built to intrinsically carry the illusion of a wayward disciple, a masterless warrior-poet, a qalandering dilettante or scrapbook prophet:

> '... and I believed that I as an oldtime bhikku in modern clothes wandering the world ... in order to turn the wheel of the True Meaning, or Dharma, and gain merit for myself as a future Buddha (Awakener) and as a future Hero in Paradise.'

Why do we even climb mountains? Why do you climb a mountain? Why does anyone want to climb a mountain I wonder? To have cause is counterintuitive to the *Zenness* of stuff, right? But in order to travel further than what is considered possible, don't we need an added incentive, a sense of conquest? Heck, some people even manage to turn travelling, the most aimless and sedate pursuit of them all into a competition — the 196 Club. Maybe that's why travellers are so fond of climbing mountains wherever they travel — so they can defeat every formidable peak in their path. I'm always wary of people who keep count of the number of countries they've visited — like people who claim ridiculous things like they hate the Beatles, don't do goodbyes, or never judge other people. My own private ontological debate overlooks the midday heat, which is reined in by a rejuvenating breeze.

Well after I stop playing games in my head I suddenly emerge from the jungle. As I hulk into the bucolic encampment Carlos's amigo Rojilio comes to greet me. El Tintal is a large clearing with a sizeable hearth and outdoor *cucina* sheltered by a flat timber roof. There is also a prominent water tower behind the *cucina* and a number of rustic benches scattered around which evidently service a large number of tour groups and archaeologists.

Rojilio escorts me to the far side of the camp. He points to a large concrete foundation under a corrugated tin roof, which I gather is where I'm supposed to pitch my tent. I explain to Rojilio I'd just seen his compadre Carlos on his way to Carmelita. Rojilio acknowledges this by simulating being on bike.

'Si, bicicleta.'

'¿A que hora llegar?' I reply, curious to know how long it took the locals to wistfully travel between the Carmileta and El Tintal on two wheels in the gloaming darkness.

Rojilio shrugs.

'Siete u ocho, más o menos,' he says while wavering a flat hand to accent the estimate of Carlo's return.

'¿Del a noche?'

'Si, si, esta noche.'

I was astounded to hear Carlos would complete the return trip, including errands and carrying whatever provisions prompted the trip on two wheels in less time than it took me to hike one way. With a broad ingratiating sweep of his hand Rojilio beseeches me to sit at one of the wooden benches for dinner. I take my cue and tear my empty 1.5 litre water bottle from the side mesh pocket of my rucksack.

'¿Posible aqua?'

Is it my rueful disposition, or did Rojilio's expression just ripple with disapproval? He complies however and returns with the bottle one-third full of chalky water. I don't care that it's blatantly less than full — half a litre put me back in the hunt to make it to El Mirador. Assuming I would not source any more water on the trip I calculate another half-litre would see me through the evening, and if I had in fact consumed close to three litres on the day's hike from Carmelita and continued to do so, my remaining six litres would at least get me back here in two days. Given the lightness of my pack at this stage, no matter what degenerative state of thirst I suffered I would always be able to drag myself back to Carmelita.

I examine the dubious tincture of the water.

'¿Esta okay?'

'Si, si, no problema.'

'¿Necessito purification?'

'No, no, lluvia,' Rojilio replies, pointing to the clear sky to clarify the water source.

I go check out at an old wooden tourist placard erected in the middle of the camp. Although I can't read the notice, an illustrative map shows the archaeological sites of El Tintal and the surrounding region. A flicker of satisfaction that I was right about El Tintal is gazumped by the realisation I've been trekking through an immense ruin since Carmelita. The entire jungle basin is a collection of connecting Mayan ruins like an ancient state, to which El Mirador is its showpiece.

While there's resolve left in my legs I take my leave to pitch my tent, and again collapse in a recuperative state. It seems somewhat redundant to trudge all this way into the jungle and sleep on concrete but I was way beyond tired to give a shit. When I wake the sky has darkened and the surrounding jungle is monochrome with infant shades of grey. My sleep had been restless and shallow, filled with my consternation over water. I feel a need to be hospitable and join Rojilio for dinner but my body and mind are spent and I can't bear another session of awkward, strained conversation filled with misunderstandings, repetition and confusion.

I made dinner where I sat in the portal of my tent. I try to take my mind off things and savour the cool change to the jungle at night. Mindful of the fundamental issue of water, I disregarded the basic consumables favoured by hikers on multiday treks like rice, pasta, oats and other slow release energy meals that required water for cooking. In fact I opted for a meagre diet of sandwiches to shift greater allowance to carrying drinking water. The added advantage of bringing uncooked food was I lost the weight and space usually allocated to my pots, stove and gas supply.

For sandwiches I carried four tins of tuna in spring water, three tins of sardines in salsa picante, processed cheese slices, two tomatoes, a cucumber and large nozzle sachets of mayonnaise and habanero salsa. From past experience I knew this was ample. And part of the reward I derived from strenuous, multiday treks was the purgative qualities, both physical and mental. So I never felt obligated to balance exertion against equivalent replenishment. I also found it highly satisfying on the occasions I embarked on these expeditions to test my body and my grit — feel my muscles clawing deep into my body and expending the organic stores that had grown corpulent and lax from recumbent living.

Preparing dinner, I rub my brow and feel the mineral crust of dry sweat. I peel open a can of tuna and once more I hear Bear Grylls in my head telling me to drink the salty water — and again that's precisely what I do. No matter how little a mouthful of salty spring water replenished my electrolytes, the sense of improvising and adapting feels good. I knew now that hiking in the heat of the day as I had done was a big a mistake. It dramatically increased my water consumption and threw my endothermic equilibrium into turmoil. I resolved to do what I knew locals did to make easier their daily routine of chores. I would wake up in the crisp gloaming and cover the majority of the six to eight hour hike to El Mirador before the heat of the day took hold.

Once again sleep only harbours my worries and does nothing to quell my insatiable thirst. Keeping still, wrestling with sleep I sense the gumminess in my mouth build. I let it grow unbearable, and despite vowing each time it will be the last drink of the night, I lean up, fumble around for the snorkel to my water bladder. I silently condemn my actions. It rectifies nothing — moisture after each sip is stolen away as if I was still out hiking in the daytime. I can feel water sloshing around in my bloated stomach like a ripe water barrel when I turn in sleep. It aids my discomfort and short fits of slumber which harbingers a formless sense of doom. Had I broken some internal thermostat on the gruelling day's hike? I have already drunk the half-litre from Rojilo. I'm now guzzling tomorrow's quota of water — and yet the thirst returns like an unslakeable demon and quickens the more I fret.

It's not hard to pull my tired bones up at 4 am. I heard Carlos return on his *bicicleta* in the night with a staccato announcement from his bicycle's tin bell. I channel my residual aggravation from the poor night's sleep into packing. I can now make out both men are awake and busying themselves around the hearth. I sling my pack onto my back, find the narrow trail puncturing the trees and vines at the far edge of the camp and quietly continue on my way.

In stark contrast to the previous day, I walk through the quiet chill of predawn, along a thin penetrating trail, immersed in the sonorous sounds of a jungle slowly awakening. Blighted by the dense foliage I see a train of spider monkeys crash through the canopy overhead, and raucously announce my incursion. The reinstated feeling of being exactly where I want to be is invigorating. My pack already feels lighter, and my legs are firm. The added reward of hiking at this hour is the crepuscular activity and opportunities for wildlife spotting that vanish with the daylight and heat — like it's all an illusion orchestrated by the sun.

My footsteps fall into a meditative rhythm with my breathing. I feel the dukkha of my tribulations fall away as each moment transports me to the next. Startled by my presence I see colourful turkey birds violently launch themselves from night-time roosts to make soft, clumsy landings in the dense undergrowth. The leader of another monkey tribe pauses in the sortie of his group's undulating carriage through the canopy. Spread starfish in silhouette between parallel vines he furiously shakes the branches above me in a menacing display of disapproval at my presence. I feel alive. Connected. With the jungle now working with me, acting as my umbrella and shielding me from the heat, the hike to El Mirador is much more pleasant than yesterday despite it being almost 15 kilometres longer.

Five hours later and the portent heat creeps in through the dry undergrowth to blister my conviction. My waterlust returns with its surfeit craving for quenchable relief. It's now past 10 am with a transient warm breeze. I decide if I can't source more water at El Mirador I will have to about turn and return without exploring or enjoying the magical beauty of the site. As I prepare myself mentally for this eventuality I realise time, which to backpackers is a ruthless quotient of savings versus expenditure *(determining the length of most overseas trips)* has no reference here. Exposing myself to the elements, drowning in the fury of green infinitude has revived the most fundamental measure of time and that of life — water!

I'm Mungo Man, Java Man, Nutcracker Boy and Ramapithecus as I stumble and heave through evolutions — surpassing the materialistic reality underpinning backpackers' more benign motivations. Six and a half hours later I reach a sign *(like the one at El Tintal)* announcing my arrival at El Mirador. The sense of accomplishment is profound as I take a break to examine the map and recall all the research, preparation and discouragement that got me here. Yet the relief and wonder at seeing the sheer magnitude of El Mirador quickly dissipates as there is an additional half-kilometre walk to the main camp. My thirst drives me blithely past hillocks and humps, blind to the fact the landscape blankets an ancient city. It's all a shallow graveyard of ancient structures, erected by hands like mine that has since been camouflaged, reclaimed, erased by the jungle.

I finally reach the edge of a rich wooded hillside that looks down onto a large dry clearing. I assume it's the main campground, or military runway, or both. I spot a semi-permanent security cabin with a chimney gently smoking on the nearside of a dusty expanse. I know the cabin or security won't go anywhere, and the outcome to obtaining water is already set, I just didn't know the answer yet. So like the previous day I collapse on my ground sheet to calm my excessive perspiration.

An hour later I head to the security cabin. A guard appears shuffling languidly in and out of the open hut preparing lunch on a large outdoor bench. He seems mildly curious to the point of indifference by my appearance. It makes me wonder what part of the heat or regularity of independent backpackers is dictating his temperament.

'¿Posible aqua?' I ask holding my depleted water bladder.

He throws a lazy gesture towards the cabin. The triumphant 'YESSsss' in my head felt loud enough to be audible. The hut is effectively a structure for storing water. White industrial buckets of rain water with goon pourers are stacked two deep on shelves which line the slanted walls. The only other allowance of space is given to a wooden table top and portable stove near the entrance. I fill my bladder to its turgid limit, gulp down three mouthfuls and replenish the amount before leaving. When I exit three more guards are present — two are slumped on chairs in the shade of a makeshift awning bolted to the cabin, while a third guard works on a skein of nylon attached to one of the joints. Out of a sense of gratitude I remain in the naked midday heat and chat with the guards.

'¿Qué llamas?'

'Daveeed.'

'¿Qué pais?'

'Oustraulia.'

Solemn nods follow.

'¿A que hora Oustraulia?' asks one of the guards with a flat hand zooming through the air. Flight time between the continents was a popular inquiry throughout Central America. I guess flight time gives a tangible sense of global distance.

'Ah, sí claro – eh, no lo sé,' I fumble to say with heavy gesticulations. 'Emm, posible venti... veinticinco horas más o menos.'

'Ooow – mucha grande.'

'Si, mucha grande. ¿Qué esta?' I say pointing to the man weaving nylon thread.

'Pescado.'

What irony I think — making a fishing net in the dry jungle basin of Guatemala. Maybe it's some kind of sorcery. Then I consider he might live near the coast. I heard all the personnel and supplies were helicoptered in at great expense to help protect El Petén's environment and indigenous communities. But I'm too hot and tired to give it further thought. I say goodbye and return to the respite of the shaded hillside. I make camp and wait to explore El Mirador once the sun's ferocity wanes with the afternoon. El Mirador is an immense and wondrous sight that still lies almost entirely under claim of the jungle. If you're reading this wondering 'Why haven't I heard of El Mirador?' you're not alone. It was El Mirador's infant popularity on the backpackers' stage which galvanised my infatuation with the ruins. Although discovered in 1926, a detailed investigation wasn't undertaken until 1978, and only in the last decade has major surveyance started in line with governmental stabilisation and preservation programs. From the air one would have no concept it existed, except for the small discernible bump in the flat expanse of green that is El Tigre.

Headstones and busts that have since been meticulously excavated from the tenacious vegetation are impressive. And the mesmerising panoramas inspire a climactic sense of insignificance. But the site requires a strong interest in archaeology and active imagination since so much of it still rests under Gaia's tolerant bosom. I presume this is why it had been reported people who paid for the tour dismissed it afterwards as not being "worth it". Instead they apparently championed the convenient, cheaper and incomparable magnificence of Tikal. But for me, like all true seekers of the open road the reward is always in the journey. That is why I have never been attracted to situations where I am not carrying my own gear and cooking my own food, because to do so would negate the corporeal experience that enriches and edifies an adventure.

Under a fading sky I hike up a precarious set of steps to El Tigre. Sitting atop the rocky summit I gaze out over a broccolied cyclorama of green. I imbibe the dizzying sense of disconnection that comes from confronting an illimitable void — like imagining yourself upside-down on this green-on-blue spackled planet furiously spinning through space — or floating on a barren disc of water under a firmament of night and glistening trails of salitter. I look down at the hand-cut stones under my boots. I try to comprehend the ancestral connection of where I'm standing to this unimaginable feat of human endeavour dating back two and a half millennia. I feel like rain over the ocean — without witness do I even exist? Does it make it all worth it? Undoubtedly. Well, that is at least until the serenity is shattered by whoops and hollers from a tour group presumably enjoying the sunset from nearby La Danta, technically higher than El Tigre because it's built on a rise.

I eat another dinner of sandwiches amid renewed concern over water. I consumed two more bottles of water on the hike from El Tintal. And after my late afternoon sojourn around the El Mirador site I had since drunk over half the water I extracted from the guards. Possessed once more by water, dark thoughts poisoned my sleep. I wake before dawn to revisit the El Mirador ruins. As to whether I stayed another night at the site I let rest with fate and the procurement of more water.

The ruins were well maintained with a multitude of tracks snaking around and between various sites. However, signage was woeful and I only had a rudimentary map which I printed off a tour company's website before leaving Flores. Without a guide I got lost a number of times, and by nine in the morning, with the heat infiltrating the insulated shade and undergrowth I felt done. After finding my way back to the main camp I again ask at the guard's cabin for water. Again, I sense a quiver of hesitation but I no longer care — raw and beaten, survival now compels me. This time I'm ushered into the hut carrying my pack with a flaccid water bladder and empty 1.5 litre bottle. I don't hesitate filling both to the hilt.

I return to my camp in a stew of ennui about what to do. The constant pressure over water, compounded by the physical exertion from the punishing two days to get here has formed a dry cloud of resignation. But from my past mistake I feel bound to the camp until late afternoon. I recall Camp Sunshine, a rustic clearing and unstated landmark I passed two hours prior to arriving at El Mirador. I decide to wait until 3 pm when the day starts to cool, and hike back there to camp for the night. At least I will have done something more with the day to make the next day's hike back to El Tintal easier. But by 1 pm I'm listless and bored. I imagine if I was on a tour right now, stuck in an excruciatingly slow goose-line group behind a flatulent, tick-ridden old pack mule, I would be resenting it. The thought lightens my mood. Given the short distance I choose to risk the heat so I pack and unceremoniously depart El Mirador.

I jaunt through the enervating heat savouring the renewal which comes from being on the return leg of a journey. I acknowledge with every footstep I'm drawn incrementally closer to a world of unhindered water, flowing freely via the thoughtless task of walking a few feet to a sink to turn on a faucet. I arrive at Camp Sunshine in only an hour. It's just gone 2 pm. A restored sense of internal equilibrium has allayed my unquenchable intake of water. With my body revitalised I make the rather rash decision to push for El Tintal which, given my increased rate of walking, I estimate I'll arrive nigh on nightfall.

For the next three hours I trek through the audible silence of the lowland jungle as it enjoys a peaceful siesta. Again my breathing and walking pace strike a blissful accord. The present moment is a pool of water I'm floating on which ebbs and flows on the path before me. My ego which I carried all the way to the top of El Tigre unravels in the posthumous lull following the moderate achievement. I feel it dissolve in the swell of selfless

connection and harmony with my surroundings. I don't necessarily feel lighter but more alert and no longer fatigued. I wonder
if this corrasion of self-glorification is what will save me. In the
words of Walpola Rahula from *What the Buddha Taught*:

> *'The word meditation is a very poor substitute for the origi-
> nal term bhavana ... The Buddhist term bhavana, properly
> speaking, is mental culture in the full sense of the term. It
> aims at cleansing the mind of impurities and disturbances,
> such as lustful desires, hatred, ill-will, indolence, worries and
> restlessness, sceptical doubts, and cultivating such qualities
> as concentration, awareness, intelligence, will, energy, the
> analytical faculty, confidence, joy, tranquillity, leading finally
> to the attainment of highest wisdom which sees the nature of
> things as they are and realizes the Ultimate Truth, Nirvana.'*

By 5 pm the treeline has snared the sun and extinguished
the ambient light. I keep a look out for the landmarks I previously noted on the trek to monitor and better evaluate my
return. But nothing looks familiar. As darkness falls down
from the canopy and rises up from the undergrowth to flood
the lean spaces between vegetation, uncertainty grows that I'm
not on the same path — a path which I had never doubted
hiking the other way from El Tintal to El Mirador. The onset
of night plunges the surroundings into something alien and
sinister, where everything I'd become accustomed to vanishes.
If nightfall caught me on the track I was equipped to simply
roll out my ground sheet, slap on 100% Deet and engage in
another sleepless night. But what if I had veered onto a divergent path? I start to consider if I'm forced to camp because
of the incumbent night, would I wake the next morning and
unwittingly continue in an obtuse direction back into the
endless jungle with only a half full bladder and one 1.5 litre
bottle of water left?

A sequella to all this anxiety is water ceases to be the primary cause of my consternation for the first time on the trip. A benighted period of magic passes where in the failing light the contrast of the trail appears luminous, like grey phosphorescence lancing the undergrowth. Birds and monkeys again exalt this transitional period with a brief discordant choir of squawks and nattering. But as the jungle rescinds to conspicuous stillness I'm again forced to play the game of willing El Tintal out of the blind darkness.

I keep checking my travel clock as 5.15 pm becomes 5.30 pm and 5.30 pm turns into 6.00 pm — the time I figured I'd arrive at El Tintal. I stop to fish out my Petzl headlamp. With my sight gripped on the plaited trail I desperately look for signs of recent use to appease the dread that I am on the wrong trail. I know all of us in the West decided rightly not all that long ago *(in the whole scheme of things)* that littering is bad. I too find it deplorable seeing girders of trash sully pristine nature trails. But spare a thought for solo hikers where the odd cigarette butt, blue-metal toffee wrapper, discarded soda pop bottle and splatter of mule shit are our breadcrumbs.

It feels like I haven't seen a recent sign of previous trekkers in hours. Mules aren't this constipated and people aren't that respectful and clean. I start to doubt everything — yet the thought of backtracking is a world of second guessing that's just too terrifying to consider. I contemplate stopping, putting my head down and waiting for dawn where I'm sure daylight will solve everything. Another trail merges with mine and I realise I've been on an alternate track and bypassed a prominent ravine approximately an hour out of El Tintal. Further on I spot a plastic water bottle and a short while later a cigarette butt. Sensing I'm back on a familiar path sops my worry. Suddenly I've popped out from beyond the darkened arm of the jungle and I'm marching through the far end of the camp at El Tintal.

I hear the rum-fuelled laughter of a tour group. I hear them before I see them. As I lumber onward to the central hearth, anxious to stop and settle in sweet relief, the dim-lit windows of their camp are revealed under the shelter where I last pitched my tent. Carlos greets me with jocular surprise at my nocturnal arrival, querying with gestures had I just walked back from El Mirador. Joining Carlos and Rojilio around the kitchen are three local guides who are all acquainted. With the tour group presumably retired for the night there is a festive atmosphere and they all entreat me to sit.

Carlos points to a plate of uneaten tacos and offers me dinner. I decline since I still have a meal of sandwiches. The tacos will not go to waste and it seems absurd to carry my supplies all this way and back without consuming them. However, I join them with a sense of affinity and merit from my trials. Once again I ask for water, holding out an empty 1.5 litre bottle. Carlos takes it and returns with almost a litre – double the ration of water I received from Rojilio. I wonder if high spirits and camaraderie of hosting friends has put Carlos in a generous mood. But when Carlo hands me the bottle he points to the level with a jousting finger. I don't comprehend the details but he relates a recent encounter with an independent group of backpackers where he refused their request for water. What was it about me? Perhaps it was simply because I was solo. Or maybe Carlos saw something *simpatico* in my harrowed gaze, and empathised enough to provide me with almost a litre of smoky rain water purified by wood fire.

This time I pitch my tent on the soft clay near the trailhead leading back to Carmelita. I'm too exhausted to work out whether it's disdain or despair but I can't bear to camp near the tour group. I feel an implacable divide chivvied by my incipient experience. I imagine prodigal tents screening the latest pictures of local life captured on newly christened digital SLR cameras.

Tourists armed with telephoto lenses who get up in the grill of locals has never sat well with me. I find it a grotesque display of inequality, watching them click away at colourful portraits of squalor and poverty — as if everyone is desperate to capture the same National Geographic cover shot like they need to own it — which they then justify with some patronising bullshit about how it will help bring awareness when they're back home. I often put myself in the same scenario and question my own ambient display of wealth and providence in such humble surrounds. Although I think I feel and act differently, I wonder if locals see me any differently — did they see me as backpacker anywhere close to how I viewed myself — or was I just a walking dollar sign, another gringo tourist?

In the same vein it's why I also struggle with humanitarian projects like the 40 Hour Famine, where as kids we'd suck on barley sugars for two days and two nights so we'd know what it's like to live in Somalia. Don't get me wrong, there's value in it — just like the value of fundraising, aid work, and abstinent practices which extend to popular orthodox traditions like Ramadan and Lent. But it relies on the purity of participants' intentions. And empathetic transposal is a dangerous game — like good intentions it can be the mother of all fuckups. I wonder if I'm being a bit harsh on all the tourists and travellers who feel ascetic endowment from a shoestring budget — and see the unattached lifestyle of a vagrant wanderer is somehow more connected to a rudimentary and enlightened way of life.

Backpackers often confuse a superior sense of liberty for a divine feeling of *oneness*. Passive nihilism and nonchalance become a cheap, counterfeit knockoff for a Zen sense of *nothingness*. Yoga solves everything. And aloofness adorns us like a halo to disguise a prevailing desire towards avoidance. Not that there's anything wrong with this. It's still hard for it not to come across as incredibly condescending — when essentially all backpackers are doing a lot of the time is roughing it. But so much of an overland experience is passive and mindless. It's easy to draw a loose corollary to the meditative practice of mystical traditions, and feel yourself being guided along tangible contours of destiny and fate. And despite how genuine or misled this perspective is, it's hard to knock the effort because travel, like any spiritual endeavour, promotes a fearlessness to being free, to be yourself and know yourself. If I had the energy or compulsion I would have gone over and introduced myself to the tour group. But the decision to keep to myself is made infinitely easier by the loquacious soundtrack and ribald laughter that continues to perforate the nocturnal serenity of the jungle.

I wake again at four. I'm flush once again with time. There is no rush. My jungle fever has lifted — the pressures of water and survival evaporating with my proximity to civilisation. I still have water in my bladder from the litre Carlos gave me. I also have one full bottle remaining in my pack that will easily see me back to Carmelita. The bus driver confirmed the return service to Santa Elena and Flores departed at 1pm. Unless calamity befouled me, I would arrive with hours to spare.

I start to fantasise about being back in Flores the same evening — feet up in the Los Amigos Secret Garden with a king brown of Dorado Ice. I can feel the cold bitter suds molest the back of my throat and tongue in an exaltation of respite. I know everything trivial and not so trivial I shed from this arcane glimpse of what is truly important will return — but not yet. Now that I feel at ease I want to savour the sensation, let it linger as long as possible, so in the future I can recall (*at least like a dream*) a semblance of the feeling.

As it grows light and warm once more I recognise a landmark that places me two hours out from Carmelita. And like with past experiences, I have a tendency to congratulate myself prematurely thinking, 'You fucking did it Dave – you bloody legend!' Along with this pre-congratulatory ceremony I hear Han Solo's caveat from Millennium Falcon's twin turret, 'Don't get cocky kid!' And just like with past expeditions, it perfectly foreshadows the moment when nature props back up to give me a final figurative flick of the balls.

I stop for breakfast and empty my final water bottle into my bladder. I smear some mayonnaise and habanero sauce on the last stale pieces of bread. I have nothing else because before departing I gave Carlos the last tin of tuna and sardines to thank him for his hospitality. I glance down at what looks in passing to be dirt on my right arm and elbow. I actually start thinking how jungle dirt got there since I hadn't fallen over or been messing about. As I blissfully recount the morning events, trying to find a logical answer, I see the patch of dirt lift and rearrange itself before settling again. I look closer then closer still.

It is a fucking nekton of ticks — thousands and thousands of them languidly settling themselves into some minute rivet in my skin before sinking their chompers in to start sucking blood. I panic. I get out my 100% DEET and douse them in it. This only seems to makes them drowsier and harder to brush off. They stick to my skin like grass prickles to socks. I quickly resort to my Swiss Army Knife tweezers and start picking them off my skin one by one. I discover a dissident colony has jumped ship and are merrily enjoying exile on my left forearm. I inspect all the other areas of my body. I think if I was a tick where would I want to live on Dave? I inspect the back of my knees, my groin, and through my shirt I check my armpits. I peel back my socks to examine my ankles and who the fuck knows how but an outcast party has regrouped at the bottom of my shins.

It's funny how ticks make you very fastidious about grooming. I must have sat picking ticks off me for over half an hour, careful to twist and pull so the heads don't detach and continue mechanically burrowing into my skin. I'm not even sure of the medical validity to this technique — I just vaguely recall a TV episode from my childhood, which stuck in my memory because of murderous burrowing tick heads paralysing some poor sod on some medical drama. I know the delay won't prevent me making the service back to Santa Elena — but back out on the exposed 4WD track in the oppressive midmorning heat I feel done with the jungle and I'm glad I'm almost out of it. I spend the last leg of the trek fretting over what possible incurable diseases I may have

contracted from the ticks. Did ticks transmit Japanese encephalitis? I couldn't remember. I don't even know if Guatemala has
Japanese encephalitis, and if I'm inoculated for it?

Sweating profusely, I pierce the jungle's belly and trample
clear on the final leg of the track. I plod across the dry expanse
surrounding Carmelita to a marching rhythm:

*Beer-beer-war-ter-beer* —— *Beer-beer-war-ter-beer*
—— *Beer-beer-war-ter-beer.*

As I amble towards the general store a final indignation drives
by in a spiffy 4WD belonging to some NGO. Two indigenous
locals grinning in the back seat poke their heads out the open
window, and one holding a digital SLR snaps my wretched figure.
In my head I shout out, 'Un quetzal, un quetzal,' in drollery to
local kids' claim for payment when foreigners photograph them.
I mean to say it out loud but I'm too buggered.

I sit for a couple of hours on the wooden verandah of the
general store with a tick-infested dog slumbering at my feet. As I
wait for the bus I sink two Tecate, savouring its archetypal Mexican water-beeriness. I check again for ticks and find a few strays
hiding down in my socks. I have time to evaluate and crunch
numbers. I work out I walked into the jungles of El Petén with
9.5 litres of water. Four days later, I'm back with half a litre having
consumed somewhere between 15 and 16 litres. I get on the bus
back to Santa Elena with the same acquiescent driver who took
me to Carmelita. It's a somnolent, resplendent journey — free of
all the anxieties that plagued me before embarking. Back at the
Terminal Nuevo de Autobus I gladly accept the appeal of the first
tuk-tuk driver who grabs my attention. At night, back on Flores
Island, I relax with a Dorado Ice in the hostel garden while airing
a plum-sized blister on the heel of my left foot.

I now appreciate the dulcet charivari and mellow merrymaking
at the Los Amigos, unsure whether it was a change in me or the

guests. But like my final night at El Tintal, a feeling of dislocation lingers overhearing the fuss about a lack of weed, dilemmas
regarding the next budget destination to stave off the inevitable
conclusion to a trip, and deliberations over where to earn money
to prolong the twisted dream.

I want to share my experiences. But for tonight I remain alone
savouring the seminal experience while it lasts. I was never close to
mortal peril and don't claim to have some exonerated, new vision
for life from a harrowing tale of survival. Perhaps, I do indulge
in a brief bout of self-righteousness. I ponder the moments that
map our day — and how rarely we save a single thought for the
luxury and blessing of each new day: from when we wake up and
turn on the shower, go to the toilet while waiting for the water to
heat, flush the toilet, shower, run the basin tap as we brush our
teeth, administer a handful of vitamins down our gullets with a
gulp of uncontaminated cold water, boil the kettle, get dressed,
put on an urgent load of washing, settle with a brew to read the
daily news full of celebrity gossip and sport fixtures, and finally
compose ourselves to confront another day.

It's fair to say we all appreciate shit a bit more when we're away.
We understand how crucial running water is when it's shut off
due to contamination or maintenance. Over the next 36 hours we
learn discomfort as the shit piles up *(literally)* in the communal
toilets, and we're unable to wash the grime off ourselves because
we've just returned from a hard day's hike. It's fun for a while
and provides the perfect excuse to start drinking beer when the
hostel runs out of bottle water — but then we can't even brush
our teeth. We also curse the blackouts from regular power cuts
because we've just paid quadruple the price of dormitory accommodation to afford the relief of an air-conditioned hotel room.
We praise the leftover urn of breakfast coffee and free shelf in
the hostel kitchen while waiting for a Western Union money
transfer because of stolen credit cards. Squatting on a drop toilet
we reminisce over simple creature comforts while staring down

into an adjacent shit-stained cavity. And with holy gratitude we cherish our own fortunate upbringing when encountering the bloody and tragic repercussions of human rights atrocities as a result of despotic rule and civil war. But like my 126 kilometre trek to El Mirador and back, all these prophetic moments are fleeting. They may resonate, but only briefly as our throwaway ambivalence is restored.

The irony in Zen practice is while it preaches direct experience with life itself over theological or academic processes, it also emphasises the continual need to study and practise. As Buddha himself said, 'Realisation lies in the practice.' I wonder if this is why we laud the virtues of a simple life on the open road, yet we so easily discount luxuries upholding modern standards of living once our trip ends. Our reluctance to think about anything too much is part of the human condition that gets us through the day. It holds our sanity, and keeps backpackers on a random path globetrotting the world. Sometimes I think it's because many of us fear we have a limited supply of integrity, so it's a case of preserving the amount we all have for when we need it most. Again I'm reminded of *Zen and the Art of Motorcycle Maintenance*'s sutra on mountain climbing and the selfish motivations which inhibit human endeavour:

> 'When you try to climb a mountain to prove how big you are, you almost never make it. And even if you do it's a hollow victory. In order to sustain the victory you have to prove to yourself again and again in some other way, and again and again and again, driven forever to fill a false image, haunted by the fear that the image is not true and someone will find out.'

Seeking your true Self and seeing it as something you attain, rather than a desire, is a sticky conundrum Zen Buddhism navigates by acknowledging it is part of a natural process. And through devoted practise aspirations inhibiting the practitioner's true potential will eventually transform into a pure pursuit towards enlightenment. In contrasting fashion backpackers by rite embark on a new journey with colourful congeries of desires and delusions; and while weighing you down they can trick you into thinking you're light and free. This is why personally I feel a need to evolve both in mode and manner to find reward from each new overland journey. I have to transcend the fickle pressures of chasing shadows and ghosts cast by fear and expectation — like getting to a destination before airports and others ruin it, travelling a route before it becomes popular, attaching value to that which I don't have and gamble it against all that I do have. To be still while still moving. In the words of Saint Francis de Sale in *Traité de L'amour de Dieu*:

> '... *only God has repose without movement, because he is sovereignly a pure and substantial act.*'

# CHAPTER 9

# FRIVOLITY OF DETACHMENT

The longer a journey stretches a routine of movement and sense of withdrawal settles into place. Colours, rituals, shapes and smells blunt as landscapes blur and destinations blend into each other. Travelling digresses into an idle exercise. Reasons are no longer relevant. You become a slave to movement — transferring to the next hippie haunt of lakeside, riverside, jungleside and beach-side bamboo bungalows. Sun over the yardarm rises earlier and earlier like an elastic summer and beer o'clock becomes sacrosanct.

This order of detachment nurtured by the open road is as fickle as the personalities and destinies which flirt along it. While it infects some backpackers with a blithe indifference, it invites ruminative introspection in others. And celebrating this disengagement or divorce from regular life with the freedoms of open-ended travel can invite more serious alterations with who you are, and who you want to be. I have seen countless backpackers clearly playing a role, trying out new identities — switching characters like they're showing off a new wardrobe to see how comfortably each one fits.

It's amusing to recall when I first considered travelling how I conjured such a precocious vision of sailing across the globe

— connecting, communicating, exchanging ideas, learning and expanding with every new person I met. The reality is speaking only one language which happens to be English is a beautiful demon. Most notably world wars, the worldwide web and now globalisation have blessed English speakers with one of the most widely taught and understood languages on the planet. But in most parts of the world it is spoken as a second or third language with bare comprehension outside of what's necessary to sell gim-crack to tourists. And my cultural awareness grew just as much inside hostels meeting English-speaking travellers from all other parts of the world, as it did in the outside world.

Being on the road for indefinite periods, hostels become a surrogate home. The walls change, kitchens move, rules differ, the vibe varies, dormitories and beds expand and contract, but the concept remains. Hostels are a retreat when the continually fresh, weird, wonderful and intimidating world outside gets too overwhelming. When my legs are spent and my brain is tired I take it slow on my way back to the hostel. I buy food from the markets, and a few longnecks. I sit in the kitchen and make a sandwich. If I've decided to stay a few days I may buy groceries to make salad or cook dinner because even a minimal shop usually provides a couple of days of leftovers.

In this setting of hostel common rooms and courtyards, and all the remote, quirky rest stops in between I've seen the most radiant and shiny image of travellers emerge. I've met Shamanic Warriors of the Souls, Spiritual Samurai of the Universe, God-desses of Water and Wind, Starwalkers of the Imagination, Valiant *Nefelibatas*, Defenders of Misadventure and the X-treme, Disci-ples of Cosmological Vibration and Intergalactic Peacekeepers. Whether these characters were truly on the way to enlighten-ment I couldn't say. They all seemed somewhere in the middle and still too caught up conceptualising some grand notion of rebirth rather than engaging a sincere shift in perspective. How-ever, I enjoy these encounters for the earnest sharing of beliefs and challenging conversation, along with the panoply of multi-coloured threads that are a prerequisite for creative personalities. The most conflicted, confused and downright peculiar of these travellers tend to be backpackers who are so clearly desperate to be the apogee from whom they actually are. And in this situation the amalgamation of the two can produce the most intoxicating performances — like an amateur dance which swings wildly between a tussle and a tango.

In my experience, the more remote or untravelled destinations also yield a disproportionate ratio of chameleonic and eccentric characters. In this regard the Karakorum Highway in the Northern Areas of Pakistan doesn't disappoint. I arrived at the Madina Guesthouse in Gilgit and could hear Walker Bradley before I spotted him. The tranquil garden setting revealed him sitting among a table of taciturn Europeans carping on about some political agenda — the eristic yap of people who think they're smarter than they actually are. I was checked into the same dorm room as Walker. Later, as I'm spreading out a laundry load on my cot, Walker enters and introduces himself.

Walker talks about his travels in India which led him to cross into Pakistan and travel along the Karakorum Highway. He goes into detail about how he now has 10 days to reach Kashgar in Xinjiang, the eastern province of China bordering Central Asia. I reveal my plans to embark on a hiking expedition in a few days. My intention was to travel through Skardu in Baltistan to the Hushe Valley and trek along Humbrok Meadows to glimpse a view of K2 and the Masherbrum massif. I also wanted to make a detour on my return to Gilgit, to hike Fairy Meadows to the base camp of Nanga Parbat. All up I calculated the trip would take at least six days, barring unforeseen delays — and this was the Gilgit-Baltistan region where delays from rockslides and engine failure were commonplace. Walker spins like a turncoat and insists on joining me. It doesn't seem to bother him that if we arrive back in Gilgit on schedule he'd only have two days to get to Kashgar — something I didn't think was possible. But it's not my trip and I'm happy for the company and economy that travelling with other people provide.

Two days later we're packing on the night before departure. Walker's true journey became clearer when he complains about the formal attire he's still carrying.

'Fucking hell, can't believe I'm still carrying a dinner tie around.'

'Why are you carrying a tie?'

'When I need to wear a dinner jacket.'

'Sure... um, sorry Walker – when do you need to wear a dinner jacket?'

'When I have to go out to dinner,' Walker replied.

Walker's catechetic manner suited his patronising tone so our conversation proceeded accordingly.

'Okay... sorry Walker – when do you need a dinner jacket to go to dinner?'

'At hotels,' Walker quipped. 'My granddad took my jacket, but I forgot to give him my tie.'

It turns out for three weeks in India Walker was on a deluxe, all-inclusive tour with his grandfather. When it ended his grand-father flew home, Walker headed for the Pakistan border, and in the same day travelled nonstop to Gilgit. My impression of Walker was that he was already a weird guy. But I was impressed he wasn't dissuaded from travelling through Pakistan when his own country's uncompromising political and military stance inflamed the pro-Islamists of Pakistan and the Middle East. It was an aggressive foreign policy which the American tourist paid a price for — albeit nothing too intimidating. Just the out-of-pocket expense of a tourist visa that was triple the cost of what a citizen from a neutral country like Japan or Switzerland might pay.

After spending a day gathering supplies we broke away from Gilgit in the crisp predawn light, crammed into the back of a Suzuki. Traversing the immense awe of Baltistan (otherwise known as Little Tibet) was memorable, but not for the right reasons. It proved difficult to enjoy because I was pinned next to Walker for the duration of the punishing all-day ride — and Walker talked a lot. Walker talked and talked, and didn't seem to mind whether people listened or not. I suppose it would not have been so intolerable if, like Walker, I too was fanatical about military history — and in particular the civil war period of the United States. He had either been a Marine, or tried to be a Marine, depending on whom he talked to. And how he left the Marines was equally unclear, with adumbrative stories that alternated with each new audience. He told me he left voluntarily because one day he looked around at the corps and couldn't see a single Marine he was willing to die for. Walker didn't clarify if this was a precondition for fighting in the Marine Corps but I presume you need that! Other backpackers said Walker confessed he flunked out of the training, but whether that was basic training or something more elite was also vague.

Walker's clumsy subterfuge demonstrated how public the process of inward change can be for independent backpackers — and how swiftly *(if unchecked)* it reaches the penultimate extension of a total personality overhaul. He also exemplified why travel and personal transformations coalesce so agreeably. It's the perfect testing ground to flex your experimental self without exposing or jeopardising anything — and only requires necessary victims like the moon, mercury retrograde, dietary intolerances, a medical condition, an unfortunate childhood, and a disorder or two. And even if transplanted parts of your personality start to fail and you feel mounting rejection from those you meet, the open road is a mobile sanctuary. It's a kerbside doorway offering a traveller the basic contingency of escape; to restore and reboot anew at the next place along the way free of suspicion and judgement.

I guessed Walker was in his mid-twenties, even though he retained the infant adulthood and vernacular of a college graduate. He admitted if seriously threatened by terrorist action he would abscond to Afghanistan. He theorised retreating to a country at war was the optimal choice because the large US military presence could protect him. From all the military talk of war strategy it appeared Walker was struggling with his own personal coup d'état — to replace the person he was with the person he envisaged himself to be. And I guessed this idle strategising in some ways appeased Walker's general state of anxiety.

Skardu had as much faculty and as little aesthetic as you'd expect from a frontier trading post. It brought back memories of Mongolia and the epic circuit I hitchhiked with Maccas — dusty, single-road towns with cowboy promenades, and sleeping in fear of legless drunk Mongolians on clapped-out cots in flimsy, back-of-house establishments. We got two beds in an outhouse extension of a cheap hotel intended for layover drivers and passengers such as ourselves. At least in Skardu and Pakistan there was no threat of a crazy-drunk Mongolian staggering back in the middle of the night and tearing the place apart to find more Genghis Khan vodka.

We woke early the next day keen to get all the way to the trailhead of the Humbrok Meadows hike. But first we had to reach Khaplu, a quaint rural village of stone and timber and the last accessible town before the Hushe Valley. I assumed the sizeable international community devoted to conquering the world's highest summits *(or like me sneak a peek from afar)* would translate into regular transport in gateway areas like Baltistan. But our attempts to secure early morning transport for the uncompromising 103 kilometre winding climb alongside the Shyok River fail. I forgot to consider 9/11 had effectively killed tourism in Pakistan. I had seen evidence of this from the guest books in guesthouses I stayed at throughout the Indus Valley region. Frayed old leather-bound books filled with reams of unbroken, tabulated names, nationalities, dates and signatures virtually ceased precisely on the eleventh of September 2001.

We spend all morning kicking up dust in Skardu before the Suzuki to Khaplu is full enough to leave. By then it's so close to lunch the majority rules and everyone disperses to eat first. When we finally get away it's the early afternoon with hope of getting to Hushe Valley quickly fading. We arrive in Khaplu late in the day. Eager to keep moving we quickly gather a confusing array of reports about the apparent lack of shared transport to Hushe Village and the start of the hike. I read only 4WD vehicles could travel beyond Khaplu. But contradicting our guide books is a general consensus that there is no shared jeep service. More troubling are the gesticulations of a few locals. They shake their heads while indicating something prohibitive *(presumably a military check point)* is positioned out of sight on the road ahead. It addresses an underlying concern mentioned in the *LP*. At the time of publication it warned military police in Khaplu were preventing all foreigners from travelling to Hushe unless they were accompanied by a guide. Our only other option is to pay the extortionate hire of a private jeep which we're both reluctant to do. With another impending night waylaid because of transport we search for accommodation.

Walker fusses about the costly delays and the impact on his rigid itinerary while I begin to regret letting Walker come along. To me it seemed insane to embark on this sort of journey, only to then enforce unreasonable limitations on it. I leave Walker to go in search of food and stroll through the bucolic elegance of the town. Nestled 2600 metres up the Khaplu Valley, the township's ingenious irrigation system cultivates a fertile oasis. There is a sense of purity and freshness in the air that is mildly invigorating and the bracing wind incites my senses. I wander up the rugged track leading out of town. I see the immeasurable icy ridgeback of the Masherbrum Range peer over the far side of valley. The spectacular scenery feels both immortal and young here, as if the elements that helped shape it are still as insolent and mettlesome as they were at the dawn of time. I realise whether I make it to Humbrok Meadows and spot the lancing tip of K2 or not, being here, right here, right now had made the trip worth it.

We find a cheap dilapidated chalet to stay the night. The promise of the establishment — the prestigious features and unfinished fixtures reinforce the tragic demise of Pakistan's tourism industry. The owner is amiable enough and tells us one shared jeep sometimes leaves daily in the morning if there are enough passengers. When I ask where it departs from he gestures vaguely out the front entrance to somewhere or anywhere along the main street.

The following morning we stake out the main road while seated outside a cafe. We debate the speculation regarding the fabled communal jeep ride. Walker confesses he dreamt last night about drive-by-shootings in Khaplu's quiet backstreets. He then admits since arriving in Pakistan he has been plagued by a reoccurring dream where he is kidnapped by terrorists, only to escape and kill them all single handed. Did Walker embody the American conundrum — the abyss between personality and character? Beyond the conflicted portrayal of a laidback and brazen backpacker, I started to wonder if Walker was also deeply distressed at being an American traveller abroad and alone in an Islamist theocracy. It was obvious to me Walker was running from something. What it was I couldn't tell — most probably himself. But I think Walker was yet to realise that to find what you're looking for you first have to admit you're lost.

I get up to take another look up the main street and see two Pakistani officials riding tandem on a moped. They putter to a stop along the kerbside, dismount and waddle over to us. The officers disclose they are employees of the Intelligence Department and ask us to write down our passport numbers. This wasn't uncommon in Pakistan. There are numerous check points for security and drug trafficking concerns, as well as for the benefit of tracking tourists for their own safety when hiking alone. Hushe was also the gateway to climbing the Baltoro Glacier and Masherbrum massif, which contained seven of the planet's 25 highest peaks including K2 *(the world's second highest peak)* which required separate permits to reach the base camps and summit. By now we'd been in town almost 24 hours. Local Intelligence seems relaxed. They bait us by suggesting we're planning to hike above permit required altitudes. I laugh and drolly invite the officers to inspect the minimal gear we are carrying for the overnight trek to Humbrok. They refuse and smile as they shake their heads. We all appear to be enjoying the banter. I look across at Walker Bradley who is paler than death — struck frozen in paranoid silence at the sight of the two officials with a white-knuckled grip of the table. As I catch Walker's fear, I realise he is compromising us both by looking genuinely guilty of doing nothing.

'If they're intelligence officers, why aren't they wearing military uniforms?' Walker whispers to me.

'Jesus Walker, nobody said they were from the military. Calm down – it's just a formality.'

Walker breathes deeply, exhales loudly and tries to contain himself while I dig through the top flap of my rucksack to find my passport. I can't work out if Walker's bizarre reaction is the result of his overactive imagination. I imagine he has convinced himself this perfunctory encounter with local officials is his worst nightmare finally coming true. I can see the brainwashed martial arts montages flashing through Walker's mind where he is compositing Chuck Norris, Bruce Lee, Jackie Chan and Jet Li into one furious set of fists and pair of legs that are ready to liberate him in a bloodied exchange of blows. There is nothing wrong with idle boyhood fantasies of superheroes and martial arts masters. I'm a prime culprit of comic book fantasies — and have been waiting a really long fucking time to get struck by a magical lightning bolt, bitten by an irradiated arthropod, fall over and realise I'm levitating, or have a mysterious unknown uncle bequeath me his billions and mansion which by chance has a bat cave beneath its foundations. But there is a time and place for everything — which makes me sound a bit like my Mum, but she is right. And Walker's behaviour is turning him into a liability that has the potential to get us into some real trouble.

'Can we see some identification?' Walker asks.

I look up and see the two officers' lymphatic shrugs, followed by two crumpled, laminated ID cards diced across the table like they're expired video library memberships. Compelled to follow through, Walker picks one up, pantomimes a thorough examination then nods absurdly with over-proofed approval. I order Walker to find his passport and write his details below mine before false suspicion causes a real problem. Satisfied with our passport numbers on a scrap of paper the two men get back on their moped and ride off.

The shared jeep does arrive, unannounced two blocks up the street. By the time we realise, gear up and rush to meet it, I can see through the open tailgate that it's already impossibly full. But the driver standing atop the laden roof rack beckons us to hand him our packs. As we stand outside the jeep waiting for the driver to strap down the luggage, wondering how we can possibly fit in the back of the jeep passengers again start shaking their heads while pointing up the road. The driver appears to listen then unties the luggage straps before returning our packs. And while we debate with each other and the locals sticking out the back of the jeep, it drives off without us. Unable to reconcile another idle day in Khaplu we look for transport back to Skardu instead.

Our contrite return is as captivating and rewarding as the journey there — and again interrupted by Walker's zeal for confiding in strangers. He divulges the reason for the Kashgar countdown is to catch a 52-hour nonstop train through Ürümqi to Shanghai. There he tells me he has an old school friend who advised him there's nothing to see or do in Shanghai. So Walker prebooked a flight back to Delhi the same day he arrived in Shanghai to catch a connecting return flight home to America. Confused? I was.

It takes time to digest the idea that Walker was ostensibly travelling the breadth of a continent in a taut nonstop endeavour to catch his return flight home from Delhi. It was even more baffling when I considered our current location, and that India's capital was essentially a short trip *(as the crow flies)* back over the Himalayas. It certainly added an absurd flavour to Theroux's insightful observation that 'all travel is circular' and a grand tour of the world is just the 'inspired man's way of heading home'. While I'm getting used to and growing weary of the manifold of inexplicable things about Walker, he still holds a beguiling curiosity which makes me want to inquire further.

'Walker, if you need to get back to Delhi why don't you just travel back the way you came?'

'Why?'

'Because it's much quicker.'

'No retreat, no surrender.'

'You know that's the title of a bad eighties martial arts movie?'

'It was one of my favourite films growing up.'

By the time we arrive back in Skardu we've missed all onward transport towards the Karakorum Highway and Gilgit. And once again we're forced to spend the night. I don't mind. I wander out of town and snake my way down to the dry basin of the Indus River. Grey clouds steal all colour and contrast and smear the valley with a diffuse light. I stumble across an old graveyard. The only sound is of the wind howling down the ancient glacial footprint. Meandering around the headstones that catch shifting sands like a dead crop I know I am somewhere distant — so distant I feel I'm standing on a lifeless, desert moon.

In lieu of failing to reach the Hushe Valley I shift my intentions and determination towards Fairy Meadows and the Nanga Prabat massif. Known locally as Diamir, it's the world's ninth highest peak. This time I'm prepared to pay for the expensive private jeep to get to Jhel and the start of the trail. The bodacious 1320 metres ascent up a gnarly 4WD track skirting a dramatic cliff face can otherwise be accomplished on foot. But there's no way I'm wasting a day hiking a 4WD track which the *LP* suggested was for the 'weak of heart'. I'm also not going to pass up a ride described as 'legendary' and 'heartstopping'.

The next morning we catch an early minibus ride heading to Gilgit. Walker revives his favourite subject, the military brilliance of General MacArthur, his favourite general. The journey is long, made longer because we're returning. And Walker talks interminably. He segues to musings of home and family and friends. All the talk about America reminds Walker he has solutions to all of its problems. He lists them, which isn't hard because they are all based on the DIY energy efficient devices installed around his house in Boulder, Colorado.

Walker's diatribe lulls me into a soporific state. I stare out the window. My eyes follow the majestic causeway cut by the Indus River and trace the serrated skyline with a tranquilised sense of awe. I hear Walker continue to pontificate how if he was president he would prohibit all the dumbasses from voting. I guessed Walker came from a privileged upbringing. He sounds educated to the dangerous point of confusing it with intelligence. I let his voice fade into white plangent sound in my ear. In my private reverie I imagine Walker as an arriviste President of the USA. It's plausible vision of terror.

As we near the Karakorum Highway Walker complains about not being able to afford the private jeep to Fairy Meadows. I see the person Walker wants to be and the person he is — and watching the pair compete is oddly mesmerising. The divergent intensity expands and contracts with each wrinkle of consternation across his furrowed brow as he renews his concerns over his strict itinerary. While Walker appeared uninitiated to life on the road he does display a modicum of survival instinct — and with creative continuity and practise he has the native ability to fashion a disguise to withstand the rigours of the open road and inquisitive minds. However Walker didn't greet new experiences with any integrity, fortitude or openness — and this is the openture with which backpackers confront new experiences and places. It's what treats us to the raw spectrum of wonderment on arduous overland journeys. The conceit of seeking out the unfamiliar to find deeper connection and understanding on the open road echoes through religious study. The emotional cultivation *(of which is seldom warranted or sought after in regular life)* is the stuff that stirs us towards a more profound and personal sense of realisation. Christianity shares Zen Buddhism's pillars of faith and doubt by describing faith as what allows someone to travel beyond what they know and trust. And it makes sense to me that discoveries found abroad or at home lie in the process of alienating ourselves to see what we take for granted and what really matters.

I admit I did exploit Walker's enfeebled conviction to accompany me on the trek to Nanga Prabat. Sharing the cost of the impending jeep ride alone saved me the equivalent of three to four days of travel. But as time grows short before we have to alight I change my mind. Walker doesn't want to be here and I don't want him with me, distraught the entire time we're at Fairy Meadows. The traveller in me also doesn't want to see Walker fuck up his itinerary *(no matter how illogical)* if I could help it. So I stoke his doubt. It's not hard since everything Walker expressed is true. As he stresses about making it back to Gilgit in time to get onward transport to cross the Chinese border, I concur saying his remaining time to reach Kashgar is alarmingly short. I also appease Walker's commendable, yet misguided and wavering loyalty to the trip. I tell him I have no issue if he is uncomfortable with the situation to remain on the ride back to Gilgit.

When the minibus stops at the highway junction, I get out followed by Walker who's holding a volatile takeaway of inner turmoil. He juggles it impatiently while waiting beside me for a minibus heading south. It accompanies him onto the minibus with me when I wave down a Suzuki destined for Chilas. It carries us the short distance back down the Karakorum Highway to the Raikot Bridge, which marks the start of the jeep track to Jhel and Fairy Meadows.

From time spent with Walker it's evident that like me, and the bulk of the backpacking nation, he's enamoured by America's literary tradition of vagabonds and drifters. But Walker overcompensates, trying to convince himself that he's some modern day Kerouac or Mark Twain, when in reality I think Walker is a conservative type — and despite criticisms of his homeland Walker was no manumitting revolutionary, medieval bard or rucksack sadhu on a floating zendo with all the other Japhys and Rays. He talked about America with fierce scary pride. I didn't know whether Walker would find the affirmation or contentment he blindly sought on the open road by hanging out with his buddies drinking Bud Light back home. Part of me thinks so — and hopes so.

Beyond the inherent perils of trying to become someone you're not, the more disturbing trend of travellers like Walker is they don't see that by offering less and less of themselves they end up with nothing for others to seize onto and to connect with. There is an emotional anaesthetic to the process I have seen many backpackers hooked on. It protects them from getting too attached to *(or hurt by)* the people they meet. So they avert potentially awkward goodbyes by telling you they're just heading to market for food and never return, or say they'll see you at breakfast before heading to bed and instead wake up at the crack of dawn to catch onward transport. They do this because they can. There's no fear of recrimination because you'll probably never see them again. And it's ironic how many backpackers say they feel the most alive and free while on a trip, even though they behave in the most defensive and divisive manner. I guess it's because in any mode of living it feels right to first teach ourselves how not to get hurt. And it's easy to believe we put ourselves on a path less followed, but how do we know we haven't veered off into mediocrity? Is a new direction going to challenge and scare us in the right way — in the way Pema Chödrön sees fear as an artful tool of discovery:

*'Fear is a natural reaction to moving closer to the truth.'*

What Walker didn't seem to appreciate is stories and people need honesty and authenticity, or a version of it otherwise what is there to invest in? He tried to discard himself so thoroughly that he left himself with nothing real or sincere to concoct a new self out of. He made the mistake of thinking what he was searching for *(consciously or otherwise)* was something to acquire, when it is only reached by thinking the opposite — to look at a map, confess you've no idea where you're heading to, acknowledge you're stuck even though you keep moving, expose yourself to perilous vulnerabilities, and admit you have found no answer to any of it in the cruel madness of the world. George Harrison clearly knew this. From *Any Road* released on his posthumous album *Brainwashed,* George sings:

> *But, oh Lord, we've got to fight*
> *With the thoughts in the head with the dark and the light*
> *No use to stop and stare*
> *And if you don't know where you're going*
> *Any road will take you there*

The minibus stops on the highway opposite an old jeep full of supplies. The driver and his partner are milling about, checking the undercarriage. There are no signs. I assume they're parked by the start of the track waiting for paying fares like Walker and me to make the trip worthwhile. Walker follows as I head over to engage in negotiations. He reacts with panicked eyes and pensive undertones to the fee being bargained — as if he's trying to legitimise a reason for not going any further.

I agree on a price with the driver's partner but when I consult Walker he talks incoherently about regretting not staying on the previous ride — and how he has jeopardised his intercontinental nonstop plight to get his indirect flight home. Tapping back into the vein of the Karakorum and gorging on the endless black strip of tar seems to redeem the prominence of Walker's onward trip. It spends his remaining resolve. We watch a minibus approach, presumably destined for Gilgit. Walker apologises for nothing in particular and rushes across the highway possessed — as if part of him is trying sabotage himself. Then he's gone like a phantom provocateur at the end of Hollywood thriller.

I was thankful Walker didn't come to Fairy Meadows and pleased he made a sensible decision considering his ludicrous schedule. But most of all I was glad to know he was returning to where I believe he felt the most secure. And I was certain Walker Bradley would return to Boulder, Colorado and tell his friends he conquered the breadth of the Asian continent *(even if he didn't catch much of it)*. That night, I sat in the portal of my tent pitched on the lush green pastures of Fairy Meadows. I ate steaming noodles straight from my pot while watching the white fin of Nanga Prabat blush like chrysanthemum against the setting sun. The cosmic palette matured into sun-spoilt papaya before gently fading into midnight pewter sheeted by chiffon clouds of smoky lilac. I recall thinking this is exactly how things were meant to be.

After the Fairy Meadows hike, I got back to Gilgit and journeyed north to Karimabad. Through the hooded glow of candlelight on my first night at the Old Hunza I heard an Englishman exclaim, 'Walker Bradley.'

'Did someone just say Walker Bradley?'

'You know him?'

'I met him in Gilgit.'

'We just met him in Kashgar–'

'Fucking crazy guy,' added a second Englishman.

That night around a communal bench of international travellers the two Englishmen and I swapped stories about Walker Bradley. It turned out Walker made an indelible impression along the Karakorum Highway — and not just because he had a surname for a first name and a first name for a surname. When I got back to Gilgit I heard he didn't even stay the night, opting for a night bus to Passu which must have placed him in Kashgar two days later. The English backpackers went out for beers with him, suggested he was light with his drink and doubted he would get up at 8 am for his train ride across China.

In everyday life or on the open road, mystical revelation and luminal moments inherently require trumping fear and doubt. Echoing Zen philosophy, at some point on a trip a traveller must put themselves on a path which goes beyond the limit of trust. Again the rewards of faith and travel are entwined. It may be as simple as accepting a ride from a stranger, or a more literal leap of faith off a bridge, over a waterfall, out of a plane or tethered to a bungee cord. The shame of it is the dukkha which filled Walker's discriminating mind could have been extracted if he had taken the plunge and opened the door within himself and not just pretended to.

I felt Walker's desperation to race across the Asian continent matched a subconscious drive to be back home, *(or at least not a place where a portion of the population hated the USA)*. And I was just as sure he made that train, as I was that he would find unmatched assurance back home in Boulder, Colorado — and slip comfortably back into the person he was and forget this travelling-man folly.

# CHAPTER 10

# PHILLY AND ROCKY

I boarded a flight from Bogota to Orlando with a decade old pledge — never *ever* return to the USA without a car. On my previous visit in 2001 I arrived into LA with grand plans built by a lego imagination. I was going to hit up Yosemite and Yellowstone national parks, head out to Joshua Tree and White Sands, hang out in San Fran, Seattle and Denver, inhale the crush and roar of the Atlantic in the Redwoods of Big Sur, swing by the Grand Canyon, put it all on black in Las Vegas, cross the Badlands and the Great Divide, visit Cape Canaveral, hop on freight trains up to New York and Maine, and coast through obscure mountain towns in the Appalachians — basically caper about, camping and hiking in the summertime. But without leaving West Hollywood I quickly realised the USA wasn't at all like the Europe I was acquainted with. It lacked the sophistication of cross-mode public transport — a neural network delivering souls to any park entrance, trailhead, mountain top and obscure destination imaginable. North America was more primitive, with clumsy ugly termini in the middle of industrial backwaters. It was like my homeland *(only much more densely populated)* where open highways with a tank full of petrol, four wheels and a metal skin ruled.

I knew without wheels in the USA it was impossible to reach all the forgotten places in between, which is where I want to be. So why was I was breaking my own oath? Well, it turns out I was in exactly the same predicament as last time. I had neither the budget to hire a car outright, nor travel buddies to split the cost. Back in 2001 I did what any penurious backpacker would do — I bolted for the Mexican border. Accommodation and food in Mexico was cheap. But travelling on the *primera clase* and *ejecutivo* bus services to prevent my luggage from being stolen was more expensive than overland travel in the USA. So after a month I crossed back over the border into El Paso, Texas and travelled on Greyhound up through Albuquerque and Santa Fe to Denver. I then headed back to the west coast where I travelled from Frisco up to Seattle and into Canada. Travelling on my wits in my twenties and being exposed to the galaxy of characters and smells that is the Greyhound was a riot. However, over the years I have grown accustomed to eschew metropolises. I favour the intimacy of rural dwellings that persevere on the cusp of nature's benevolence — which is why I will always trade cosmopolitan hopscotch for any excuse that gets me into the wild. This is the freedom you buy when you have private transport. So what do you do when you can't afford to rent or purchase a car?

Before leaving Colombia I designed an itinerary not based on travelling. I figured any effort to do so without a car would only cause undue frustration. Orlando International Airport played me. Like a lot of modern cities across America and Australia, it's easier to cross Honduras into Nicaragua along the Mosquito Coast than it is to get in and out of the airport on a budget. I couldn't even work out how to get out of the airport without hiring a car or private shuttle. I got a car for 48 hours. I navigated on Google Map memory to a Days Inn in Titusville. The following morning I visited the Kennedy Space Center. I slept in the car that night in the back of a hotel carpark off the I-95 and dropped the car off the next day in Savannah, Georgia. From then on I decided the most logical way to avoid any disenchantment of not having a car this time round was to totally ignore nature — and shunt from city to city up the east coast. I turned to the couchsurfing community to host me. It wasn't just a budgetary consideration. I liked the idea of discovering cities again without the partial veil of a tourist's gaze — have their wonders and secrets revealed through eyes that come with living and working in one place. And although I've seen Couchsurfing adopt the scary fetishisms of a cult since joining in 2006, the community as whole remains incredibly lenitive and welcoming.

I spent almost a month jaunting up the coastline, all the way from Florida to Massachusetts then back to Philadelphia. I treated the short transitions of rest in each city like video clips which danced between fact and fiction — sequences rebooted from the nexus of cinematic stories connected to the sidewalks, subways, parks and cityscapes which surrounded me like waking dreams. The quixotic feeling of being on a quest is a lure of international travel that is impossible to ignore. And on daily sojourns through urbane jungles of concrete and glass with towering hives full of people I imagined myself in the sequels from identifiable films — where I was the hero, the saviour, the kindred spirit chasing the one who's getting away. It's an indulgent folly that for me makes city exploration infinitely more enjoyable.

The idea of eliminating delusions and desires, which in Zen Buddhism is necessary to remove all the dukkha clouding your mind, is a tough one for everyone. Delusions are like ex-lovers. Sometimes they're really hard to get rid of without fearing you'll pull out a bigger part of yourself that's attached (that makes you unique) — the part of you which believes in one-in-a-million chances and an exquisite match of oddities can conquer all. In the gallery of globetrotters, youthful hearts through to nostalgic veterans pack a kit of playful delusions and desires. Much like other avocations such as gastronomy and heavy thirsts, they are quintessential hobbies to stay sane and combat the daily vicissitudes in a backpacker's kerfuffle to cross vast foreign lands. They are also the very tools responsible for propelling a travelling bhikku and bhikkuni out into the world, to seek out a new path.

I like to entertain the notion that backpacking may elicit a grand solution to my life. There is a part of me that will always remain on the lookout for my Shangri-La — a place that I will fall for like a woman with a foreign accent, move to, and spend the rest of my life there. Otherwise, I conjure a debonair billionaire playboy slumming it in youth hostels. I make such a favourable impression on him when we meet that he declares I'm just the man to sail his boat from Antibes back to his holiday house in the Virgin Islands. Forget that I have no experience, it's no bother. I'm cool and he trusts me and is so fucking loaded we'll just design another boat together if I crash his current one.

What remains constant in travelling circles is a private belief in possibilities. Personally, I'm sceptical that backpacking as a contingency offers any real answers or atonement to the heavy lifting of the soul. But to think backpacking will reveal some remarkable turn of fortune or unknown destiny is a fallacy which plays into the fantasy of the open road. And as a nostrum for the stresses and malcontent of modern living, independent travel has become a one-stop cure. Why shouldn't it? Just like any phenomena of subjective validation, it's hard to resist the signs when every day you wake and open yourself to possibilities.

So, I let these pleasant fantasies reside in a quiet compartment of my mind because like superstitions, I find them fun to engage with from time to time — to entertain myself on the long space travelling between places. But to give it any more room would ultimately lead to disappointment. This is why the USA rules — beyond the titillating glitter and schmaltz there is an impermeable belief in the unbelievable that sits alongside the limitations and harsh reality of life. For me it's expressed in its rich filmlore that is evocatively preserved by its equally enviable landscape of iconic architecture. This is thanks in part to modern visionaries like

Bernard Goldman, Eero Saarinen, Gordon Bunshaft and Phillip Johnson who laid iconic urban landscapes in many of the country's capital cities. And it helps make the USA fertile ground for escapist forays while ambling through the capitals.

I actually had no intention of visiting the state of Pennsylvania or the City of Brotherly Love. I wanted to go to Chicago where I'd already hatched a plan to follow the itinerary of Ferris Bueller on his day off. However, from Boston I thought the cheap bus networks which serviced much of the northeast would stretch to Illinois. But there was no way to get from Boston to Chicago *(at the time)* on a moderate budget. Compared to Amtrak and Greyhound's archaic and exorbitant pricing structures, *(which offered a convoluted array of multi-day punishment)* I found domestic airlines in the USA provided much better value for money. However, even the airline tariffs were in excess of my end-of-trip insolvency. So I gave up on my Ferris Bueller dream. And to avoid backtracking through New York and Washington DC I bought a $20 ticket for a six-and-a-half hour journey on a half-empty bus with extra leg room and wifi. This is how I ended up rather unwittingly in Philly.

Exiting 30th Street Station I was struck with the fragile sensation that everything was very familiar and very foreign at the same time. I looked around the stark concrete surrounds of the Amtrak station. There was a portent sense of winter in the air, complemented by a lone pretzel vendor dressed for the conditions in a cardinal red jacket, fingerless gloves and beanie. A biting wind blew off the Schuylkill River and a tenebrous light permeated the charcoal sky to accentuate the austere grey landscape.

I realised I had not yet encountered such sullen weather on my trip in the USA. It reminded me of Manchester and I wondered if this was the reason I was already enamoured with the city of Philly. I tried to recall all that I know about the largest city in the Commonwealth of Pennsylvania. Given that I'd basically ended up here because of a cheap bus fare made me question why I hadn't met anyone so far who cared to mention or recommend the city.

I rode the El on the Market-Frankford line east down to 5th Street. My couchsurfing request was accepted by Fishtown residents Eve and Melinda. But they were both tied up with work until the evening so I had the whole day to burn. I ambled around the Historic Waterfront District. It elicited vagaries of Dublin's Temple Bar infused with the downtrodden bohemian spirit of Manchester's Northern Quarter. I wandered down to Penn's Landing where the Delaware River divides Pennsylvania from the shores of New Jersey. The steady flow wasn't the lamp-black stagnant slick of Manchester's canals but was sufficiently maculated by waterfront industry to remind me again of the north of England. I walked back through the compact business district, meandering between the tall, bold buildings reminiscent of downtown areas in America. I still can't shake the feeling there's something distinctly European about Philly. This feeling lasts until I head back up to Independence Hall and visit the Independence Visitor Center. There I realise I'm diametrically wrong.

It turns out Philly is steeped in modern American history. It goes back 300 years when William Penn amicably settled the Pennsylvanian colony with local Lenape Indians by the convergence of the Schuylkill and Delaware rivers. Philly was the meeting place where the Founding Fathers of the United States signed the Declaration of Independence and acted as the nation's interregnum capital while Washington DC was being built. It's also home to the Liberty Bell and how could I have forgotten, fictitious heavy-weight boxing champion from Kensington in North Philly, Rocky Balboa. In fact much of Philly's proud working-class spirit, famously captured in the Oscar-winning series of *Rocky* films, is identifiable all around Philly.

With a legacy over three decades old it's easy to undervalue Rocky's sense of courage, mettle and desire for personal betterment. But this is precisely what makes him so unique and universally adored. For me what makes *Rocky* such a venerated series is it captures human merit without resorting to nuclear threat, deadly mercenaries, ballistic weaponry, incendiary reprisals, super villains, spaceships, intergalactic battles, time travel and the undead. *(Luckily, Sly saved those for his other movies.)* Rocky shows the power of the underdog spirit, and it does so through an equally humble journey of a debt collector resurrecting his boxing ambition.

I spent the night with Eve and Mel enjoying the ambience of Northern Liberties' former industrial area. We ate $1 tacos and drank cheap beer. We bought red wine and headed back to their house where I met Eve and Mel's short-term housemate Dante. The following day I was invited by Eve and Dante on a walking tour of the city streets. Dante led us to the Italian Markets, instantly recognisable from the rousing *Gonna Fly Now* montage in *Rocky*, the original Oscar-winning film, and the more memorable reprise in *Rocky II* — where an army of kids materialise behind Sly and chase him while he's jogging, which inspires him to leap over park benches outside Independence Hall. Stopping at Paesanos's sandwich bar on 9th Street, Dante, a Temple University graduate and barman elaborates on the bizarre affair between Rocky and Philly and movies and real life.

'It's weird cos I've spent my whole life here – I grew up just outside of Philly and Rocky feels like a real person here. I can't help thinking one day I'll turn a corner and bump into him.'

As a film graduate, I also found the connection between the fictitious southpaw, Rocky Balboa, and the city of Philadelphia palpable. The next day I wander through Fairmount Park. Walking in the warm mizzle through America's oldest and largest landscaped parks I'm mindful of how fact and fiction can melt, meld, blur and bind. Nowhere in Philly is this affinity between fact and fiction embedded more deeply than where I was heading — the front steps of the Philadelphia Museum of Art. Offering an unbridled view of Philly's skyline, the forecourt at the top of the front steps directs one's attention down the Benjamin Franklin Parkway *(an American Champs-Élysées)* to Philly's Town Hall, an iconic structure with its own national and architectural importance. Even at the time of completion it was a feat of construction, being hailed as the tallest inhabitable building in the modern world.

The image of Rocky atop the steps of the Philadelphia Art Museum is such an iconic cinematic image it was used both on the original *Rocky* movie poster, as well as *Rocky Balboa* AKA Rocky VI. The front steps of the Philadelphia Museum of Art are so synonymous with *Rocky (appearing in five of six instalments that span 30 years)* they have long been dubbed the "Rocky Steps". For an unofficial air of cultural legitimacy, check out Google Maps where the Rocky Steps are clearly labelled in Fairmount Park, separate to the Philadelphia Museum of Art.

In the training montage of the original film, and again in the sequel, the steps embody Rocky's tenacious battle to reach peak physical fitness and strength in readiness for his championship bout. So much so the steps have come to be regarded as a symbol of perseverance, determination and Philly's fighting, underdog spirit. In fact, the term "Rocky montage", commonly used in the lexicon of cinematic terminology illustrates how indelible Rocky's legacy is both culturally and in real life. While training montages are a well-worn motif, open to homage and parody in martial arts and sports films, their effectiveness persists. There is a *Zenness* to them because they eminently delineate the process of stripping away all that you know to start over and learn anew *(at least in a physical sense)* which many of us aspire towards. It's no wonder the Rocky Steps have become a place of pilgrimage for film and sports fans from around the globe. It draws thousands of visitors a year to the Philadelphia Museum of Art to complete the iconic run up the 72 steps. This is highlighted in the highly self-referential last instalment *Rocky Balboa* with an end credit sequence showcasing a collage of real life people duplicating Rocky's sprint up the steps to the rousing theme song — thus completing the omega from fiction to fact and returning to some sort of *facttion*.

Arriving at the museum's east entrance a holler pierces the robust serenity that attaches itself to places of culture. Am I surprised to see a group of Eastern European men taking turns filming each other running to the top of the steps and bouncing about and shouting in front of a water fountain to impersonate Rocky's "champ dance"? Mildly. Did I visit the Museum of Art while I was there? Fuck no! It cost like $20 which I didn't have. And I'm pretty sure the Eastern European lads didn't go either. But it turns out Philly has the biggest public art collection in the country, and it brings to mind the end of *Rocky V* where Rocky arrives at the top of the steps with his young son Robert in a scene of reconciliation:

*'Look at this. I've been running up and down these steps for 20 years and I never knew there was valuable pictures in this building.'*

But across six instalments there are many examples in which the films curate Rocky's legacy as it evolved in the real world — further corrupting the line between fact and fiction. So what of the Rocky statue, unveiled atop the Rocky Steps in *Rocky III* in a citywide tribute to Rocky's achievements?

In another twist of fact and fiction it was Sylvester Stallone who gifted the city with one of two bronze cast statues commissioned for the film following its release in 1982. So am I disappointed to see a water fountain in its place? No — because movies are often way better than real life *(except for* Rocky V — *it sucked)*. And to think reality will play out like movies — that everything is certain and everything explained, invites the kind of disappointment that makes people want to binge on movies and junk food.

Over a decade earlier, staying in a village just outside Paris while backpacking through Europe I visited the Père Lachaise

Cemetery. I saw the graves of dead people that influenced me as a young man — Max Ernst, Molière and Oscar Wilde among others. But the express purpose of going to the cemetery was to visit the grave of Jim Morrison and sit in vigil by the head bust shown at the end of Oliver Stone's cinematic biopic *The Doors*. And just like the film, I naively imagined the same gravesite — adorned in graffiti, burning joints and incense — accompanied by two or three swaying hippies I expect will ask me to join them in a trip or some other hedonistic journey while in Paris.

I could happily accept the fact there were no hippies or spliffs to pilfer. But discovering a modest plaque diminutively set in the ground between two overbearing headstones was deflating. At the time it was irrelevant that Stone's biopic accurately portrayed the original bust by sculptor Mladen Mikulin, which was stolen following the tenth anniversary of Jim Morrison's death. This was because I obviously learnt all this later. So I stood at Jim Morrison's grave feeling the excursion to Pére Lachaise Cemetery was a bit of a waste of time. But I learnt my lesson — never travel with high expectations.

The "Rocky statue" dispute lasted over two decades and saw the statue move numerous times — where it was briefly returned to its natural home atop the Rocky Steps for filming purposes. Bizarrely, I learnt not just for subsequent Rocky instalments — it was also moved back for other projects such as another Oscar winner *Philadelphia* with Denzel Washington and Tom Hanks. In the long-standing debate some museum officials saw the statue as merely a movie prop. And by allowing it to reside at the top of the Rocky Steps, the proximity of popular culture to fine art threatened to insult the museum's exalted reputation. Meanwhile others saw the silver lining — and shrewdly observed people *(like Rocky)* who had never been inside a museum at least now got closer to the entrance.

It made me consider another mythical prop of sorts, housed inside Philly's Independence National Historical Park — the

Liberty Bell. Cast from a flawed hunk of metal out of London *(that for some reason many people I met in the USA thought was gifted by the French),* it has over time come to symbolise freedom and independence and, well… everything else in between.

The fact that Philadelphia officials decided the Spectrum sports arena was a more suitable home for the Rocky statue only seemed to further galvanise the fictional boxing champ's place in the real world of star athletes. *Rocky Balboa* perfectly distilled this controversy when Paulie jokes about Rocky's desire to return to the ring at 60 years of age:

'*Ya mad because they took down your statue?*'

Not knowing any of this at the time I sauntered down the steps on my way to the free Rodin Museum, which was guarded by Rodin's *The Thinker.* Upon seeing a few people milling around the bottom of the steps, I went to investigate and discovered the Rocky statue!

Only in September 2006, on the thirtieth anniversary of the original *Rocky* film and the eve of the final instalment's release was the statue contentiously returned to Philadelphia's Art Museum — albeit at the bottom of the steps. I guess that's called compromise. Reading about the inaugural ceremony sounded like some repeat-reversal of *Rocky III (which is a film of repeat-reversal)* minus Clubber Lang AKA BA Baracus AKA Mr T. Over two thousand people attended to enjoy live music, as well as a free showing of the first Rocky movie from 1976. And once again Sly, ahem I mean Rocky showed fact and fiction can be hard to separate.

For the next two days I hung around Philly while figuring out where to go next. I grew increasingly captivated with the city while exploring the gentrified areas around Northern Liberties and Fishtown. I emailed the couchsurfers I had corresponded with in Chicago and apologised that my awry plans would now bypass the Windy City due to budget constraints. The following evening I ventured north of 30th Street Station with Eve on our way to dinner then bluegrass night at a bar in West Philly. A familiar sense of Manchester returned staring out the window of the El. The stark low income areas around the university district carried a drab flavour of housing estates where I worked on the original cult television series *Shameless*. Eve reiterated warnings of crime and violence conveyed to her when she first arrived in the city to study at Temple University. But Eve was Croatian, and quickly disposed of talk about the dubious area we were heading to with the lightness of a curtsey.

We ate dinner at an authentic Ethiopian restaurant called Abyssinia because it's on the street front below Fiume, a legendary bar renowned for its diminutive size, live music and obscurity. The bar was packed, which wasn't hard. It had the ambience of a house party being hosted in a single bedroom flat. My soul foot stomped to the music. I would have literally foot stomped to the fiddle, double bass and washboard — but because of the neighbours downstairs, the crowd was routinely castigated for doing so by the barman. Beer and bluegrass lingered in our legs as they swayed in tantalising unison on the El back to Fishtown. However, the wistful flirtation of public transport quickly dissipated when we got home and discovered the pets had staged their own household mutiny.

Melinda's satanic terrier I named Lord Voldermort shat in Eve's bedroom which made her scream, *'Bassst-tard'*. This was only discovered after Eve went to the toilet and yelped in fright at one of three mice lying surgically garrotted with its entrails missing on the bathroom floor. I ran upstairs to investigate the sound of her distress and that's when I smelt shit and later found the terrier that shan't be named had pissed again on my backpack. Dante's gecko was presumably okay, since he was at work and wise enough to shut his door. The two feline residents of the house were sat at the foot of the breakfast table in the kitchen. Their smug gaze taunted the murdered rodent's two cousins. They stood quivering, stuck on top of the microwave — still probably trying to figure out why the fuck the deceased tried to escape through the cardboard patch we later discovered at the back of the aquarium.

The hubris of my imaginary world had Eve and I sidestep the psychopathic savagery of nature with a resurgent desire to be together. Aroused by the mortal coil of life we'd embrace, find standing a bore, and head back upstairs *(wary not to step in any dog shit)* to Eve's bedroom and close the door before the beer and bourbon wore off. In reality I helped reinstate domestic amnesty before Eve said goodnight. And this was how it should have been. I was already smitten with a girl I'd just met whose heart was daring as it was timid — a Lowcountry heart to which I had vowed to return to at the end of my trip.

I knew I was back in danger, gambolling with potent fantasies that can easily trick you into not knowing which realm you're in. This is possibly why I skulled three raw eggs after seeing *Rocky* for the very first time and made myself really fucking sick. It's funny when I thought about Philly because it was utter pragmatism that got me to the USA in the first place. I had just spent five months in Central America, travelling by bus, boat and plane to find myself in Leticia in the southwest corner of Colombia. Nestled on the tri-border of Peru and Brazil, I was well beyond the end of the road. Leticia is only accessible by boat or plane with the river journey rumoured to take a minimum of two to four weeks. There I stood on a figurative and literal border in my life — symmetrically placed to see equally where I'd come from, where I was and where I was heading. There was a physical lyricism to match the border crossing. It took the form of the grand Rio Amazonas flowing like a giant causeway into Brazil and out into the Atlantic Ocean. Fresh from an *ayahuasca* ceremony with Jimmy, the local Medicine Man, I glimpsed an arcane conflation of things that seems to visit me on every overland adventure I undertake — usually involving me staring down at my feet or gazing across a vista, marvelling at how I got there. I couldn't ignore the feeling that I'd reached the fulcrum of my seesaw life. It felt predestined. I chuckled, knowing I was right because I was literally standing on the Rubicon's edge of my journey. I had every intention of jumping on a boat downstream for 8–10 days to Manaus and onto Belem on the coast, but for the first time ever I hesitated with cash still in my pockets. I was mindful about returning to Australia to help promote my first book. So in an unprecedented manoeuvre I suppressed my insatiable onward desire by flying up to the USA — to give myself a few weeks of American culture and comfort before I flew out of LA. Three weeks came and went. It passed while I was in Boston — and I still had every intention of returning to Rosie and Charleston then swing further south to Nola and maybe across to Austin and White Sands in Texas.

I checked my emails before bed and had received a couch-surfing reply from Maribeth Joy in Chicago. Her name alone sounded like a theomorphic incarnation who reverses misfortunes and grants wishes to downtrodden travellers. She offered to give me a $129 travel voucher from Southwest Airlines which was about to expire. She said she would happily email me the redemption code details if it would help enable me visit her fair city. I realise sometimes we feel the need to justify fate's existence when its presence is most doubtful. We burrow down through a sequence of events and blow the dust clear of all the missed chances to examine them closely for signs of connection and a guiding influence. Then there were times like these when the divine forces just shout out:

'Oi, come get it you fool!'

The gracious offer from someone I had never met floors me — strangers connected simply by a passion for travel and meeting new people. I am back in a film but with me as the protagonist. Maribeth, a backpacking diviner had championed the forces of fate to keep alive my ultimate goal of merging fact and fiction in reliving Ferris Bueller's day off. With the voucher I still had to contribute just under a hundred bucks. I would also have to call Rosie and hear the disappointment and doubt in her voice when I tell her I'm still coming, just not now, and not from Philly. But I would do both these things because I couldn't ignore the providence of Maribeth's gesture. So before going to sleep I emailed Maribeth, got the redemption code and booked a flight back north to Chicago.

# CHAPTER 11

# FINDING FERRIS IN GOTHAM CITY

I contemplated my imminent arrival in Chicago while waiting at Philadelphia Airport. Since arriving in the USA I had devised the grand plan of following the itinerary of Ferris Bueller on his day off. But the promise of returning to Charleston and to Rosie was stuck in my thoughts. Part of me regretted that yet again I had sacrificed the possibility of something for nothing in particular. I wished Rosie was beside me like Sloane, sharing in the thrill of the moment. A messy and sentimental goodbye with Eve was avoided. Familiarity reinstated as I skulked out of a beautiful stranger's house and into shitty weather and uncertainty — with a mild hangover obscuring the ineffable grace of the open road and wonder over whether I'll ever see these people again. The reason the entire household got hammered and were all still in bed when I left for the airport was prescribed by antics the night before — and the diabolical success of celebrating Dante's twenty-fourth birthday at the El Bar, a student dive under the metro arches by the Girard stop. It's funny how departure lounges administer a strong belt of loneliness along with the anodyne of being alone and free. So I drank in the *resferber* of hopes, dreams, trepidation and soul-crushing dejection vented by the vagaries of the heart in departure lounges.

Between Charleston and Philly I passed through a number of cities along the east coast mainly using Amtrak and a number of cheap intercity bus companies. Before Charleston, I spent time in its sister city and twin jewel of the South, Savannah. It evoked a ubiquitous mis-en-scéne from vague, affluent settings in period dramas set in the South. I was disappointed Savannah didn't reveal a sense of *Garden in the Midnight of Good and Evil* — one of my prime motivations for visiting the city. But I also recognised the uniqueness of characters is what formed much of Savannah's personality in John Bernedt's bestselling novel. And it is only with time or luck that you are able to ingratiate yourself in a place the way Bernedt did to capture a place of such captivating style and class. Charleston was Bill Murray spotting. My best shot was at the Joe but the minor league season was over, where Riverdogs' co-owner and Director of Fun, Mr Murray regularly attended. And I didn't have the funds to frequent the upscale bars around Market Street and late-night bowling alleys where I was unreliably told Bill hung out sometimes.

Washington DC was... well DC. I could imagine a giant alien saucer hovering over the commanding Capitol Hill and US Congress Building. I know in reality alien craft always hover over the White House. But I could never be arsed walking there after a day at the Smithsonian museums, plus both buildings were white and sort of looked alike anyway. I spent a number of taxing yet highly rewarding days exploring the immense museum complex. I found the nation's capital bustling and fun, but *(like my own country's capital)* bereft of an intangible vivacity that I guess happens when you clone a capital city.

Boston was predominately an Affleck-Damon affair with *Good Will Hunting* and the emergent subgenre of Southie crime thrillers such as *The Departed*, *The Town*, *Mystic River* and *Gone*

*Baby Gone.* In New York I walked through a reincarnation of film highlights while strolling along 7th Avenue and Broadway. I passed by elaborate police dramas being filmed on location on the streets of Harlem, and again just off Times Square. In Central Park I gazed up at New York's unforgettable cityscape — immortalised in too many films to list, but Woody Allen invariably comes to mind. Looking across at West Central Park's Historic District I recognised the striking Art Deco behemoth with an uncanny ziggurat top rising up from the greenery, better known as the Ghostbusters building or Shandor building. So, I stood for a moment on the grass and tried to envisage CGI darkness swirling overhead to envelop the sky and foreshadow the coming of Gozer, the Sumerian God of Destruction.

The Windy City could be considered a diminutive rival compared to the chiral twins of American movie making, Los Angeles and New York. However, sweet home Chicago is a formidable opponent of cinematic pre-eminence with its own signature sights and prestigious skyline. It also has a long history of usurping its competition. In 1890, much to the chagrin of rivals New York, Washington DC and St Louis, Congress awarded Chicago the honour of hosting the momentous World's Columbian Exposition. A World Fair was held only once before in you guessed it — Philadelphia. Chicago's World Fair in 1893 celebrated 400 years since Christopher Columbus set foot on the New World. It had a pronounced effect on arts, architecture and Chicago's identity. It set an indelible precedent in theory and implementation for the future of town planning and modern living, which strongly influenced the beautification movement of urban areas in North America. The Fair also unveiled the Ferris wheel, the first fully electric kitchen and Pabst Blue Ribbon, without which I would not be nursing a fragile disposition from the $3 boilermakers at the El Bar the night before.

I suppose my fictive sparring on the streets of Philly with Rocky did render a moral of sorts — discovering the Rocky statue, and reading how Philly put the statue back *(well as near to where it should be)* mitigated the cynical side of me which thought sometimes real life can surprise you. This was of course then totally eclipsed by Maribeth's offer to help fly me to Chicago. However, it's still a precarious and often disappointing path to follow in the footsteps of your idols — especially since *(and speaking personally)* for most of us malingerers of Generation X they exist only in fiction, whether it is celluloid, canvas or print on paper. To quote DJ Happy Harry Hard-On AKA Mark Hunter, played by Christian Slater in *Pump Up the Volume*, Alan Moyle's iconic Gen X film about disaffected youth festering in Arizona:

> *'You see there's nothing to do anymore. Everything decent's been done. All the great themes have been used up, turned into theme parks. So I don't really find it exactly cheerful to be living in a totally like exhausted decade where there's nothing to look forward to and no one to look up to... that was deep!'*

Chicago wears so many masks from so many memorable films. So I had to be discerning with the fictions around Chicago I intended to revive. The city also boasts the tallest building in the country, the Willis Tower where Ferris notably suggests, 'Anything is peaceful from 1353 feet.' Formerly known and still referred to as the Sears Tower, it held the mantle as the tallest building in the world for a quarter of a century and is currently the seventh tallest free standing structure on the planet. Then there's the Chicago Board of Trade, or as I prefer to call it, Wayne Enterprises, Wrigley Field, and of course Goldberg's inimitable Marina City — a prerequisite to incorporate in any Chicago-based film *(so don't knock Captain Ron)*. Blessed, not only with an unbridled view of the cityscape from Lake Michigan, the Chicago Loop also embraces the eponymous river. To gain a sense of the city's photogenic versatility one only has to traverse any part of the Loop's 18 bridges connecting the Narrows to the rest of the city

— which will probably make you want a Batmobile even more than you did before.

To be fair, a Batman-themed visit to Chicago would have been my first preference without doubt. But I had to be a bit reasonable. Without the costume and cape, access to an Applied Sciences division, Morgan Freeman *(or even a Desmond Llewelyn)*, and billions of dollars to afford those wonderful toys, *Batman* was impossible to emulate. *The Blues Brothers* were out because I didn't have a Bluesmobile. And anyway *Ferris Bueller's Day Off* was the perfect fit. I realised since seeing the seminal slacker movie by master Gen X filmmaker, John Hughes I had actually spent my life trying really hard to live by Ferris's fundamental code of conduct — which as turns out isn't far removed from the guiding principle of Zen and most backpackers:

*'Life moves pretty fast. If you don't stop and look around once in a while, you could miss it.'*

Even though Maribeth was my unofficial Patron Saint of Chicago, she was away at a farmstead wedding the weekend I arrived. Ukie Village couchsurfing host Lena who reflected the sang-froid cool of the hipster haven came to the rescue. That afternoon, hanging out with Lena off Damen I could happily convince myself into thinking that I was in some kind of *High Fidelity*. Then the wind picks up and rain sets in at the louring end of the day and I'm back in Gotham City.

I was surprised by Lena's positive encouragement when I disclosed my plan to follow in the footsteps of Ferris Bueller. Lena had a migratory itch of her own and had lived in six cities in the last decade. But since she now called Chicago home I thought my idea *(especially to her)* could be verging on lame — caught precariously between Ethan Hawke's post-irony and Chevy Chase's tourist bumpkin. After all, I was knocking about between Wicker Park and the Ukraine Village — carbon copies of hipster enclaves that seemed to be taking over the USA and gentrifying great swathes of impoverished, multicultural boroughs with absurd, apathetic, vagabond cool.

I knew the doubt I nurtured over my life's direction *(or lack thereof)* was making me question my thirst and perseverance for life on the open road. However, I didn't feel the new wave hipsters and I were that different. I imbibed the renewed zeal for speakeasies and prohibition cocktails, and embraced the psychedelic dream rock and indie folk revivals. It would appear I endorsed the resurgence of vintage hats, outlaw beards, moustache twirls and shaggy-chic because I owned the trend since the age of 17. Back then I worked out the easiest way to uphold a basic standard of casual dress and hygiene was to hide it in a beard and under a hat — and the way to do that was to study media/arts. As a result it made the large spat of time since graduating university appear terrifyingly short because I was still single and just as fucking skint as an undergraduate. The new generation of hipsters and iBackpackers wore their apathy like a summer shirt they could effortlessly slip on and off, whereas my generation wore it all year round like a prickly old coat. Maybe that was the only difference — some of us are more committed to pretending.

However, while staying in Williamsburg and Bushwick I wondered if the new young hipsters had their shit way more together than my own generation, which made a career out of wallowing in self-disillusionment. Maybe they had created a meta-ironic parody of Gen X that smote irony altogether? I doubted it since it sounded a bit too post-postmodern and complicated. And the more I thought about it I felt my mind swallowing itself up into deep, muddied layers of a Charlie Kaufman film which hurt my brain. Anyway, hipster villages were full of supportive folk who all reiterated that they'd never thought of re-enacting a film. So by the time I arrived in Chicago my imagination had brewed the positivity surrounding my objective into something much more grandiose.

Mimicking the progression of the film, I saw the day beginning in a rather modest circumstance. Maybe I've convinced Lena and a couple of her mates to skive off work in tribute to Ferris Bueller. And we enjoy a mimosa breakfast before embarking on the day's agenda — complete the exact itinerary of Ferris Bueller within a real day. As I had arrived in Chicago on a Saturday it didn't seem right to embark in the footsteps of Ferris until it was a school day. So to preserve a semblance of truancy I decided to wait until Monday morning. It would also give me time over the weekend to research the primary locations in the film. Failure and disappointment greeted me immediately *(which was not unexpected or surprising).*

Firstly, it turned out the Bueller household was in Long Beach CA. Also in LA was the pizza joint Edward R. Rooney, Dean of Students goes to in search of Ferris, as well as the interior of Chez Quis, the snooty, or snotty fine dining restaurant that serves pancreas. The googlemachine did tell me the filmmakers matched the restaurant's exterior in Chicago. But it was a private residence and had since been remodelled — so to hell with that!

The Cubs' home game season ended a week before I arrived — so scratch Wrigley Field. Then there was the Chicago Board of Trade building, where Ferris proposes to Sloane in the viewing gallery overlooking the trading pit to a soundtrack of dripping water courtesy of Cameron. In the past the Chicago Board of Trade advertised a visitor centre and granted public access to the gallery. It was kindly hosting Occupy Chicago during my visit, but had since closed down its visitor centre. It also prohibited public access to the viewing gallery for security reasons. Permission now was only given through prearranged appointments that were reserved for academic or industry affiliated groups, or a visiting dignitary like Bruce Wayne — so fuck them too!

After much googlemachining I worked out it was possible to get to Glenbrook North High School. This is where Ferris avoids a test on European socialism by licking his palms, faking an illness and hijacking Cameron's dad's Ferrari 250GT California Spyder to break out his girlfriend, Sloane from said school so they can gallivant about Chicago for the day.

The school is renowned for another of John Hughes's most acclaimed and quotable films, *Breakfast Club* — albeit primarily for its interior and end-shot freeze frame of John Bender's fist-punching-air under the football posts. Without a car, not even a piece of shit car, the journey from Union Station on light rail to Northbrook took an hour. Then there was a mile long walk from the train station to the school. So fuck trying to get to Cameron's house — the stilted wooded bunker of glass-panelled panoramas in Highland Park, which by way of coincidence also shared its notoriety with another seminal eighties movie of teenage free-dom, *Risky Business*. What was left was less than daring, yet an achievable day's itinerary.

On Monday morning I woke in the style of someone planning to skive — late! There was the less than auspicious distinction to the start of the day's undertaking — I'm my own alter ego. Lena had to work and her friend Avery, whom I met on Sunday at a sex-themed spoken word night at the Burlington off Logan Square, also declined. I wondered if it was my fault for not inspiring people like Ferris. Walking to the Damen stop, the unequivocal answer I kept arriving at was, 'No way!'

I caught the Blue Line to Clinton. By the time I cross on foot to Union Station it's past midday and I've just missed the noon service. I stop at the Metro Bar and sink a pint of Goose Island Pale Ale. Sitting at the bar waiting for the next service, I appreciate there are much more depressing situations in which to imagine and find yourself in. But I can't help shake the feeling that there's something obscenely wrong and pitiful about embarking on a reimagining of *Ferris Bueller's Day Off* by myself. I'd have to let loose all my narcissistic tendencies on real people — which would make me a righteous arsehole, right?

The journey through Chicago's outer boroughs to Glenbrook North is dull. I examine the Milwaukie District North Line schedule. I calculate that unless I leg it the two miles there and back in one hour I'm looking at a logistical nightmare of wasting a total of three hours of my day just to see the fucking school. The only other reward of such a timely detour was the iconic "Save Ferris" water tower stood right by the Northbrook train station. But as I said before, transplanting movies into real life — transposing fact for fiction, indulging too often in delusions, or spending too much time living in the past or future breeds disappointment and is ultimately unfulfilling. This is why you should always *always* travel with low expectations. The problem with this is it's fucking hard to do — because even the idea of travel raises expectations to the rafters!

It's a strange committee of feelings finally arriving at Northbrook and seeing the water tower. I'm encouraged by finally clocking the first location of the day, yet deflated by the reality it doesn't look like how it did in the movie. It has since been repainted in the colour of a public swimming pool. And without the moniker "Save Ferris", or Jennifer Grey's original nose in the foreground, the water tower just doesn't look the same.

I trundle along a wide, manicured sidewalk, beside a dual carriageway through spitting rain to Glenbrook North High School. Since my vocational past involved securing permission to film on locations for media productions, I'm well conditioned to how hazardous pulling a camera out near school property can be these days. I'm prepared to announce myself, and my project to the school administration, and humbly request to take a couple of exterior photos. When I finally reach the school I can't see an administration entrance anywhere to follow professional protocol. So with the clock ticking *(encouraged by the imagined din of Special Forces deploying around the school perimeter along with the whir of charging Tasers tickling my ears)* I dart down a carpark entrance to the Performance Arts Building. It was on the steps of this building where Ed Rooney quotes the Book of Common Prayer to console Sloane's bogus bereavement. It was also this scene which consolidated Ferris's mythical status in every schoolboy's mind at the time — by succeeding in his highly audacious ruse to bust his girlfriend out of class then ask Mia Sara, 'Have you got a kiss for daddy?'

Compared to its onscreen persona, Glenbrook North High School justifies itself well in its affluent surroundings. The setting in real life once again appears decidedly different, but I know that's because films have long lenses and people like me to clear carparks. I reach the position of where Ferris stands to await Sloane's arrival. Even though it's clear Ferris parks at a distance to obscure his identity from Ed Rooney, my proximity to the school is already making me deeply uncomfortable. After all I'm a heavily bearded 35-year-old man, wearing a beanie and cargo pants, with a camera pointed at a school full of children. I can feel laser pointers dancing about my torso and forehead. So I get a quick photo and schlep it back to the train station in time for the next service back to Chicago.

By the time I arrive back at Union Station it's just gone 3 pm. So far what I have accomplished with the day doesn't extend beyond the first act of the film. Fretting over the lack of business hours left in the day I'm halfway up the Union Station steps onto Canal Street before I realise where I am — *The Untouchables* memorable Union Station shootout where Brian de Palma honours the famous Odessa Steps sequence from Sergei Eisenstein's *Battleship Potemkin*.

I had completely forgotten about *The Untouchables* in reference to Chicago, yet it's another iconic film capturing the quintessential Chicago during the prohibition era. Looking down at the intransient stone steps bowed by use reminds me of climbing ancient ruins in Mexico and Peru. It gives a visceral sense of just how many bodies past and present have scuttled up and down this staircase and evokes an arcane sensation when I consider such a young nation showing so much wear.

I cross the Adams Street Bridge to the Willis Tower. To say I'm not a traveller normally motivated by sightseeing is a heinous understatement. Rocks shaped like waves, buildings that aren't straight *(unless I'm watching bad Superman straighten them)*, mountains defaced with heads of past Presidents, the tallest *this* and the smallest *that* doesn't really 'pump my 'nads'. So it's with a fair degree of disconsolation and personal betrayal that I hand over $17 and take an elevator to the Skydeck of America's tallest building.

The Ledge, a boastful series of four glass-bottom boxes weren't around in 1985. But they're packed anyway with loud Russian kids and meek Koreans all vying for a fresh Facebook profile pic. So I go old skool like Ferris. I wait for the security guards to pass, get up on the railing, lean my head against the glass and see if I can see Cameron's dad because 'shitttt... the son of a bitch is down there somewhere.'

Given my aversion to tourist traps and entrance fees I have to admit the Skydeck offers a breathtaking view. Staring out at the vast Meccano landscape of human accomplishment a paradox of diminutive supremacy possesses me — like I'm the miniature master of a toy world. Below me, geometric monuments of dominance sprout upwards in a compact and uniform portrait of absurd beauty. The futurist dream is splashed in belts of sunlight and shadow. There is neither sound nor movement. I feel an omnipotent intimacy to the silent world below me. Ferris is right! Everything is so serene at 1353 feet! I have to keep reminding myself this is a living picture and not a still canvas. I surrender to the intoxicating contradiction of standing aloft in my own world and feeling at once both so close and so far away from everything that's important. My eyeline traces the straight flat shoreline of Lake Michigan north until it's lost in the hazy orange glow of the horizon. As the grey cracked sky projects shafts of lights and spills dim puddles onto the industrial carpet far below I start to feel lost in myself. I could get used to feeling like a god. I think I would be a good god, a just god — like the king from the Ween song *What Deaner Was Talkin' About*:

*If I was king*
*I'd wear a ring*
*And never hurt my people*
*I'd stay alert*
*And dress to kill*
*I might even slip you something*

My gaze sails over the grand structures of downtown, which fall away quickly into endless tracts of residential housing divided by gridded lodes of highways and bypasses. It's hard to believe but for the first time I find myself in a place that fiction and cinema have utterly failed to replicate. I wonder why in 1985 John Hughes didn't use the overwhelming awe of this vantage point to better translate the sense of dislocation in the blundering life of a teenager. Instead he pretentiously chose the Chicago Art Institute and the neo-impressionist movement to trigger an existentialist crisis within Cameron.

I notice the daylight starting to rot so I head back to the street view of Chicago to join the rest of the peons on the planet. My ears pop three times on the way down in the elevator. By now Chicago's notorious wind and rain have advanced in from the lake and settled over the city. It channels burred gusts along avenues and between buildings and lashes the downtown in short, sharp spells of drizzle. It tarnishes my mood, and like Cameron I feel tired and dejected, and I doubt that I have in fact seen anything good today. It's also way past beer o'clock. But I persist and continue down to the Art Institute of Chicago. My spirits rise briefly passing under the city's distinctive L Line. I imagine Jake and Elwood flying past in the Bluesmobile, bringing a whole world of mayhem in their wake. But by the time I get to the Art Institute of Chicago it's already 4.30 pm.

It hardly seems worth $18 admission for the last remaining hour that the museum is open. I briefly enter to get out of the rain. I peruse the museum gift shop and spot a calendar for sale with a print of Georges Seurat's *A Sunday on La Grande Jatte* on the back decorating the month of May. So with a fraudulent sense of success I tick the box of having a renowned piece of pointalism peel away layers of my soul in a montage.

I return along Jackson Boulevard, mimicking the majority of city dwellers at the end of their working day. As I turn onto Dearborn Street I imagine a throng of disciples start to swell behind the penultimate stage of my pilgrimage. The crowd continues to build, converted by the essence of Ferris's free spirit which I've resurrected by retracing his itinerary. Pedestrians alongside poor suited slaves exiting office buildings and subway stations are swept up in the infectious atmosphere. We pass Calder's iconic red Flamingo in what feels like a revival of the real life American-German parade Ferris joins nearing the climax of the film *(which also explains why all the ladies on the float around Ferris were wearing lederhosen)*. Over final credits we all march onward, drunk on Buellerism down Dearborn Street to fill Chicago's karaoke dens with renditions of Wayne Newton's version of *Danke Schoen* and *Twist and Shout* by the Beatles — accompanied by highly choreographed eighties-style dance montages.

In reality I limp past the Flamingo which is shrouded in construction fencing. I'm so delirious with exhaustion reaching my final destination, I'm not even sure it's right. It's the carpark where Ferris leaves the Ferrari with two questionable professionals. Who the fuck cares anyway — it's a carpark! As I stagger back on the El at Clarke/Lake I feel drained with hollow achievement, like I'm drinking light beer. I guess the moral to the story is if you're going to follow your idols do it properly:

i.  *Make sure you have mates: failure and disappointment can be fun as long as you have company to share it.*

ii.  *Steal a Ferrari 250GT California Spyder because they are so choice — otherwise you just spend the whole fucking day on foot and public transport, and don't even get to eat pancreas!*

iii.  *Booze 'n' drugs are okay, m'kay! I'm pretty sure I'm not wrong about this — freedom of youth IS booze and drugs and peer pressure. I'm not condoning that you get preloaded before a pilgrimage. All I'm saying is just because your idol doesn't drink and do anything more hedonistic, illegal or anti-social than steal cars, shit on his best friend, and cheat and lie to his loving family doesn't mean you don't have to.*

iv.  *Just because you're following in the footsteps of your idol doesn't mean you have to do EVERyThing they do: well, it kind of does, but who the fuck would really go to an art museum when they're skiving off school? I think what's most important when summoning your idol by re-enacting their deeds is to elicit the essence of your idol, rather than compete for some sense of exactitude.*

John Hughes did later admit there was a fair bit of self-indulgence with Ferris Bueller's visit to the Art Institute of Chicago. But since I skipped the Philadelphia Museum of Art I returned to the Art Institute of Chicago the following day. I spent four hours there. Seeing Seurat's masterpiece with naked eyes, as opposed to a print in a gift shop calendar was a surreal highlight. But when I discovered I still hadn't touched on the upper level's extensive collection of European Art before 1900, or the ground floor galleries dedicated to Asian, African and Indian Art of the Americas, I finally left under duress of suffering cultural catatonia.

Beyond the inevitable challenges and hazards underpinning any pilgrimage *(self-designed or otherwise)* there is the tendency for travellers' constitutions to grow fixated on hardship and sacrifice to feed a meritorious sense of worth or reward. In a religious context, the Protestant sect of Christianity strongly rejects even the concept of pilgrimages as being a blasphemy of sorts. The irony under Protestant faith is no matter the spiritual clarity found in mortification and sacrifice of a pilgrimage, in attempting to become more devout the aspirant becomes an apostate — unwittingly performing an action which nullifies the need for their Saviour to die for our sins. As such, the aesthetic layers of traditions and rituals are seen much like the sin of idolatry — cultish seductions which lure Christians away from the true foundation of faith. I identify with the wayward pilgrim but find value in this doctrine to keep in check the feeble idea of proving yourself before others — which many travellers like to shine and gloss when bragging about the risks and perils of their latest misadventure.

As a final salute to the enigmatic and perpetually shifting line between fact and fiction, Lena sent me a link on Facebook a week after I left Chicago. It was an article from the *Chicago Tribune* titled, 'Ferris Bueller's Day Off to be shown at Wrigley Field'. It announced a screening of *Ferris Bueller* to launch the stadium's inaugural season of weekly film nights and coincide with the film's twenty-fifth anniversary. Beneath the link Lena wrote, 'Look what you missed! Xxx'

# CHAPTER 12

# CONFORMITY OF CHARITY

Backpackers work very hard to maintain a balance of chivalry and nonchalance while traversing vast continents. It's an enigmatic synergy which serves to promote a sense of *oneness*. Like a mantra it's a constant exercise — suppressing emotions in a dry bag of composure that's all wrapped up in the apophenia of delusions and desires. It enables us to coast along as spectators in the perpetual swell of crested highlights and plummeting misfortunes from unforeseen turns of events. Affecting this harmony are elements of self-preservation and personal growth. But while they often consult backpackers travelling from one remote place to another, striking an accord can be messy — especially when the charitable gestures and enlightened outlook sought after on a long journey are clipped by the pragmatic reminder of long work hours, overtime and other sacrifices to afford a global trip.

It must be said that not all backpackers radiate altruistic vibes. At the darker end of the travelling spectrum, the covetous yen to remain free to roister unhindered across the globe grips backpackers like any pernicious addiction. And these selfish motives are blue kryptonite — turning some travellers ungenerous and dishonest to the point of petty thievery, fraudulent insurance claims and other illicit actions in their desperate bid to stay untethered from ordinary responsibilities. But no matter how beneficent backpackers seem, skirting the developing world, all of us at one time or another succumb to the accusation that we're all secretly super-rich cheapskates. Aldous Huxley addresses the inherent duplicity of charity in *The Perennial Philosophy*:

> *'Charity, of course, is essentially spiritual, and a love of this kind can be no more than its first moment. It is too much bound up with the senses, unless we know how to make use of it with prudence, and to lean on it only as something to be surpassed.'*

This viewpoint usually expressed by mendicant locals and vendors goes with the territory of being a fiscally challenged globetrotter. Yet, like anyone who feels underappreciated, vexations simmer from the recurrent misconception — because we backpackers work really fucking hard to be able to stand at the Pyramids, Machu Picchu, Rapa Nui, Angkor Wat, Teotihuacan and Palenque; cross the Eurasian tundra and circumnavigate the Antipodes; visit the Dome of the Rock, the Golden Temple, the Taj Mahal, the Imam Reza Shrine, the not-so-forbidden Forbidden City and Echmiadzin; touch the Sahara and swim in the Dead Sea; cross the Caribbean, the Adriatic, the Aegean and Caspian seas; traverse the Tibetan Plateau, the Pamirs, the Hindu Kush and the Tien Shan mountains; hike up the Rockies, the Andes, the Alps, the High Tatras, the Atlas, and the Carpathian mountains; see stars so luminous you feel you could jump up and grab them, and see the sun when it doesn't set.

It usually surfaces haggling over the price of goods or services — handlers who insist on being tipped when they don't do anything, and juvenile gangs antagonising us with demands for spare change. I often hear exasperated backpackers say, 'but I'm a backpacker, not a tourist.' They implore the locals to appreciate the difference between us, which beyond body odour and type of luggage and uniform is a debatable issue — distilled down to philosophical outlooks as much as finance. Flippant responses are made about how the sums of money asked or begged for are a pittance to us gringos or *farangis*. We lash out. We accuse locals that they don't know shit — we holler that the West isn't some fucking fantasy land where candy grows on trees and clouds rain money and that life is fucking tough everywhere.

Travelling through the scalding Balkan summer I met Tom and Howard on the Croatian island of Korčula. Tom was a magnanimous young Aussie in the ugly postmortem of a long-term relationship. Howard was a rakish New Yorker blessed with ambiguous ethnicity. He had invested in an IT career only to be utterly disillusioned with it three years on. At the time I had already lived in Manchester intermittently between travels for half a decade — bouncing around bars and student digs. I'd worked at some of the city's iconic establishments including Johnny Roadhouse, the Cornerhouse, and Kro Bar — and danced *(well sorta)* to the north's soulful breakbeats, meeting amazing people, getting higher than high, and falling in and out of some kind of love. And right when I felt like escaping again, Charles, the older brother of my best mate Felix gave me the chance to assist him on local film and television productions.

At the time I was a *maestro chasquilla* living off a base hourly rate. From high school and university through to living in the UK I had carefully amassed an abundance of skills. And between intrepid overland journeys I was confident the following experience would keep me forever employed on minimum wage: cash handling and till operation; letter dropping; stocking supermarket shelves and packing boxes; chopping wood; pruning; digging straight trenches; fishing and killing shit; baking, slicing and boxing pizzas; concocting the perfect margarita, whisky sour, and dry martini; pouring pints and frothing milk; selling fine wine; shelling shellfish and shucking oysters; reading maps; packing luggage; looking and sounding sincere and attentive when someone was really boring the shit tears out of me; making myself known with the finesse of Dr Marcus Brody in every village from where I stood to Sudan; surviving on the dole; and conceptualising without implementing how my life could be better.

Charles's offer gave me the opportunity to justify *(if somewhat erroneously)* my Bachelor of Arts in Creative Writing and Film/Television. I also fancied seeing what it felt like to earn more than £5.50 an hour. So I dedicated the following 18 months rather sensibly *(which is unusual)* to working in media production in Manchester. I'm glad I did. I worked with Charles for Company Films on two series of the original cult TV show *Shameless,* which was one of the most memorable and demanding working experiences of my life. *Shameless* illuminated the real side of *Mad-chus-ter* without which I would have left the birthplace of the industrial revolution with an unenlightened student existence — shuttling between work and leisure along the thin corridor connecting the city to the student haunts of Fallowfield and Withington.

I enjoyed the old skool nature of media production, the diverse people I encountered and the unpredictable and challenging nature of the job. I met some outstanding individuals, but after a while I started to despise the fissiparous nature of film crews. My exposure to the industry began to taint my impression that it was essentially plagued by a scourge of arseholes and burning martyrs. I'd also had enough of doleful Manchester and the splenetic north of England. I felt done. Like my time spent previously in London, I again wanted a change but didn't have a better answer than take the decent wedge I'd saved, pack my shit and hit the road on an overland adventure.

Tom, Howard and I decided to travel together back to the mainland to visit Dubrovnik. At the time Croatia lacked a hostelling network of any kind. Tenacious grandmothers, pruned and cernuous with age scrimmaged for our patronage at bus stations like we were bread, lard and cheese, which made accommodation easy to sort. And they typically charged flat rates for double and triple-bed rooms so it was economical to travel in groups. Apart from the financial advantage, Tom and Howard were easy company, and we held a healthy rapport from correlating circumstances that all had us using a backpack as a diversion and escape from our lives.

We strolled around the infamous walled old town of Dubrovnik, empathising with each other's predicament. We discussed our shared hiatus and ambiguous futures — debating if any real insight can come from the escape of backpacking. I'm guessing Tom was in deep reflection over this issue, possibly ignited from a fresh correspondence from his ex-girlfriend when we entered a *slastičarnica*. I can't remember who wanted gelato. It wasn't me — I wanted another 40oz plastic bottle of beer. It must have been Tom, because he paid €4 to a poor acne-blighted kid who joked how Croatian prices must feel like everything to us was virtually free. Tom popped. And recalling the gruelling overtime and monotonous split shifts endured to afford the trip, he vented a parlour of frustrations at the insolent presumption.

The adolescent kid was so repentant Tom walked out with free ice cream, colourfully decorated with sprinkles of his own contrition. It's sophism to contemplate such altercations in terms of right and wrong. It happens all the time — especially when heat and recent bad luck suborn an undercurrent of aggravations. It's all about perception. And while evasion is the chief architect behind someone strapping a backpack on and hitting the global circuit, self-preservation dictates a tacit conformity in backpackers. So there are no rich backpackers, no matter how big the budget or inheritance — in fact the term "rich backpacker" is so contrary it's virtually an oxymoron.

Our penniless status also lets us pass legions of homeless the same way we pass emaciated, crack-head beggars — convinced that a couple of dollars can't help — and who are we to decide the good fortune of one desperate soul over another? We multiply a couple of dollars by every dire person in need in every decrepit place we travel through. The maths is not difficult. It's easy to approximate because it's like counting stars. A day of goodwill would blow our entire travel budget. And given the overwhelming futility of the situation, we maintain a righteous position of neutrality to justify giving nothing. But what happens when a fellow backpacker is in financial trouble and the situation is compounded by their own stupidity or negligence?

Arriving in Tallinn while travelling the Baltics a year earlier I met Gabe, an Irishman who exemplified a backpacker's self-resilience. He had lived and worked in Australia on a travel visa. He then backpacked for six months up through South East Asia and China then along the Trans-Mongolian before punching out of Russia to arrive in Tallinn. Unlike the Irish mode of pack travellers I'd encountered previously, Gabe was a lone wolf. And by the time I met him in Tallinn it would be fair to say he had completely surrendered on the long, lonely journey to self-interests. When the occasion arose he would say,

'I look after one person – me!'

This in no way affected my opinion of Gabe. Travellers understand the importance of self-sufficiency — the trick as it has always been since the time of scriptures is finding the balance. After all, harmony and interconnectedness is the fulcrum for all religious schools and esoteric thought — to embrace the dark green spirit and stare into the void, past the illusionary reality of *I-me-mine* to find universal happiness, compassion and enlightenment.

Gabe was great craic, mixing a robust blend of doughty and bonhomie flavours. With a merry band of other backpackers I met in Riga we travelled at the same time up to Tallinn. We had a grand time exploring the old town and discovering a chthonic city of hidden coffee dens and bars buried behind and underneath the superlative medieval facade. We jammed in the hostel with guitar and drums, chilled in the hostel banya, and we drank. It was late November and we drank the way the locals drank away their Baltic winter, which incidentally was not that different from the way they drank to their summer.

It was Saturday night when Lewis, a glaikit young American from a German university exchange arrived at the hostel for a weekend holiday. He attached himself to Gabe and me on a routine nocturnal escapade. The invigorating cold air and strong dopplebock we downed at the hostel before leaving infused the night with an intrepid feeling. We started at Levikas, a subterranean bar just up from the hostel with such a notorious reputation for being a den of misfits, miscreants and roughnecks even tourists knew about it. And we were warned by hostel staff not to go there.

It was hard to avoid the Neo-Nazis sitting on long stools at the bar. It was even harder to ignore the Brobdingnagian sailor, who later apologised for his racist countrymen while telling us how he'd just returned from training exercises in the USA and couldn't stand taking orders from the 'fucking American niggers'. Yet it was virtually impossible for Gabe to repel a middle-aged, self-proclaimed witch who was fresh out of the clink and hitting on him hard. Her story was sketchy. It involved two years' incarceration for assaulting a man. But as Gabe continued to thwart her physical advances, the story's relevance gained traction with the speed in which she became aggressive. And with mounting spite she incited the locals around us — goading their nationalistic tendencies into telling all us foreigners to fuck off out of Tallinn and Estonia. Lewis, with his maladroit lankiness and long, limp hair appeared oblivious to what was clear to Gabe and me after a short time — if we didn't get the fuck out of Levikas we would most probably end up in a fight.

We drank up fast and exited with knuckles and noses pleasantly intact. My Dutch courage escorted me across the street to where two local girls looked to be in a friendly embrace against an old town rampart. It turned out one girl was holding the back of the other girl's hair while she hurled onto the pavement.

Dauntless, I inquire if they know of another bar nearby we might frequent for a quiet dram. The girl who isn't spewing says they're heading to another bar just outside the old town and we should follow them. So we did.

Being much more expert at walking through the freezing, snow-crusted Estonian night the girls walk ahead of us a short distance out of the old town to an Irish-themed pub. I lead the charge as we enter a peculiar office style foyer which connected the street front to the pub. Passing an indifferent doorman I proceed through to the bar to survey the desolate scene, turn around to Gabe and Lewis, and discover I'm alone. I walk back out past the doorman. From the foyer I scan the barren snow-laden sidewalk through the glass. I complete a disorientated Indiana Jones spin before saying aloud, 'Fuckers left me.' As the sharp resolute feeling of the end to the night descends *(not an unfamiliar feeling for those of us more inclined to revelry)* I hear the doorman address me.

'Toilet,' he says and motions to a separate entrance up a couple of steps in the back far corner of the lobby.

Gabe then appears from the toilet, grinning a merry grin with a jolly Irish saunter. With the night resurrected I turn to re-enter the bar but the doorman stops me.

'Cannot – friend too drunk.'

'What?'

As I turn back around Gabe is shuffling down the couple of steps towards me. Then I see Lewis, who has somehow miraculously appeared behind him, collapse to his knees on the first step and trickle down the remaining stairs on his shins and arse. In a fluid B-boy transition he spins himself around on the tiles and is back on his feet again, barely acknowledging the physical faux pas.

'Okay,' I say as I turn back to the doorman and ask very politely if I can explain the situation to the two girls who are expecting our company, which he agrees to.

'What's going on?' Gabe asks.

'I'm just gonna tell the girls we're not allowed in.'

'What?'

I signal with a look to Lewis, who as yet shows no sign of awareness of anything around him.

'Jaysus!'

Jesus was right. Jesus never let shit get in the way of a good time. I wondered what Jesus would have done with Lewis as we schlep back through the old town to Hollywood, an upstairs nightclub in the heart of Tallinn. Jesus would have been welcome company considering where we were going.

Hollywood was a facsimile to an evening's last resort that exists in every town across the globe — the nightclub everyone bagged, but invariably ended up at from time to time. It's my round when we get to the bar and the boys want vodka and Redbull. So I keep it simple in the deafening tumult of the club and order three vodka Redbull doubles. As Gabe and I turn around, drinks in hand, and lean back to settle into the bar and gaze over the dance floor pulsating with a glistening panoply of Baltic women, Lewis downs his highball like he has gills, slams the glass back on the bar and disappears into the thick energetic crowd.

Gabe by now has a steam up and is claiming Lewis is a liability that we should rid ourselves of before he gets us into serious trouble. He is right of course. Given backpackers proclivity for a drink and appetite for other substances, it's little wonder this is a prevailing provocation for confrontation and trouble. And the one thing in all walks of life most of us actively avoid is confrontation, especially when backpacking. It would be a nice thought if it was because all of us are endowed with *ahisma* — and since all life is sacred harming others only harms you. But in the case of solo travellers it precipitates from primal concern that there's only one person you can rely on to have your back, and that's you — so by default you are always outnumbered. It also seemed Tallinn had a talent for dispensing trouble. The night before last in the same nightclub a crazy Austrian traveller named Walter exuberantly lifted a young woman up off the ground on the dance floor on his way to the toilet. A local man followed Walter into the toilet and went *pop, pop* with his fists — and Walker exited with panda bear eyes and a terrorised look on his face.

Gabe and I held no loyalty to Lewis. And while I didn't disagree with Gabe's staunch display of self-perseveration I grew up in Australia. I was ingrained with the Aussie ANZAC drinking philosophy of never leaving a man behind. But after half an hour of discussing the matter, Lewis hadn't returned. And this meant he'd broken the sacrosanct rule of Australia's drinking culture — he hadn't got the next round when it was his turn.

'Fuck him,' I finally say and with Gabe's firm support we leave to head back to the hostel.

Lewis was an early topic of conversation the following morning. From the crew who were already awake and milling about the kitchen eating cereal I learnt news of the unfortunate end to Lewis's evening. Apparently he woke up at some unspecified hour in the early morning to find himself beneath two large bouncers at the bottom of the staircase by the front entrance to Hollywood minus his wallet.

Given Lewis's apparent allergy to steps, the news didn't surprise me. Recalling the debate with Gabe over our duty of care to help Lewis get home safely, I did feel a lightness of compunction flicker briefly. But Lewis seemed pretty philosophical about the event when Gabe and I saw him later in the day. He possessed an insouciant naivety bordering on laxity that comes from a privileged upbringing. I imagined a family home in the Hamptons, skiing holidays in the Swiss Alps and summer vacations in the Bahamas. Lewis was leaving that night back to Germany. Although he said it would have been nice to have spending money for his final day in Tallinn, the only place he could get money wired from his parents was at the airport, so it seemed a bit pointless.

No matter what path of inner or outward illusion or elusion propels independent travellers, constant self-reliance in any frame of life is exhausting. It's why all of us employ some degree of conformity. You only have to witness the changes in a back-packer's attire the longer they're on the road — see the practical zip-off cargo pants, sensible cross trainer footwear, breathable under layers, and versatile synthetic fibres employing Polartec and Gore technology succumb to trampoline trousers, loose linen threads, ponchos and messiah sandals. In a similar vein, whether a backpacker naturally possesses a humanistic spirit or not, it's rare to see self-interests outweigh the *Beat Zenness* backpackers brandish about in the company of others.

So it was amusing to observe the competing forces in a common room of travellers when hostel staff announced a whip-round to solicit a taxi fare to get Lewis to the airport. Some backpackers like Gabe were clearly opposed to rewarding stupidity and donated the shrapnel of loose kroon in their pockets. But a primary element of conformity is not looking like a dick — so everyone chipped in some amount. Lewis departed, only to blissfully reappear an hour later. Lewis blamed his ignorance of the 24-hour clock uni-versally used across the travel industry to avoid such confusion. And to an incredulous audience he explained how he missed his flight because it left at 1025 not 2225. Fortunately, since Lewis actually got to the airport he was able to secure a wire transfer from his parents. As I pondered what string of freak happen-stance got Lewis out of his own country *(let alone to the capital of Estonia)*, I realised I was starting to enjoy his company. And although Gabe found himself at odds with Lewis, they weren't that different. They both had no capacity for pretence, which flowed steadily through the backpacking fraternity. And I hoped at least that part of Lewis wouldn't change.

Travelling veterans might mock the misfortunes of the uniniti-ated, but to me calamitous stories of innocence abroad are worth the price of admission. Backpackers have a gift for recounting tales of woe with self-deprecating mirth and charm, and usually it sees the solicitude of other travellers sort them out. When I met Chloe, a delightful and guileless Tassie at the Hump Hostel in Kumming she was stuck there. She was stuck in Kumming, the Yunnan capital in southern China because she'd handed her passport in to the Vietnamese embassy to apply for a travel visa but had left herself without enough yuan to pay for the visa and get her passport back. And without her passport she had no identification to verify a wire transfer from her father to pay for the visa. I presumed she had plastic that wasn't compatible with the Bank of China's ATMs but asked the question anyway.

'Why don't you just use a credit card and get a cash advance from an ATM?'

'I don't have a credit card.'

'Why didn't you get a credit card before you left home?'

'I don't think I can get a credit card.'

'Why?'

'I don't know.'

Chloe's quandary makes me think of Henry Morley in Kerouac's tale of climbing Matterhorn Peak in *Dharma Bums*. Despite insisting on bringing an air mattress because he bought it expressly for the hike, Morley forgets his sleeping bag. Then shortly after commencing the hike he realises he's forgotten to drain the crankcase of his little English car. Concerned that the radiator could blow if night-time temperatures dipped below zero, Morley decides to put his mind at ease and returns to redress his oversight — a roundtrip of eight miles, which turns out to be unnecessary as the day and night remain mild. Even though Morley eventually catches up with Japhy and Ray, he opts out of joining them on a belated attempt at the summit. But the irony isn't lost on Ray that poor old feckless Henry is the most sage and Zen-like of the three:

*'I looked down at the small lake where Morley was lying on his back with a blade of grass in his mouth and said out loud "Now there's the karma of these three men here: Japhy Ryder gets to his triumphant mountaintop and makes it, I almost*

*make it and have to give up and huddle in a bloody cave, but the smartest of them all is a poet's poet lyin down there with his knees crossed to the sky chewing on a flower dreaming by a gurgling plage, goddammit they'll never get me up here again."'*

Man, Chloe's cute — and her naivety only adds to her appeal. I felt a Jungian conflict of parental and sexual desire and want to embrace her with both. As the evening mouldered away with a copious supply of sangria that fails to veil the hideous taste of cheap Chinese wine, the opportunity presents itself. But I'm not too into it. I had a beautiful Swede on my mind who was travelling from the real Shangri-La to rendezvous with me in Kumming in the next day or two. And I was helpless to the deceit she caused in my mind and heart. So I play the gentleman and offer to pay for Chloe's Vietnamese visa then fall asleep, upright in a chair with the sediment of cheap wine in my mouth.

More recently when I backpacked from the Yucatan to the south of Colombia, I noticed a chronic swell of insubordination and entitlement in the travelling world. Backpackers *(it seemed)* were simply refusing to return home when their funds expired. And they were using any method of family extortion to remain abroad. A recurring concept in Buddhist text, and emphasised in Zen practice is when we discover our true nature *(on the path to enlightenment)* it evokes the sense of having returned home or rediscovered our long-lost home. It is not surprising Beal, as quoted earlier, uses the terms *nostalgia* and *homesickness* to describe our desire to put ourselves in context of a sacred story.

Maybe I was getting old and couldn't recall my own youthful obstinacy to keep travelling when I couldn't afford it any longer. Or perhaps this was the corrupted legacy of the older generation of overlanders — who championed the rewards of prolonged transcontinental journeys. But it had me question what was instructing travellers' wilful trend to avoid home at all cost? Was it because they were on a completely different path?

Or were they yet to realise the trick isn't finding what you want, it's about not getting distracted by looking too hard for it so you notice it when it comes along.

I had witnessed the introduction of cheap airlines during my first years living overseas in the UK. With the collusion of the internet I watched a broad sense of wanderlust awaken the general public and popular media. And with it I saw the widespread passion for independent travel rise to meteoric heights. Coming from Australia which had a long history of airline monopolies and prohibitive ticket prices, I also felt the cheap airlines alleviate an unconscious pressure to stay away for one or more years — and it made me respect even more the travellers who under their own graft still aspired to embark on grand overseas odysseys. I wondered if the younger generation who had been ushered into this opportune period of budget travel took it all for granted the way children of any era grow up — blind to the fact they are the product of what preceded them.

Youth wasn't an excuse for Luke, a Queenslander I met working at Yo Mama's Casa in San Pedro La Laguna on the shores of the Lago de Altitlán. Unlike the majority of supine young backpackers proselytising from their hammocks, we were similar in age. Yo Mama's let me pitch my tent on a small patch of bull grass. It was out the back of the hostel, adjacent to a row of dilapidated double cabins where Luke stayed. I heard him wake each morning hacking a packet of cigarettes and dope from his throat while another year had fastened to his face from a night of intoxicants and lack of sleep. Luke was friendly enough, until he turned truculent and tiresome from the night of free beer awarded to him for working a shift. I assumed free beer and accommodation was the only payment for working at Yo Mama's Casa. And like most hostel employment it was a simple exercise in prolonging a journey.

Lago de Altitlán is a mountain lake in the central highlands of Guatemala, with a crenellation of Mayan villages nestled between lofty volcanic peaks. And the celestial waters make San Pedro about as idyllic as backpacker haunts get. As a result the town served up all the gringo fixings to ensnare independent travellers for a long time. There were bamboo bars and hippie hangouts; late-night dens with free DVD movie nights; menus replete with fruit salads, yoghurt, granola, health shakes, hummus, cheese, pizzas and other western fare; coffee shops serving export quality beans rarely retained within Guatemala due to overseas demand; spiritual retreats; and a myriad of land and water-based leisure activities. I still had itchy feet after hiking Volcán San Pedro so I continued on my journey. Three weeks later I was in León, a historic colonial city of Nicaragua. While exploring on foot I ran into Luke again with fellow Lago de Altitlán compatriot Jordan.

Jordon described how they just got into trouble with the law after Luke tried to buy weed off the street. The drug dealers turned out to be undercover cops. They kept the bribe Luke offered them then extorted the remaining money they were both carrying, and finally searched their daypacks for anything else of value which included Jordon's sentimental pocket knife. Luke admitted he was almost out of money, but insisted he would be fine. He outlined an elaborate plan to pry money from his estranged brother back in Queensland. And with a disturbing amount of forethought he described in detail how it would require a number of ingratiating phone calls before he eventually requested financial aid.

I found it hard to have any sympathy for Luke or his situation — especially given his contentment was derived entirely from a weed stash, bottle of suds and roof for the night. The places themselves seemed irrelevant. Sharing my opinion that Luke was becoming a serious liability, Jordon followed me down to Granada on Lago de Nicaragua, which rivalled León's pristine historical legacy. We journeyed to Isla de Ometepe, the indelible twin volcanic island in the middle of Lake Nicaragua to climb the formidable Volcán Conceptión.

Staying at Hotel Central in Altagracia, we encountered two Kiwi sisters who Jordon had volunteered with at an orphanage near Rio Dulce in Guatemala. Their salacious youth and recent litany of global adventures, including six months teaching English in Moscow, made me wonder how travellers so young could amass such sustainable earnings — especially when their penchant for party hostels had them patronise each one from Guatemala to Nicaragua. But they'd now run out of money to fly to Brazil. There they had a friend of a friend who had offered them jobs in the bar of a new hostel on the northeast coast near Belem or Recife. They were stuck! Or were they?

'We're not stuck! We just can't afford to leave.'

Jordan and I shared a quizzical look.

'So you're stuck.' I said repeating Jordan's initial claim.

'No, we choose to be here – that's why we're not stuck.'

'So how are you going to get to Brazil?' I asked.

'Wellll... I was going to apply for a loan, but we'll probably ask our dad first – because I think he'd prefer we owe the money to him rather than a bank.'

The rationale was irrefutable. I couldn't help but think of Jack Nicholson's Oscar-winning performance as the misogynistic Melvin Udall in *As Good as It Gets,* and his laconic response to a kowtowing receptionist:

Receptionist: *How do you write women so well?*
Urdall: *I think of a man, and I take away reason and accountability.*

The following day I bathed in sublime exhaustion after completing the most inspirational and diabolical hike to the infernal nose of Concepción. Nursing a longneck of Victoria beer after the eight-hour trek I thought again of the two Kiwi sisters. When did this tendency to stay away from home become an obsession? Or was this sense of entitlement symptomatic of the post-millennium's updated new order — where time and distance lack digital potency — and were now idle concepts of convenience or inconvenience? Perhaps the mania has always been there, to placate a traveller's fear that they may never get the opportunity again — so we keep going onward to somewhere new — and never *ever* look back.

Only three weeks before I met Jordan and the two Kiwis I had the veritable sensation of being stranded when my email accounts were hacked. I was staying in Antigua, a colonial treasure of Guatemala, prized for its beauty and vibrancy. I knew my accounts were compromised after three attempts to withdraw money from nearby ATMs failed. At first it didn't make any sense. I had just checked my finances the day before at a local internet cafe. I rushed to the closest cafe and that's when I realised I'd been hacked. I couldn't log on to any of my accounts and as my Paypal account was linked to my email address, which in turn was connected to my credit card, all my finances were in jeopardy. It led to a rack of fraudulent internet purchases that battered the savings out of my account. I cancelled all my bank cards and made an urgent request to my sister for a wire transfer. Being financially shipwrecked on the other side of the planet is a horrible stew of helplessness that's hard to digest. Yet, seeing how my sense of liberty was reliant on the impotent plastic and 40 quetzales in my wallet gave me pause — and made me thankful it was just a matter of money.

I felt sore but not sore like a victim. To live the life of a Beat Zen hobo, to seek out rawness in the world invites vulnerability — to earthly elements, as well as experiences which freely fluctuate between the depths of a destitute void and the soaring heights of sukha. This is what happens when you give value to people and things — they require faith and faith doesn't come cheaply. I'd lived in Manchester where getting robbed and mugged was an annual event — and I'd been through this shite way too many times before. Some would see the fact that I've been mugged and robbed 13 times as an omen of bad luck. But what's the point of falling down if you don't learn how to protect yourself so you're not hurt as badly the next time it happens.

That's why I carried a final contingency in my rucksack like any experienced rogue agent. My last resort was so well stashed in my daypack I had to unpack everything to find it. When I inspected the immaculately folded greenback I took it as a good sign that the $50 bill was decorated with United States President Ulysses Grant. And old serious looking Ulysses didn't disappoint. It got me across the more challenging coastal border of La Hachadura, El Salvador, and supported me over a weekend of frugal living in El Tunco before I received a Western Union cheque the following Tuesday. But this wasn't some unconditional handout. And apart from the rare exceptions of truly emancipated individuals, backpackers are lying, ignorant, or unappreciative if they don't believe their sovereignty is moored the emotional and financial support of good friends and family.

In our current climate's crusade for third-party accountability I wondered if some backpackers had lost the onus of personal responsibility. Maybe it's an inherent part of travel and before now I was too young to see it. Either way, it's a corruption to treat the art of travel with exclusion. In all facets of life, self-interest and solicitude need to find harmony and conformity with those around and nearest to you — because like everything else in life, travelling draws value from appreciating where you've come from and where you're heading, and the sacrifices and rewards that come along the way.

# CHAPTER 13

# THE REALITY OF ARRIVING

Touchdown and disembarkment, no matter how foreign or familiar can be a daunting experience. Overseas trips for many are a dream of a lifetime — a fantasy which can percolate for months or even years. Then the impending reality approaches all too quickly. As the cabin crew prepares for landing, the final in-flight crew announcements summon a liturgical air of deliverance to the onboard congregation that's busting to alight. Amidst the clamour of screaming kids, a revival of nerves ushers in the impending new reality.

For me, the reality of arriving is the counterpoint to saying goodbye. As the aircraft banks sharply to the right the premonitory reckoning of dharma and karma fairies rally for attention — still buzzing from the short awkward departure lounge embrace which tried to undo everything it couldn't. This is because it's hard to board a plane after saying goodbye to someone special without a mutiny of feelings from all the things you meant to say but didn't, or did say but fucked up. The aircraft yaws steeply back to the left to correct its approach vector and the cabin lights dim. Trepidation accompanies the mechanical jolt and whine of landing gear being extended under foot. And an asinine rhapsody of insecurities and self-assurances adds to the hubbub of the cabin on final descent.

'What am I fuck-ing doing?'
'This is a bad idea.'
'I'm exactly where I'm meant to be.'
'Shouldn't I be trying to buy a house?'
'Life's too short.'
'What if I'm injured or kidnapped and killed?'
'No regrets.'
'What if I die right now in a plane crash?'
'I am a falling raindrop.'
'What if people don't even call my death a tragedy?'
'The weight on my back reminds me that I'm free.'
'What if I fail?'
'Stay the course.'
'Shouldn't I get a proper job, a family, settle down and forget about all this Beat Zen rucksack revolution crap?'
'Come back to me – the real me, the best of me who waits for open roads, and mountain tops and the spaces between places.'
'I have nothing.'
'I am nothing.'
'I am the whole of a doughnut.'
'I am the i in A-'
'I am a rock – I am an island.'

The bump, soft skid and shudder of landing breaks the mental spell. But for dissenters of rigid itineraries and noble separatists to suitcases and conventional living, tarmac touchdowns also signal the most pragmatic drawback to air travel — the onerous airport procedures. And in the post-9/11 reality of flight travel it's fair to say much of the former glamour of international travel has been lost. Whether luggage is pushed in prams, pulled by wheeled trunks, or harnessed to the back, the *resferber* of arrival quickly stymies from the tracasseries of airport protocol. And the residual thrill of being feet on the ground in some place new suspires in long static lines with pensive hands clutching a passport and relevant documents.

There is however plenty of time for new reservations to take hold in the exasperating processes of airport immigration, baggage claim, customs, currency exchange and scouting out economical ground transport from the terminal building. You're rich in the idleness that compels you to recheck that all the fields on your arrival form are filled in correctly. You reconfirm the PDF printouts of your flight booking are in your laptop satchel, and fish out the tourist visa payment receipt, which is still in the front pouch. You fumble through your cargo pant pockets for the shopping docket from last-minute bought toiletries, which you used to scribble down the hostel address of an even more last-minute booking. And once again you pull the guidebook out of your daypack and take a mental image of its central location on the downtown map.

For added excitement maybe you've refrained from booking onward passage because why would you? You're a leaf in the wind. So before departing you ignored internet forums which warned about recent immigration changes. The procession of émigrés ahead starts shuffling forward. The relief that felt so sweet when you checked-in without needing proof of an onward ticket returns now with a weary and sickening sense of perfidy. Consternation grows as you're drawn agonisingly slowly towards your impending and uncertain fate. Like an encore to the vigorous crescendo of neuroses provoked by the plane's arrival, you now start to entertain a new palette of qualms.

What if the government has had a gutful of gringo-grunge radicals? Perhaps escalating unrest has aroused suspicion over bohemian insurgents spreading free-spirited practices? Or maybe the newly instated usurpers are actively discouraging the scourge of tourists and travellers, believing them to be partly responsible for the kleptocratic practices of an ousted government?

You question whether you've been too arrogant and dismissive and curse yourself for not booking a cheap disposable one-way bus ticket across the border. You search the snaking line for the consolation of another raffish filibuster, or knave to the open road. But all you see are frazzled families and red-eyed couples mustering Samsonite luggage with armpits of thick transparencies and airline sponsored compendiums of travel documents. To appease your concerns you start rehearsing your story to immigration officials.

'I'm a writer… no, not a journalist, a writer… an author-'

'My brother's a pilot so I fly standby… Yes, it's no bother booking another flight at any time.'

'No, because it was standby I was only confirmed on this flight an hour before it departed – so yeah… no, I didn't want to book another ticket until I knew I was on this flight to avoid any date change penalties.'

'Yes, I've got over five grand in savings and a credit card.'

'Yes, I had a travel book published late last year.'

'About five hundred copies-'

'Yeah I know it's not many-'

'Copywriting and proofreading contracts-'

'No, not a lot – but it's a good fit cos I can work remotely and travel at the same time.'

When you finally arrive at an immigration booth the perfunctory inquiry about the intention of your trip is almost disappointing in light of the creative energy spent in line combating all manner of interrogatory questioning.

'Ah yeah just tourism – backpacking cross-country for the next six months.'

*Chk-ddk – Chk-ddk*

'Enjoy your stay sir.'

'Thanks.'

The sound of a passport being inked is as sweet and golden and reassuring as the exquisite whir and flutter of an ATM approving your withdrawal. It almost reignites the thrill of arrival — where the wallop of the immigration officer's entry stamp is the starting gun heralding a new trip and adventure. But then you're corralled into the baggage claim hall and a final luggage search at customs where inevitably you're picked to unpack your hard drop Tetris-stacked rucksack. The stifling commotion of the arrivals halls reminds you you're in a foreign country where everybody speaks a language different to you. The nearby ATM is broken and the currency exchange counter is closed because it's after business hours. The information desk predictably has no concept of the world beyond the automatic doors of the terminal building. So you exit the arrivals hall into the sticky heat of the night and hump like an acolyte between prehistoric terminals in search of a working ATM. The raw sting in the shoulders from a crippling backpack is exacerbated by the cumulative weight of a daypack, digital SLR and acoustic guitar. Fatigued, frustrated and tackling a new language on cabin swollen feet, you realise you still have no idea how to get into the city without paying a budget-breaking cab fare.

Debate over the reputations of countries and airports with the most draconian customs and immigration is a savoured subject among international travellers. While this kind of discussion provides a luxury of officious treatment and raving injustices, the stories soon turn repetitive. Australia, USA and the UK usually take honours as highest ranked leading rivals. However, what remains undisputed is in the post-9/11 epoch of global travel suspicion reigns supreme. And all us errant scholars and scoundrels, soi-disant reformists and backpacking rebels — we're the mushahadeen to captious airport personnel.

Hell, I was once ushered through airport security arriving back in my hometown because my subversive beard and long hair didn't match the short cropped and shaven thumbnail image of respect in my passport. It was entertaining enough watching the immigration officer's studied glare oscillate from the onscreen display to my passport and back again. So I tentatively joked,

'Last time I was in Australia beards were still legal – if I had known I would have shaved before departing the UK.'

'No, no – it's fine,' the female officer absently replied before launching my passport into the air with an outstretched arm and hollering, 'SECURITY!'

'Is everything okay?'

'Yes, everything is fine – you just need to follow the security officers.'

'Who?'

I spun around in the opposite direction to two uniformed officers approaching. They emerged from the mischief of passengers who were regrouping with stray family members following their own personal ordeal of airport arrival. The officers snatched my passport like a relay baton. With sober-baked expressions and an implicit directive to follow, I was chaperoned to a nearby service counter where my passport was transferred to Federal Police for further scrutiny over my identity. The absurdity over how difficult it was to re-enter my home country compelled me to joke more freely with the officer behind the counter.

'It's funny you know – I was sat next to two Scottish backpackers on the flight here and as we came into land I said the irony of Australian customs and immigration is you'll probably have an easier time getting into the country than me.'

The dour female officer looked up from her computer terminal with a blank stare.

'What's your mother's maiden name?'

'Hahahaha – you know that's the security clearance question my bank asks me?'

Disbelief that standard interrogation was well... so standard was met with stiff silence.

'Just answer the question.'

In light of the harmless questioning I was disappointed. My mind was filled to its fertile limit with espionage make-believe. And I've always secretly craved a lethal challenge of wit and intellect. But instead of trading 007 double-entendres I fatefully waited for the officer to photocopy my passport, stamp it, and sign it with undiluted severity then send me on my way.

Despite the gauntlet of airport arrival, backpackers are valiant insubordinates. We are the hamburger filler in the queues — adaptable and malleable we push through the quibbling repartee, accusatory looks and aggressive interrogations with a stolid grin. But what if a port of entry symbolises something more than just another vay-kay or escapade — what if it represent a new life with someone sweet and crazy and too easy to love who's patiently waiting on the other side of the terminal?

I knew my luck was running low as I strode up the carpeted gang plank to the vacant immigration booth at George Bush Intercontinental Airport in Houston. I was well schooled in the reality of arrival. This was my third consecutive re-entry into the USA and I held a doctorate in the Imperial Lord Vader tactics and treatment traditionally conducted by US airport customs and immigration officials. I'd previously used the ESTA visa waiver free program. But the last time I entered through LAX a pedantic customs officer pulled me up for a previous overstay of less than 24 hours and rescinded my ESTA privileges. So I returned on a H1/H2 visa — even though a visa meant shit to US port of entry officers. In fact a US visa is a contradiction of sorts because it guarantees nothing — and the amenable staff at the US consulate confirmed as much when they granted my visa.

The reason I keep coming back to the USA is because of Rosie. There's also an unrealised road trip I've been dreaming about since I was a kid. It's potential lingered in the supernal days and weeks of previous visits that I spent living and writing out of Rosie's downtown Charleston flat — and now rested with the Subaru Legacy I bought during my last visit, which was parked and waiting at Rosie's flat for the big adventure.

Rosie and I had been together, more or less since we first met 18 months earlier on my travels up the east coast. We were

introduced through Sienna, my Couchsurfing host who accepted
my request hours before I boarded an Amtrak service from Savannah. Sienna's presence glowed warm and golden and sage as the
sun. I was Siennafied in less time than it takes to hold moments
together — which is altogether too rare and dangerous for a
traveller because then you never want to leave *(trust me!)*.

To say our first introduction was less than auspicious would
be an understatement, as well as a gross injustice. After all, this
is the real world remember — where flirting with disgust and
loathing are just as legitimate vessels for true love as smitten
neon-lit, rain puddle gazes. I arrived midmorning when Sienna's
day of classes and work commitments commenced. Not that I
minded. A new destination beckoned and as always on arrival
in some place new my legs barked to be stretched. So I spent
the day exploring the incomparable antebellum elegance and
postbellum charm of downtown Charleston. When I returned
to Sienna's vintage Spring Street houseshare, Rosie was sitting
knees-on-chin on the lounge room couch. It wasn't that I didn't
notice Rosie. It was just that she didn't say anything — cloaked
in diffidence like household camouflage.

I had also been living a solitary existence for the past five months
as I backpacked through Central and South America. Travelling
on my own I built up fresh congeries of contradictions — which
stemmed from a sense of exclusion over the masquerade of emergent
travellers, and where I fitted into the new mix. My libido was out of
order. And my analogue radar broadly attuned to signs and signals
of mutual attraction suffered. Askance glances, bang flicks and hair
tosses, petite sips, winks, and nervous heel-toe-rockers had packed
it in before I even made it across the Nicaraguan border. But to be
fair my Kerouacked ego has always been rather shit at discerning
the attentions of the affectionate kind without high gravity input.
And while I try to stay positive, I'm easily discouraged. Rosie later
admitted she was struck silent by my Australian bravado — the broad
accent, the McCartney beard, and the healthy Hibernian curls. 'The

full package,' Rosie called it — something of fantasy she'd gathered from movies and cultural references which made me love her more.

As I hand over my passport opened to the page with my visa I remain optimistic. I remind myself that loves knows no border — except of course love that's been barred by the curmudgeons of US customs and immigration. A resistant old Turk shakes his head as he flips through my passport then speaks with diction still thick and fresh from his homeland.

'No.'

'No what?'

'You cannot do this.'

'Do what?'

'Keep coming here.'

'I can't keep coming to the United States as a tourist and spending all my money?'

'No.'

'Why not?'

'Because you cannot.'

The old boy brusquely flips through my passport again like someone who looks at their watch without noting the time.

'Stand here.'

The explanation, which sounds a bit flimsy *(and which I hope is just a limitation of his pay grade)* ends with an abrupt gesture of where to stand. The officer places my passport on an open surface at the back of his booth for collection. Déjà vu rains. A few minutes later a short, perky Vietnamese man joins me. Then a passing officer collects us and our passports like supermarket items as he browses the row of immigration booths. After he's amassed a sizeable group of nervous sightseers, we're escorted to a fluorescent white room. It has a soulless veneer and ambience reminiscent of places that dispense migraines and tragedy such as hospitals and government buildings.

I shuffle along a vacant row of chairs. The same Vietnamese man follows me and we sit down in the middle with two empty chairs between us.

'Are you on the boat?'

'What boat?'

'The cruise boat.'

'Are you on the cruise boat?'

'Yes,' the man nods. He gestures inclusively around the waiting room and adds, 'we all have job on boat.'

'Oh... I'm just a backpacker.'

The man nods again, agitates in his chair then ditches me for safer company of three other Vietnamese men sitting in the front row. I scan the room and realise besides me it's comprised solely of young Vietnamese men conversing in their own tongue like hopeful applicants before an exam. By now my nerves should have been pored over with worry. But I'd been operating solely on complimentary in-flight booze and three temazepam doused in minimal sleep for the 42 hours it took to get here. I reconstitute the silliness of it all with the sentiments of Lin-chi, Zen master of the Rinzai school of Zen Buddhism:

> 'Friends I tell you this: there is no Buddha, no spiritual path to follow, no training and no realisation. What are you feverishly running after? Putting a head on top of your own head, you blind idiots! Your head is right where it should be. ... Stop turning to the outside and don't be attached to my words either. Just cease clinging to the past and hankering after the future.'

So I shut out the heavy luminescence that imbues all waiting areas. I let my mind stroll along meditative shores induced by open-ended travel. I think about the apprehension John Steinbeck expressed when planning his trip with Charley — that in all long-range preparations for travel we hold a private conviction it won't happen. It makes me think how rarely the point of departure coincides with the jolt of awareness your long-awaited trip has begun. It's funny that the fears which hinder trips and naked insights are the same fears which attach themselves like barnacles and come along for the ride. I look down at the scuffed up tips of my hiking boots set against the polished enamel flooring. I try hard not to think about what had got me here and what is waiting for me. But so much promise is waiting, it's hard not to.

My first night in Charleston still felt like yesterday — a wild trance spent with Sienna and Rosie trawling the bonhomie banya of midtown bars along King Street. It was like a time of yore, prior to mobile connectivity — and we were a tight trio of potulent funambulists traversing the social telegraph of downtown venues with aplomb. We reached the high street shopping district of lower King Street. We stopped at Mellow Mushroom and filled up on tofu hoagies and vegetarian pizzas before bursting into the Upper Deck. I was soon drunk on this paradisiacal coastal enclave of Lowcountry liberalism ensnared in the conservative South.

The Upper Deck was dead so we headed back up King, stopping in at a couple more bars to see who was about. We ended the night at the Rec Room AKA Recovery Room, the epitome of a last orders dive bar that also boasted a rather intimidating reputation for having the highest volume of 12oz PBR consumed out of any venue in the nation.

Back at Sienna's I helped her topple a campaign placard erected in the vacant property across the street while Rosie kept lookout. Sienna's punch-drunk plea argued the bullshit sign of local politics was an eyesore that had blighted her street front view for the last fortnight. I struggled to see what view Sienna was talking about as I tumbled over the iron fence behind Sienna. Landing softly on a bed of overgrown grass I justified my actions were not vandalism, rather job creation. But this sort of sane thinking had no place in the current mission at hand — which was in the here and now, and to which I'd been training all night to build up my rye-tanned courage. In fact as Sienna and I rocked the heavy banner loose of its foundation I was mystified as to why my cavalier and drunken demeanour was so greedy to impress. But that's because it often takes retrospect to see it's standing on the other side of the street — perched in stealth with hands cupping elbows and an owl-eyed stare.

The next day I reconvened with Sienna in the late afternoon. Rosie was there in the same spot on the couch like before. I was happy to see Rosie again following our enduring bond of anarchist collusion. She had a silent eloquence and alkaline temperament that fitted our collective aura like esoteric curves of candlelight and fēng shuǐ. Rosie felt familiar, but not in that way people typically describe first connections — feeling like they've known someone forever. To me this is a cosmic tragedy. I fear the all-knowing, having its divine machinations revealed like the prestige of a magic trick. I enjoy the bravado — the idea of knowing everything. But in reality knowing everything would suck. And when the novelty wears off where are you supposed to find the inspiration to re-know and rediscover someone or something you already feel like you've known for a lifetime? I have no idea — but then I'm a glutton for inspiration and get bored way too easily.

I guess I just figured Sienna and Rosie, or Rosie and Sienna was how they rolled. Hell, for all I knew Rosie was gay too. I didn't know because she had given so little away and said nothing about herself. But after spending the majority of the past 24 hours at Sienna's I didn't expect Rosie to linger too long. I figured she surely must have shit to do elsewhere. I wanted her to stay though — like pluming a horizon, Rosie's company at least gave me a vision of possibility. The evening attached itself to the late afternoon, as is the way of Charleston and the South — and gestated with talk and promise over the onset of new nocturnal frivolities.

For Rosie's benefit I waxed lyrical like a regular Dave Dundee from the hackneyed script of Antipodean tall stories. She remained demure and attentive as a dormouse. Occasionally, she interjected with questions, curious about Downunder like it was a mythological land. Meanwhile Sienna mined the cornucopia of social connections on her iPhone, germinating possibilities and charting infatuations for an evening of fresh interactions.

Housemates, Wes and Oliver circulated between the dilapidated front porch and the insulated pet sounds emanating from their respective bedroom. And we regularly shifted from the lounge room to the front porch for a fag. It was as if the old pink Single House and everyone in it was thrumming to an impromptu yet intricate dance, which was beholden to the halcyon stillness of Charleston's summer after dark. Preparing to leave Sienna, Rosie and I stood in the vestibular kitchenette downing shots of Fireball. I felt conscripted with such a sense of comfort and belonging I had to keep reminding myself I had only been in Charleston one whole day. As I threw back a second jot of mingin spiced whisky I realised this feeling was something much more profound than simply being moonlit by hopinated suds and cinnamon-infused liquor. The *goya* or suspension of disbelief I originally felt from immersion in an opportune moment was being gently deposed by something more fragile and permanent.

Maybe it was all because I was just shy of my thirty-fifth birthday, which I was keeping schtum. Perhaps this is why for the briefest period I felt a quantum dimension trying to reveal itself — like when you're intercepted by crazy coincidence, or find yourself traversing infinitesimal bridges of perfection extended between seconds. I watched the dregs of the Fireball bottle orbit around me but I declined another shot.

Midnight was upon us when we left Sienna's. We headed back to Upper Deck where it was decided we would arrive at a much more respectable hour for the late-night venue. As we turned onto King Street a cool breeze lifted to gently comb the wooden gables and tiered piazzas of downtown in light relief. I asked Rosie the time.

'Ummm... five past twelve.'

'Well, it's official then – it's technically my birthday.'

'Whyattt?' And suddenly for the first time I saw Rosie in technicolor — all lit up like vigil candlelight.

'Are you serious?' Sienna added.

I nodded.

'I love birthdays more than anything,' Rosie said and I believed her.

As we passed Marion Square and crossed over Calhoun I tried to explain my own reluctance to announce or celebrate my birthday. It was a familial disposition — but also for those of you not born under a Virgo star sign September birthdays can be a fucking popularity contest. And I have never been attracted to the spotlight. Anonymity is my counsel. I'm an introvert who shows off solely for the attentions of girls — preferring obscurity — sitting out of earshot at the end of communal tables, lingering behind a rollicking pack on the way to the next watering hole, and hovering outside circles for the strategy of a quick exit. Indulging my eccentricities, Rosie seemed to carry the celebratory spirit of my birthday for the two of us like the burden of a feather. She was still glowing with the news when we arrived at the small overhead sign on King Street marking the off-street entrance to the Upper Deck. In a township of extravagant transparency the Upper Deck was a small dose of avant-garde concealment which cities love to boast about — even though everyone *(at least in the alternative scene of Charleston and the college circuit)* knew about it.

We file down the graffitied corridor and up the steep, rickety staircase. In through the back door entrance we cross the eponymous wooden decking. It's the size of an intimate lounge room and has a healthy midnight capacity of emos, geeks, stoners, nouveau riche hipsters, karaoke junkies, kitsch addicts and smelly cute urban yoga-hippies. Rosie and Sienna's unrestrained and indeflatable enthusiasm for cinnamon whisky and birthdays is contagious. We hook onto the small bar squashed between the dance floor and the toilets.

'What do you want Dave?' Sienna asks.

'No way Kangaroo José – you're hosting me. This round is mine.'

Sienna leans into my ear and whispers loudly, 'Dave you might have guessed – I'm not a poor student so let me buy you a drink.'

In the short time I'd been at Sienna's I did notice the random boo radleys who buzzed her place at odd hours — entering as if they were already trying leave. I sensed Sienna's fierce maternal spirit came from a childhood that was auctioned early. And the fact that she was resourceful enough to build up a fortress of independence by selling dope while putting herself through college made her even more awesome.

'Okay, um… beer then,' I reply.

Sienna is soon sucked into the Sapphic world of brightly dyed hair, bold undercuts, inked skin, full lips and avaricious eyes. Left standing at the bar with Rosie we smile the way people do when things they want to say stay stuck in their heads. We lean into each other's ears to combat the din and try to converse in short broken observations and questions while I drain my plastic beaker.

'We need birthday shots!' Rosie sharply announces with her polished Southern lilt.

That's when Rosie had me — had me in headlights. I'm not going to lie — buying me a drink would have been enough. It's not the gesture alone even though I've also always found gender reversal undeniably sexy — especially when offered by a princess from a faraway place. Through the dim lit bar I see Rosie framed with an ethereal expression of fearless damage. Soaking up the euphoria of the moment makes me realise Rosie is a destination of woman I have never encountered before.

I lean back into Rosie's right ear and bellow, 'You're not buying anything – you're a student.'

'Pshhhhshhhh-'

'Well you know there's an Australian tradition called rounds?'

'Whyttt?'

'In Australia we never let a round go unanswered – it's actually a gaolable offence.'

'Oh, I love that – I think we have that here too-'

Rosie orders two shots of tequila. I respond with two more shots and a chaser. Sienna crashlands back into the bar, gushing with cinnamon-spice details of a girl-on-girl shakedown in the ladies which turned into a provocative and steamy encounter. The culprit is Annabel, a reckless sea-glass Cinderella with a formidable reputation according to Sienna.

Annabel and her panache of household cohorts now gather around us at the bar. To be fair, I have no idea really what the fuck is going on inside or outside the dive bar female restroom — except for the irrefutable fact that I'm missing out and can't enter the kingdom of understanding even if I try because I'm a dude. What I do see in Sienna and Annabel are two equally brash street warriors, armoured by ardour. I hear them hatching an onward plan when Rosie orders two more tequila shots.

'Did you just order two more tequila shots?'

'Uhhuh!'

'We're leaving-'

'Whyatt?'

'One for the road then. How are you so wise in the ways of us Antipodeans?' I say beaming a golden agave grin. Unsure of the joke Rosie shrugs and bites her lip but latches onto my smile with one final toast.

By natural persuasion we find ourselves spilling out of the Upper Deck onto King Street with a much larger attaché. But the seditious nature of large travelling groups quickly manifests itself in the short walk back to Marion Square. By the time we reach Calhoun Street, the Rubicon of downtown adventures, Sienna is moaning about the walk home — and debating with Annabel over hailing a pedicab. The general sense of entitlement by everyone else to express their own views in a loose pack on the corner of Calhoun and King conveys a sharp sense of agreement that everyone is piling back to Sienna's place.

My senses however, are far from sharp. Tequila is doing its job right. That's why even now I find it hard to explain how the clarity of Rosie's softly spoken voice reaches me through the noisy charm of lesbians.

THE REALITY OF ARRIVING

'I think I'll walk.'

In the loose cobwebbed moment, the corner of Calhoun and King is my universe, and my universe is talking to me — talking through the sweet, dusty Mexicana fog of tequila. I'm reluctant to say *voice* because there are no words uttered in my ear, or emblazoned letters in my head. The words are a colour in a dream, where I automatically know the message.

*She's talking to you – follow her stupid!*

Call it instinct, the cosmos, my birthday, or a Cadillac Margarita of all three — but I reply with the verbal equivalent to an awkward yawn.

'Oh yeah – me too, actually. I'll walk with you if you like.'

It's a lie. I want a rickshaw ride. It's one of Charleston's quaint accompaniments to downtown tourism which helps keep a healthy portion of CofC graduates employed in a post-study malaise. But I want Rosie's company more. Sienna and Annabel have agreed on a romantic ride in a pedalled chariot. By design yellow bike taxis start to gather. Everyone else is still busy debating the worth of paying to be ridden a few short blocks when Rosie and I announce we're walking. Well at least that's the way I remember it. No one reacts and I wonder if everyone is in on the universe's plan. But then I think the opposite.

The walk back is moonlit taillights and I can't remember anything of what we talked about — except the awkward pressure when words and talking run dry. Before I know it I grab Rosie and kiss her fiercely up against the jail bar glass front to George's Loan Co. pawnbrokers. I feel Rosie put her heels into the brick skirting to take my weight and my lips. Her arm is around me, hand through the back of my hair. Mine are pushing on her bra, fingers through her hand then gripping the back of her neck, the other from behind pulling her hips into mine. With a smile Rosie later says how she will always remember my exact expression when I was about to kiss her. I've asked her to describe it but she says she can't and I don't know what I looked like since I was looking through Rosie.

Out of my peripheries I spot a solitary cop car slowly coast by along King Street. Through golden goggles of tequila and beer the universe's inner machinations *(at least for the infant hours of my 35th birthday)* are luminous and lucid like a runway at night. I'm struck with a peculiar sensation that I will see that cop car again. It doesn't take long.

Incidentally, the time it takes for my natural hesitancy towards public displays of affection to reach a physical abeyance is also the exact amount of time a Charleston squad car needs to turn around and park just behind us. It turns out Charleston police also don't like public displays of rampant affection either. Good for them — I like it when the United States of America and its Muslim cousins can celebrate their commonalities. All wrapped up against the side street window pane I don't hear a sound until the officer speaks.

'Alright kids – that's enough. It's time to go home.'

Unwarranted torch lights in your face are never fun — especially from men in serious looking apparel. From my anarchist indiscretions the night before, I feel a karmic pardon in the acquitting officer's tone of voice.

'Okay sir – no worries! Sorry for the trouble.'

Rosie and I exchange a cheeky grin — tacit in understanding, barely intimate we're already in trouble with Johnny Law — angels help us!

'Did you hear that – he called me a kid?'

'Shhhsh! You are a kid!'

'It's like getting carded in every bar I go to – US tourism should promote themselves internationally to thirty-somethings as a trip that will make you feel younger.'

'You're silly.'

'I suppose I am.'

We skip back to Sienna's with clasped hands swinging like a porch swing of new love. But the sobering encounter with law enforcement has by contrast turned Sienna's place into a merry madhouse of mayhem. We pass through the kitchen and lounge where I bunked on the couch the night before. Sienna and Annabelle are on Sienna's bed, bandaged in sheets and profuse in fits of rapture. Stubborn to leave, the cohorts happily linger, plastering themselves against walls and all over my crib. Our arrival gets minor acknowledgement. Everyone else has either found, or is still desperately seeking their own night-time tragic-magic that they can own. I start to wonder what time it'll be before I'll get to lay down when Rosie leans into my ear and whispers,

'Do you want to go back to my place?'

I nod, thinking when do you say no to god? Rosie lived by herself in Mt Pleasant and by the time we get back to her upstairs flat we've returned to a perfect state of drunkenness for physical undress — where clothes are a nuisance and hips make sense. They fit together perfectly like random jigsaw pieces that we are — against the apartment door, against the kitchen bench, on the armrest of the couch where I pull Rosie's knickers down and off of one leg and she spurs her heels into my back, down the hallway in a fumble, on top of one another in Rosie's bed. There's no indecision — nothing to be worked on, to be rehearsed or engineered. It's syncopated prosody as hands devour with hot breath and wet kisses. I cup her breasts and her wetness. Rosie takes me and I take her — to capture an elusive and fleeting promise. I look up at Rosie and watch the flare of ecstasy across her smile that comes in and out of view of her maple brown hair and long bangs. We're both greedy and selfless for the well of each other's limit — fumbling through movement and transition for love and climax and the simplicity of oneness.

I stayed at Rosie's from then on which is why I missed my prebooked Greyhound service to DC two nights later. Once more I took comfort in the burgeoning thrill of new love resting on the kerb of another goodbye. Three nights later we were at the Amtrak station in North Charleston. Standing on the platform outside the station building we're equally determined to deter the inevitable and prolong the impossible — the inescapability of time. I know it well — how it plays with vicissitudes of distance and fills the space between goodbyes and the next proposed reunion with ineptitude of words and conjecture.

Just like the stark disparity between the anticipation and reality of arriving, I knew the truth behind halcyon holiday romances is they hurt too. The script is the same — it's just the context which changes. And this is my life, not a movie. I admit Hollywood is adept at basing films on real life events. But Hollywood and audiences demand a recherché smorgasbord of perfectly-timed heroics and acts of redemption that are all too scarce in the real world. In reality, protagonists rarely survive endings that exist beyond the odds. Love isn't everlasting. And a frantic race across town to catch regret at the airport will in all likelihood incur hefty parking fines and a restraining order.

I've bet on the open road again and trusted the relentlessness of rail to corral me back on my premeditated journey up the eastern seaboard. But of course I still have to try. I am the underdog up against insurmountable odds in a glutted up world of cynicism and scepticism. So with the same fanatical vulnerability I give to the open road, I give to Rosie. I put my untouchable faith in the cosmos and its undertow into the void of an uncertain future — knowing it could well be playing the hand of tragedy. I hold Rosie in my arms with hands on her arse, which makes her blush. I never make promises I can't keep, which is why I rarely make them but I promise Rosie I will be back — it's one I keep making and keep keeping.

Three hours on the ground in Houston tick tock by. It gives me comfort knowing the glorious spectacle and distorted dream of the United States of America was built by the underdog. Tolerance and perseverance are my Camelot and Lancelot. I remind myself of the guiding premise to Eastern philosophy, which is balancing great doubt with great faith — and realise it doesn't really matter what you're into. Past the metaphysical nitty-gritty it's still light and shade, faith and doubt, logos and eros, harmony and chaos, me and you, form and formlessness, shamatha and vipashyana, nirvana and samsara, oneness, nothingness, allness and emptiness — just slightly different ways of perceiving it. As Ram Dass expressively states:

> 'The art of life is to stay wide open and be vulnerable, yet at the same time to sit with the mystery and the awe and with the unbearable pain — to just be with it all.'

I wait a further half hour in the small white waiting room before I'm granted a short interview with a polite immigration officer. Satisfied by my visa and the amount of money I am travelling on I'm unceremoniously let back into the USA. Originally, I had decided to spend the night at the airport like a true backpacking limpet since my Charleston connection was scheduled early the next morning. But now I reconsider. I book the cheapest room I can find at a nearby Days Inn using a courtesy telephone. I spend another 40 minutes outside in the furnace of a sublevel pickup zone, trying to comprehend the frenetic system of complimentary shuttle buses. I finally find the right ride to get me to a sacred bed for the night. In two weeks Rosie will graduate university and look to embark on her own travels while also threatening to join me on mine. I have arrived but in no way do I feel like my adventure has begun. With the same uncertainty I also know the road trip I'm about to embark upon will linger long after it is over.

# CHAPTER 14

# WATERFALLS AND ARCHES

To witness the yin and yang of tourists devouring their annual quota of nature, one has to look no further than the Uffizi of sculpted canyons and rock formations which is the Colorado Plateau. Located on the Four Corners of Colorado, Utah, Arizona and New Mexico, nature has spent millennia shaping a canvas of desert and blue sky into something astounding. Containing the greatest concentration of national parks in the country, its epicentre in the state of Utah is the regional city of Moab.

Swelling in vacation periods with the chaotic throttle and torque of outdoor enthusiasts, Moab is a peculiar little irrigated mirage of civilisation. I was halfway converted by the silence of stone when I rolled into town on an empty tank. Crossing New Mexico I'd been drinking in the holistic vibe resonating in the numenia of colossal sunburnt monuments. Passing through Henry Ford country into southern Utah the dry wind cartwheeling through the Canyonlands massaged rooftop memories of Rajasthan — sinking Kingfishers with a pageant-faced American named Heidi, who liked to linger on her own after holidaying with her mother.

Inside the Canyonlands' southern entrance I pitched tent on the vast uninhabited tracts of BLM land. The resident heat and glow of dusk exhumed a familiar sense of isolation as a kid on coastal summer holidays — riding my bike through small townships of Cervantes and Jurien Bay which were always deserted in the daytime due to the heat. But that was all about to change. Ahead of me were the Arches, Capitol Reef, Bryce Canyon and Zion national parks — cardinal wings of a colossal open-air sanctuary know as Glen Canyon.

Ironically, Glen Canyon's undiscovered magnificence turned out to be its curse when facing the unmitigated destructive might of Western progress. In the 1950s, conservationalists led by Sierra Club founder, David Brower, successfully fought a highly unpopular proposal to dam Echo Park in Colorado's Dinosaur National Monument. Although it was a major victory, Glen Canyon was ignored in the process and became the viable scapegoat for a much more expansive scheme than originally planned. At the time the compromise with the Bureau of Reclamations was even endorsed by the Sierra Club. Brower, who visited the region before construction began, later noted that it was one of America's most regretted environmental mistakes. Good intentions and all that shite I guess. Sadly, it's also nothing new. When I travelled through China in 2007 the plaintive echoes of 'see it now before it disappears' resonated in reference to the Three Gorges, the controversial dam which finished construction the previous year. The dam has already caused devastating environmental issues. And it seems China doesn't give much of a shit about its people or legacy either since it displaced well over a million people in the process. But it's funny how tourism, often considered a pariah defiling the chastity of fragile habitats, can also bring awareness to environmental causes.

Damming the Colorado River eradicated the natural ecosystem and much of the Glen Canyon's serene splendour — sealing its fate as a lost paradise. A new generation grew up in the area with the recreational benefits of having a big-arse lake in the middle of a desert — as if it had always been there. But with climate change, chronic drought and a steady increase in tourism, opposition against Lake Powell and the damming of the Colorado River Storage Project has persisted — with renewed activism to pull the plug and restore the natural order of things *(if that's even possible)*.

However, all this was rather difficult to see as Tog, my Subaru putted and stalled into the nearest gas station. Moab isn't shy at showcasing the diversity of avid borrowers of nature — all seeking to harvest restorative fruits from its plentiful orchards, which is hard to source living in big cities. But while everyone is on their own hunt, everyone's doing exactly the same thing. So on first impression Moab resembles a Wacky Races refuelling station — a less-than-holy crossing for the phenomenal spectrum of tourists and travellers.

There are the perpetual drifters with winter coats tattooed to their packs who move with the weather and the reflexive Zen of Forrest Gump. Then there is the budget coalition of couples on rented road trips, and facsimiles of me a decade ago who still dare to ride Greyhound and hop off silver-lined coaches wearing lost and determined expressions of a novitiate. I'm part the lucky upgrades, scruffy raconteurs and open-road warriors with four-wheel autonomy. We travel with our lives on display in the back of a station wagon like a Vietnamese spring roll — the messy order of bedding, clothes, maps, cheap tinned food, dry lentils, nuts and trash open to inspection through dusty tinted windows. Next are the adrenalin junkies and aggressors to gravity. Finally, the holidaymakers which include retirees who sold up their stake in the American dream for the mobile version; tour buses full of senility and dream bubbles; and family litters of tired eyes and forced smiles led by Frankenstein fathers of greying stubble whose harrowed conviction still believes everyone will at least enjoy the trip in hindsight. The spirited scene comes along with the hubbub of an outdoor lawn mowing convention as everyone gears up and revs up two-wheelers, quad bikes, SUVs and RVs to embark on carbon-copy holiday circuits.

To make the most out of the day I head a short distance north to the Arches National Park. Enshrined with scenic lookouts and carparks full of vay-cayers is a phenomenon of nature-trail tourism that must be tolerated — especially when it is typically attached to a hefty entrance fee. Just beyond the turnoff I pass a dude lying prone like a soldier in the red dirt on the verge of the road. He's attempting to take a macro photo of a desert flower, which is being uncooperative by blissfully swaying in the light breeze. I can't help but pity his premature show of exuberance because he has so far to go. As I pass the visitor centre rammed with family wagons and luxury behemoths and ever other blessed size and shaped automobile I reconsider. Maybe I am the one who's wrong. What's wrong with premature exuberance in the digital age — it can handle it!

I consider stopping at the visitor centre but the amount of traffic moves me on. I want to hike, to feel the timber in my legs stretch on a long walk. So I push onwards to Wolfe Ranch and the trailhead to Delicate Arch. The arch is the Venus de Milo of the park, so of course everyone in the park is already there including a newly arrived tour bus. And the three mile hike in the midday heat discourages no one. I watch the exodus of the docile herd from the bus with strange delight — enfeebled bodies holding Zimmer frames and walking aids, eager to join the ant trail going to see what all the fuss is about.

With our limited human perception it's often hard to capture the sheer magnitude and context of natural wonders. Luckily, we have aeroplanes, helicopters and hot air balloon rides for those who can afford them. The Delicate Arch is no different. Its embodiment of natural grace *(which prompted the state of Utah to emboss it on their licence plate)* is inspiring enough. But to appreciate its dramatic stance on the precipice of a rocky abyss requires a separate drive and short walk to an alternate viewpoint. To avoid the crowd I take this option — to breathe in the fragile immortality. I mill about for a few minutes. I try to frame the spectacular breadth and majesty of the scenery with a couple of photos. But capturing a hollowed-out knuckle on a cliff edge that is lost in a fossilised sea of scorched red rock is like taking a picture of a supermoon with a smartphone. Mindful of getting stuck in the dyspepsia of vehicles departing Wolfe Ranch I quickly move on.

The problem of Amerikana caging nature with admission gates and scenic looped roads of pristine tarmac is you can start to feel like you're trapped in some crap, outdated safari park. Entering the national parks in the USA is the equivalent to doing laps in a carpark with righteous scenery. And invariably you end up at the mercy of the slow moving cavalcade in front of you. There are frequent signs reminding drivers they're on a functioning road and not to stop. But many still do, taking photos like they're on an automated monorail. Thankfully, holidays and wildlife exude tranquillity; otherwise national parks would be a blood bath of road rage.

On the way out to the Devil's Garden I stop at the Fiery Furnace. I shuffle behind the other hypnotised pilgrims up the short trail to the view of a Gaudi dreamscape of rock fins and mazes that dance with sun-beaten contrast and colours of mushroom, ochre and white charcoal. By the time I get to Devil's Garden, which houses the greatest concentration of arches in the park, it's busier than at Delicate Arch.

'Fuck it,' I say to myself, 'it's all just a heavenly pile of rocks anyway,' so I keep going.

I scan the map for the most out-of-the-way place with a decent hike. It's obvious. Situated in the northeast corner of the park, Tower Arch is at the farthest reaches from the checklist tourist. Just like countries with bureaucratic visa applications and pedantic immigration procedures, I was sure nine miles of winding unsealed road and a 3.4 mile trek would cut me loose from the seasonal muster.

Slowly cruising out into desolation, over corrugated track, hearing the squeeze and pop of gravel under tyres is uplifting.

And I'm relieved to see only a handful of other parked vehicles when I arrive at the trailhead. The trek is loosely marked by ducks and shoe prints in the red sand. There's not another soul in sight. Hiking over rock and soft sand in the desert air is purifying. The silence is sanctifying. It's not the cruel and confusing-as-fuck disconnected silence we compost because we're tired of hearing excuses wrapped up in reasons. It's the loud-and-clear quiet that's meek and reflective and makes deserts the dojo-libraries of nature.

I let my thoughts unravel in the edifying heat. I wonder what it is about nature that makes us want to run off to be in it when we travel. What compels us to go out of our way to see waterfalls, arches, land bridges, flumes, yardangs, hoodoos and other odd-shaped rock features? Most of us have been there at some point on a trip. The desire is immutable — to surround ourselves in some kind of nature while on holiday, or at the very least convince ourselves we are doing so. We alight from planes, trains, buses and boats at gateway towns with the express purpose of seeking out the highest, greatest, deepest and most stupendous grade of natural phenomena previously sold to us by the internet and guide books as a "must see". Even the most sceptical ne'er-do-wells window-shop with languid poise at laminated possibilities along high street realtors peddling photocopies of the same tier packages. Not that an abundance of options ever gives a greater sense of fulfilment. True happiness generally comes from less. And it's irrelevant to the budget backpacker when confronted with a compendium of limitless options because we will invariably pick the cheapest.

When there is no choice conformity of travel beckons all breeds of tourists and travellers to board the only motorised ark to tour an outdoor gallery of masterpieces. When there is freedom away from guided tours and money to be saved, backpackers unite. From Mongolia to Australia spendthrift travellers connect with resourcefulness and zeal to fill vehicles and set off on overland tours of their own accord. Organised or not, both methods can be a curse or reward. Just like being on a cruise, or staying in a one-pub town the experience comes down to luck of how well a group bonds or curdles. I don't find it appealing being forced to get along with a bus or kombi full of motley strangers — along with the frequent toilet stops, onboard palaver, lunchtime buffets where everyone's greedy to get their money's worth and sunsets through tinted windows. But the menagerie of personalities and miscellaneous agendas that would otherwise rarely intersect *(except at baggage carousels)* is an entertaining sideshow to vast backdrops of barren landscapes.

It's every traveller's prerogative to want to feel like we're on our own unique quest. So we often go out of our way to preserve the feeling we are on an adventure of our own design. But I think a lot of us deep down feel we need to see everything everyone else has seen first before we spin a globe and book a ticket to the country our finger lands on. *(Call it a fear of inadequacy, or maybe it's hypocrisy.)* Of course this is impossible, especially since the next undiscovered natural treasure that's trending is in constant flux. As one "unmissable" paradise is ploughed by infrastructure and inflated prices to cope with the number of tourists, another hidden jewel somewhere else on the planet is propped up as the new "lost world".

Maybe our conformity in seeking out nature and provincial dwellings comes from the rational threat of change — natural relics pimped out and vandalised by tourist hoards, along with the disappearance of regional customs and culture. Many of us are aware as portraits of locality with their unique lyricism, rhythm and quaint anachronisms are increasingly lost, they're repackaged with a generic global brand. And this kind of ecological and cultural endangerment is what inspires a lot of us to go on a trip. I'm not suggesting the extinction of stinky cheese, fermented horse milk, or tejo *(national sport of Colombia)*. But it is certainly a mitigating factor choosing "hot spots" prefaced by warnings "See it now before it's gone!"

With a bit of distance it's not hard to see the whole affair as something profane — people shinning up rocks and skidding down ravines 50 feet from parking lots and laybys to join barricaded galleries of paparazzi tourists. The spectacle is made more ludicrous as tablets, smartphones and selfie sticks enter the foray of professional long lens kits — being held up like periscopes with everyone eager to capture the same digital image already reproduced under perfect colour and light and sold at postcard stands by kiosks and gift shops nearby. It's as if everyone is running around with Faustian zeal, like taxidermists extinguishing the last of a species from a misguided sense of preservation.

Tourists like to put a HOLIDAY in small caps — give it significance like a subheading or *ism* in their life. Not unlike the rest of us, they trade in the currency of proof, desperate for photographic evidence to update their online lifestyle. After all, a digital souvenir is better than a memory to show everyone afterwards — especially if it's all soon to be lost. And this scares the shit out of me because they may not be far wrong.

None of this seems to matter when I arrive at Tower Arch. As the largest arch in the park its stoic grandeur empties me. A small pride of travellers lay in its shadow. Presumably, they've been searching for nature's solace like me — to have Nature all to themselves like greedy lovers, and why not? The site is respected with a silent reverence given to places of worship — everyone sucking on fruit, crunching down trail mix and water, and conversing in muted tones of German, French and American. I bounce over stone, looking ridiculous as I squash my recumbent body into narrow crevices trying to frame the arch in my 28mm Konica lens. I then relax under the shaded heel of the arch. I imagine I'm standing in the crossing of a cathedral. I listen to the hallowed resonance while savouring a balsam breeze that's cooled by the voluptuous curves and permanent shadows of the gulch behind me. I lie down in a rock cradle and feel my selfness melt like cool larva into the rockwork. I get it — the stillness, the potential, the

dharma of it all — if but for the briefest moment. On the way
back I've had my fill so I do what everyone else does — I take
shitloads of photos on my old Nokia handset from my moving car.

I've been two days and nights without a shower. As I exit the
Arches I settle on finding a hostel in Moab to spend the night.
But the sun still hangs immovably in the sky and the northern
entrance to the Canyonlands is just a few miles ahead. So I decide
to make use of my weeklong pass and detour back through the
Island in the Sky before driving back to Moab. I drive along
the scenic route to the Grand View Point Overlook. I jump the
wooden railing and leap across a deadly fissure to a vertiginous
tower of rock. I crawl on hands and knees to the edge where the
escarpment curls away behind me. It provides an airplane view
over a giant basin of rocky tumours and blackened veins. I crouch
low against a gale. It bullies the camera in my hand in forceful
sets that circles the belly of the canyon. Without another soul
in sight I watch the Canyonlands simmer into the night with a
florid glow.

Again I wonder what it is about arches and natural portals
that enrapture us so much. I'm not talking about the deification
of landmarks and their ancient and animistic connections — or
the unregenerate tourist trying to access the axis mundi from a
spiritual foghorn of nature. For most of us in the West this union
was extinguished with our forgotten ancestors aeons ago. Is it just
because arches and land bridges are aesthetic and rare? Or is it
something deeper, a spiritual reverberation? Do we find a chalice
in nature to slake our bendless drive to bridge and destroy stuff,
or are we just lamenting a lost connection? Arches are, after all a
potent symbol of connection. To a traveller nothing epitomises
where we've been and where we're heading more than crossing
a bridge between territorial divides. Perhaps arches are a natural
relic symbolising something we've forgotten like a dream — we
kind of get it but can't see past the surface because we've gone
too far. So we mimic and build our own instead.

*Bridging a Gap*
*Bridging a gap*
*Crossing coulees guarded by mesas and mountains*
*Bridging a gap*
*Crossing ancient canyons and gorges*
*Breaching borders and new lands*
*on bridges over river torrents*
*Bridging a gap*
*The way nature intended*
*Yoked to the rain and seasons;*
*Arches over gulches*
*Rainbows laid up on unreachable horizons*
*Waterfalls conspiring between high plains and low valleys*
*Bridging a gap*
*The taut knee knocked distance*
*like a suspension bridge,*
*To once familiar land*
*A leap of faith*
*to her face, her lips*
*The unripe almond green of her eyes*

The Lazy Lizard hostel was the only hostel in Moab at the time and had the shitty charm and facade of a highway thrift store. The upstairs dorm room was undergoing DIY renovation which was the only reason there were vacancies. A temporary mattress between leftovers of carpentry work completed earlier in the day isn't for everyone. It suits the colourful ragtag collection of cliff monkeys and downhill berserkers who mingle well with rootless travellers and budget road-tripping tourists. This is because to travel light and on a shoestring inherently nurtures a fetish for hazards and hardship. Doing anything repetitively without incident *(including travel)* eventually loses its own reward. In the same manner the serenity of nature isn't enough for sporting enthusiasts and outdoor extremists. Decimating past and future requires an added jolt — throwing yourself off a stable perch, pelting downhill at quadriplegic speed, scaling sheer cliffs with ghost-knuckled fingers, and fishtailing down backcountry slopes through sternum-cracking boulders and woods. It actually all sounds rather absurd when I think about it in such terms, which I do. But it's all about outward ritualism — just like the ruminative, yet lazy traveller, strapping on their pack, waving *sayonara* and going in search of their next *kensho* buzz.

We welcome the passive insights that strike atop a Himalayan summit; watching a golden sun sink behind a black ocean; being caught in the warm rain and lightening of a summer storm; or staring into campfire light which dances to the acoustic rhythm of ukuleles and drums. Not that there's anything wrong with this since I'm writing it with myself in mind — spiritually invested, carrying a vague sense of deficit but not devout. Maybe that's why mysticism is such a perfect fit for the unorthodox and idiosyncratic personalities of so many budget backpackers. We're curious but not committed with an overriding credo to take shortcuts in everything other than the physical route. Is this the reason we mix the hedonism of happy hours, drug tourism and tantric couplings with monasteries, ashrams, nature retreats and volunteer work — everyone concealing an everyday desperation to forget — trying to cultivate our own botanical garden of happiness, to have real-world worries melt away to the cocktail umbrella and swizzle stick of a brittle moment?

The open road is an epithet for mediation and offers the perfect soundtrack with a litany of idyllic settings — annexed on an aquamarine lagoon with a cool beer in one hand while the other holds onto a promise that's attached to a radiant smile; sleeping under the shoulder of champagne-lit mountains; sitting on a wet rock divining the ephemeral faces in the spray of a tropical waterfall; or picking up the girl you love in San Diego, driving up to the Redwoods and seeing her sunlit delight chirp as she bites into a perfect campfire vegan s'more.

Sat in the half-lotus position at a picnic table outside the hostel I meet Seth. He resides in northern Arizona where he attends a unique open-learning college which he states is one of only five in the country. Not unlike many graduates, he is a degustation of seminal college learning and is anxious to regurgitate the rich stew of all that he's assimilated.

'Hola señoritas – Cómo estás?' he says to two young female travellers with healthy curves. They sit down at the opposite end of the bench holding a loaf of bread with cheese and salami slices.

'What? We don't speak Spanish!' says one with a thick European accent, making it hard to tell if they're annoyed or not by the interruption.

'Where are you from?'

'We are from Austria,' says the friend.

'I'm so jealous.'

'Huh?'

'I'm a rock climber you see.'

'Yah.'

'Have you guys ever been rock climbing?'

'No.'

'We like hiking.'

Effeminate, passionate and acutely sensitive, there is something socially awkward about Seth as he tries to connect with everything around him, which is why I already like him. With the fading light putting the first stars in the sky I remember the two-thirds bottle of tequila and two Mombacho cigars I bought in Charleston before I left.

'How about a couple of stogies and some cheeky margaritas,' I say to make everything all light and social.

'I've only smoked cigars a couple of times on special occasions when friends have graduated.'

'Settled then-'

I go off to my car. When I return the girls are gone.

'Where did they go dude?'

'They left.'

'I thought you were in with the blonde one.'

Seth's face contracts with discomfort.

'I'm just happy to have met them.'

I realise while Seth possesses a rigid facade of *Zenness* there is something amiss — it's pious and cartoonish like he's pretending to someone he's not. Engaging his passion for free climbing, he tells me he started at the age of 12. It's partly the reason he studies in Arizona because it's a premier location for the sport.

'Do you consider it an extreme sport though?'

'It can lead to extremism,' Seth replies while gingerly sucking on his cigar, 'and that's the danger.'

'So what part of it is confidence and risk? I mean don't these sorts of pursuits by their nature push you further and further into an unsustainable realm of danger?'

'That's why I took a break.' Seth coughs and takes a gulp of tequila with sweet and sour mix.

'Is a life-or-death scenario necessary then to acquire the pro-found insight you experience?'

'No,' Seth instinctively answers then pauses and says, 'yes, I guess so.'

He extrapolates on his experiences — the *oneness* with a rock and the climb, the perfection of when it all integrates and the mind is empty and like liquid — one limb flows over the other effortlessly, losing a degree of consciousness until you're finally atop what looked like an impossible plinth of stone — staring out over a magical desert expanse, amazed and still reeling in how your own body got you there. Then recalling the thread of the original discussion Seth digresses.

'And everything in life is risk – being here tonight, sitting here – I mean a jet engine from an airplane could fall and land on us right now.'

As I watch Seth start to trace semicircles with the rim-shaped condensation from his glass I start to wonder if he's a bit carparked and light-headed from the smoke.

'Life is concentric circles,' Seth adds, 'and we exist comfortably in the centre. But we need to push ourselves beyond that to gain experiences we can then return with to reflect on to bettering ourselves.'

While drawing his finger back and forward in zigzags between puddles of water Seth says, 'The problem with extremism is it pushes further and further out into the concentric rings without retreating to reflect.'

'Like the blasphemy of the devout pilgrim?'

'Hmmm, I need the restroom but I'll be back.'

In this tone of mystical self-indulgence and intoxication, I wonder if we need to caution our growing tendency to personalise spirituality in the West. How much is to blame for confusing, misdirecting and disguising our motives for travel — or at the very least legitimising the reason for a trip? Maybe it is why we all turn to nature — because Gaia does not judge or care. And her compassion in absorbing all our faults, insecurities and desires is boundless. Seth sways lightly as he returns to the table holding a hipflask of whisky, which he says is to complement our dwindling cigars.

'Just like art,' Seth declares as if he had never left the conversation. 'Art is about the human desire for improvement. A painting should usher you on a journey across a canvas.'

'"True creative power isolates one and demands something that has to be subtracted from the enjoyment of life,"' I say quoting a favourite line from Herman Hess.

'It's all about the doing it for the right reasons though... and being in the right head space. When I look up at a rock I'm about to climb I know I will climb it. Forgive me if I start sounding too philosophical-' then struggling for the right words Seth grips the table.

'Wait! It's like me and table – I am the table in this moment-'

From the robust Nicaraguan tobacco and whisky nightcap Seth descends further into the well-versed vernacular and rhetoric of spiritually lost young Americans trying to find themselves.

'That's why I had to take a break,' he finally says again before we both agree it's a good time for bed and bid each goodnight.

In the morning I continue west, circumnavigating the jewel-encrusted crown of the Glen Canyon towards Capitol Reef. Anticipating the car-lined charade of its scenic drive I veer north off SR-24 before the Capitol Reef Visitor Center. Over arroyos and loose rock I head out into the Bentonite Hills and Cathedral Valley. There is something unsettling venturing through the striated landscape of lichen colours — treeless mounds spored red, grey, green and blue. I stop at the Temple of the Sun and Moon. These towering mainsails add to the spooky terra firma, resonating with an ancient power that's hard to grasp or describe. Rimrocked, I push poor Tog up a talus staircase to Harnet Junction and the Cathedral Valley campsite. The campsite is empty and protected by a cove of stunted pine. Parking up by a picnic table I listen to the howl of a high plains wind while I brew a coffee and boil a packet of ramen noodles.

In the tradition of great travel writers *(who always seem to be seeking reconnection and mourning cultural degradation)* it seemed fitting, in addition to writing exhaustive lists of shit, that I name my ride. Steinbeck named his Rocinante after Don Quixote's horse, while Heat-Moon called his van Ghost Dancing to honour his ancestors' resurrection rituals at the end of the nineteenth century. Feeling pretty bloody daunted by the literary legacy before me I referred to one of my favourite childhood cartoons from Hanna-Barbera. I named my four-cylinder, white station wagon after Mighty Mightor's pet pterodactyl and trusted steed named Tog.

Tog obliges my obstinance to backtracking and we cross into Fishlake National Forest. We trundle through the eldritch quiet of dormant aspen stands and lake-studded snow. Without the restrictive rules and prices of national and state parks and monuments, the national forests in my opinion are not only the USA's greatest natural legacy, they're one of the best things about the nation. Although there are many to thank, it was Theodore Roosevelt who shaped the US Forest Service — establishing free and open refuges for anyone from weekend mudslinger to outlaw. We eventually descend from the mountain tops, connect with the SR-72 then get back on the SR-24 to intersect the scenic byway 12. I travel south through Dixie National Forest with its bounty of camping opportunities then over the Grand Staircase-Escalante. Charged by the certainty this will remain one of the most memorable drives of my road trip, I'm almost disappointed when I reach the township of Escalante on nightfall.

The following morning I'm in the courtesy shuttle boarding area outside Bryce National Park. I'm encouraged to take the free shuttle but not that encouraged since there is no reduction in the $25 vehicle entrance fee. Despite filling up on Zen after camping the night at Posey Lake, I'm piqued by the cost and in a quandary about paying for what I think I will loathe. I text Rosie who has just arrived in San Diego.

> Should I pay $25 to see Bryce Canyon?

> Of course you should!

Rosie has a moon-time kingdom of crazies and spontaneous changes of mind, but they tack on a sharp keel of shrewd certainty about what she thinks or wants, or knows to be true in her heart. I'm sold! So I line up behind a couple with eighties barnets and holiday garb to match, who keep exclaiming how they just hiked five miles in Zion to the cashier. I wait my turn to purchase a ticket and board the next available bus.

I get off at the general store with most of the other passengers looking to gorge themselves on information, refreshments and trinkets made in China. I'm no longer burred by the exclamatory voices of parents, or spoilt children who look like they're sucking on lemons when they're not sucking on candy or ice cream. I wade down into the multi-layered wonderland of hoodoos along with everyone else. The hike is glorious — everyone is smiling and saying 'Hello' and 'Howdee.' Despite hip replacements and osteoporosis even the dour grandmothers manage a grin. It's like being in the UK on the first day of spring weather. I mistakenly end up on the Peekaboo Loop from the Queens Garden Trail and Navajo Loop. I'm fleeting free. A bravura passage of sun, snow and rain occurs all within a few hours, making the amphitheatre feel alive. I eventually emerge up at the Bryce Point carpark with a burn in my legs two hours later than expected. A couple of girls dressed like college students in tricolour board shorts and tank tops arrive a short distance behind me. They suspire loudly in relief while still bouncing on their toes as they make their way back to their giant, bright red pickup.

'I am sooo hungry.'

'I'm starving.'

'I was hungry even before we left.'

'You didn't eat anything for breakfast.'

'Yes I did!'

'Yoghurt doesn't count.'

While checking the shuttle bus timetable I notice a flurry of food preparation accompanied by car doors being swung open then slammed closed. One of the girls opens the back of the pickup and drops two portable travel chairs on the ground. The other arrives at the rear of the parked car with a platter of cheese dip, grapes, olives and bread on a large chopping board. They dump themselves into legless, padded seats, which seem to have a singular purpose of protecting their butts from the carpark dirt. And on the hot asphalt by the tailgate of the vehicle, which obscures any view of the majesty behind them they converse about how amazing their experience has been while enjoying a picnic in a carpark.

Following the crowd is an inescapable side-effect of international travel. Yet as backpackers we can't help but try to break the shackles of conformity and reject popular trends. To this end the answer seems simple enough — see it all first! Fuelled by social media and word-of-mouth we get seduced by the conundrum of travel, in which the very act just makes us want to travel more. We become slaves to the horizon — and the tantalising new destinations that always sit just out of view. I'm no different. When I first set foot in Europe I ricocheted around the continent like some culture-starved lunatic, marvelling under all the manmade bridges, towers, temples, grottos, catacombs, castles, museums, mausoleums and basilicas. It was only from exhaustion and experience I came to realise I was chasing a desire I could never catch because it was insatiable — the desire to see everything *(which I guess is the point)*. Not that there's anything wrong with a budding obsession if it helps spur a greenhorn out the front door and across vast oceans and ancients seas. But I guess like everything in life, it's good to keep a healthy check on things — which is why Zen makes the strong distinction between desire and pursuit when on a spiritual quest.

For some of us nature epitomises travel, and escapades into the great outdoors is what validates overseas trips. For others nature is a friend to be taken in small doses, where booking guided tours through pristine wilderness conveniently substitute days otherwise spent in a similar fashion sightseeing on city stopovers. Some of us prefer the reassurance of company when confronted by the overgrown volatility of Mother Nature. While for others, like me, the *waldeinsamket,* or the holy solitude of the wild is the ultimate reward on challenging multi-day treks. From hobby to worship nature grounds us, gives meaning beyond our crapulous lives, and justifies us in a way that often makes modern living appear vacuous and fraudulent.

I realise I have just under an hour until the arrival of the next courtesy shuttle service. I decide to wander back over the elevated Rim Trail to Inspiration Point and catch the bus to my car from there. I stop regularly. I honour each new vantage point *(which always appears better than the last)* by photographing the outcrops of pine and rocky spires of terracotta and white talcum. I've already decided to forego the hubris of Zion. I've had my fill. I'm feeling the pinch of time and I miss Rosie like the moon. Pods of plump, grey-bellied turtle clouds glide across the sky, bedimming then flushing the arrebol basin. I realise I've been too harsh on all the drive-by tourists. And what's so wrong with avid weekend ramblers, prowling into the closeted mysteries of nature while smugly cloaked in impervious synthetic fibres to handle any extreme. Who cares — baby steps! Baby steps got us out of the primordial soup. Learning to fall, to laugh at ourselves, to be dignified and unified in a crisis helped us down from the trees and got us to where we are today. Baby steps too can return us to Gaia's forgiving grace.

Whatever your thing is, again the mode of travel is imperative. Whether it's glamping or wild camping, the type of vehicle acts like an avatar that helps shape the interaction one has with nature. It not only dictates the type of experience we have on an outback journey, it defines the dialogue and strength of communion we aim to have. To this end the classic cross-country road trip is king.

In the remote region of Western Australia where I grew up, the phenomenon of seeking out nature is a simple consequence of being on holiday. All my home state has to offer when venturing beyond the isolated capital in packed four-wheel drive vehicles is nature. But away from the white-ribboned coastline and relentless roadside chaparral, the flat never-ending terrain is agonisingly subdued. It reveals its wonders seldom, and only after covering great distances in extremely hostile and inaccessible environments. This is Australia after all — and all we've got for tourists who endure the unwavering monotone shades of farmland and desert with itchy fingers on cameras and touchscreen phones are big-arse rocks.

Due to its easy access and close proximity to Perth, it's no surprise the Pinnacles are easily the most popular and visited site in

Western Australia. Located in the Nambung National Park three hours north of the city, the Pinnacles transport foreign and local tourists alike to an otherworldly terrain. A short off-road scenic loop permits air-conditioned comfort while navigating a petrified forest of eroded limestone plinths embedded in shifting coastal sands. Most visitors will agree exploring on foot, making tracks in the rippled sand and feeling the dry wind wash over you is the best way of exploring the area. But even with the plethora of photographic opportunities and the enigmatic mystery surrounding the Pinnacles' origins it remains somewhat of a local joke. This is because the confounding awe which first strikes visitors vanishes so rapidly in the enervating heat. And as all inclination to remain dissolves in the homogenous surroundings it soon prompts one member of a travel party to voice what everyone else is silently thinking:

*'How much longer do we have to stay here for?'*

I call this the *Postcard Effect* — where the tether to stay at places of natural grandeur or human endeavour last as long as it takes to snap a photo. These places like Niagara Falls or the Xian Warriors undeniably have outstanding face value. But after scrambling up hillsides and down steps to photographic vantage points, and with very little further engagement the feeling quickly fades like a whim. So you're left feeling stranded, wondering what time the next bus is returning. And backpackers make it their daily job to lay eyes on as many ancient and natural spectacles as possible. Right or wrong, avarice or not, overexposure breeds indifference.

So it's a common sight amidst breathtaking scenery to see backpackers dozing savagely, or combating ennui at ancient ruins rather than contemplating the tapestry of their human ancestors. They immerse themselves in paperbacks, flippant banter and downloadable apps while circumventing a kaleidoscope of wondrous cultures and inconceivable landscapes — oblivious to cascading waterfalls, picture-book panoramas, jungle-smashed coastlines, mountain grating glaciers, prehistoric fjords, and Jurassic forests of Tolkien trees as if it's an aversion to their sight because they've seen it somewhere better before.

Whatever provocations and persuasions march us into nature on holiday, they're as varied and elusive as the definition of Zen itself. But if the art of travel is a spiritual exercise then the act of travel is an ode to the pacifism of nature. Not that there's anything new about the link between nature and spirituality. Adoration of nature fills the pantheon of great artists, poets, scholars and writers across every language. Wildness is the original locus for personal transformation and renewal. We may argue over evidence of telekinesis and astral projection, but the healing properties of hugging a tree, or massaging bare feet over the knuckles of tree roots to release blocked *chi* is a romantic truth most of us don't doubt. Again, I defer to Japanese for its eloquent veneration of nature with words such as *shinrin-yoko*, which literally means to bathe in the positive green energy of a forest.

As an enduring muse throughout history, the sacredness of nature also finds accord across the scriptures of Christian Mystics, Sufis, Taoists and Zen Buddhists. While Zen is champion of the *wabi-sabi* void found in the spaces between objects and places, Taoism is the ultimate patron of nature and the female. Yin is the feminine spirit symbolising shade, shelter, nourishment and water of a valley or nurturing Mother. Yang is a fierce, sun-bleached mountain. The play of sunlight over mountain and valley throughout a day sublimely illustrates the eternal dance between light and dark, green and red. In words of the *Tao Te Ching*:

'Know the male,
yet keep to the female ...'

For the overlander who is continually pocketing wildlife adventures, introspective revelations and esoteric murmurings can occur both suddenly and gradually. But the end of a trip, much like any celebrated moment of change often compels us to mark the occasion with resolutions of self-improvement. So we declare on our return we're going to learn Russian, take up basket weaving, or meditate every morning in the pre-light of dawn. Like New Year's resolutions these typically attenuate with time. So maybe the most achievable and often forgotten covenant one should make at a journey's end is a promise to Mother Earth — to not forget about her in the everyday grind, to reconnect with her more often, and to continually help protect her. In other words, let's all be more like Kerouac's Ray and Japhy:

'... *Dharma Bums refusing to subscribe to the general demand that they consume production and therefore have to work for the privilege of consuming, all that crap they didn't really want anyway ... all of them imprisoned in a system of work, produce, consume, work, produce, consume, I see a vision of a great rucksack revolution thousands or even millions of young Americans wandering around with rucksacks, going up to mountains to pray, making children laugh and old men glad, making young girls happy and old girls happier, all of 'em Zen Lunatics who go about writing poems that happen to appear in their heads for no reason and also by being kind and also by strange unexpected acts keep giving visions of eternal freedom to everybody and to all living creatures.*'

# CHAPTER 15

# THE ONENESS OF TRAVEL

Following my resistant re-entry into the USA via Houston I was back at the airport the next morning to board my connecting flight to Charleston — where beautiful, desperate Rosie awaited my return. Our relationship thus far had been built on goodbyes and reunions — so much so we turned it into a competition like when we made pizza or soup. Not that this in itself posed a problem. I cherished goodbyes. They are ruthless, self-sacrificing assassins choreographing our lives — expeditiously shaping relationships from what we don't say, or say and fuck it up in a rushed moment after a lifetime of missed opportunities to say it all. Stooped and cooped in the pigboat cabin of an old Embraer ERJ 145 I wondered how much easier it would be to love a girl from my own country — to paint without mixing colours or going outside of the lines. As we took off I gazed down at the flowering brown estuary of Galveston Bay. What a strange game we have made for ourselves. How silly the cavil of border security and immigration protocol seems when you're rocketing up over an incorporated world. What an easy target we've made of the House of Star-Crossed Lovers. Why? Because love is prey that's easily corrupted — well doesn't that apply to the sum of who we are?

The first time I returned to Charleston after meeting Rosie we drove out to Asheville in North Carolina where she called my bluff to all of it — to everything about my cheap-arse commitment free life. She went so far as to calling me some sort of international freeloading gigolo. I think she was trying to protect her petticoat heart but she wasn't wrong about most of it. When I turned the focus onto her she revealed herself to be a serial monogamist who just broke free of a two-year relationship. I didn't return to Charleston simply to fulfil the promise I made to Rosie. I wanted to spend the final three weeks of my trip there — flirt around the future while filling up on as much of Rosie as she was willing to give me. We had our own secret super powers and made our unorthodox connection our strength. Rosie was rich in time and I was rich with compromise — 12⅔ years to be exact. So we worked it out with an unconventional vow of sorts. Two and a half months later Rosie absconded from Charleston on a study abroad program, and arrived in my hometown. My very own tearaway princess.

Rosie spent the semester in Perth where she became a staunch vegan, ate raw garlic, got super skinny, drank cider, and frequently wore a feminine poncho of introversion. Meanwhile I was an oaf — inept and slow to adapt to a life involving another. I was so used to travelling solo along unbeaten paths, I didn't see how far or blindly I'd gone, or considered the inevitability of where it led. It took time to grow accustomed to Rosie's uncompromising welter, which altered silently and irreversibly like the wind. Only if asked would I realise she felt differently. But I didn't want to jinx what we had. What would be the point anyway? I didn't want to get hurt, and was afraid she would turn and say, 'No, I don't want any of this anymore,' so I stayed silent.

Perth did give us time to work one another out, rather than time apart to indulge in nostalgic fantasies. In Perth we also practised our airport goodbyes and pickups — an unavoidable ritual if we were to stay together. Rosie left on short excursions during the semester to Sydney and New Zealand. Then in her final month stay following exams she chose a yoga retreat in Bali instead of the Australian outback and me. At first Rosie was too invested, too truculent and susceptible to emotional goodbyes she didn't see the game of it. Instead of rejoicing she inadvertently filled up time before departing with the melancholia of leaving. And melancholia is a wild purple beast — tenacious and hard to tame, it can skyjack people and occasions. But from the cycle of goodbyes and reunions we got better at them. We made comical gaffes at airport security, shared awkward kisses in stalled queues, texted carry-on messages punctuated with 'fuck' and 'love' as if they had only real meaning in repetition, and let goodbye celebrations last days, to sour from longevity and excess like a prolonged afterparty. But not before I again promised to return to Rosie and Charleston.

The Embraer moaned and clucked its landing gear into place. On final approach into Charleston I contemplated the jet-lag of self-realisation following procrastinations of departure and arrival. Beyond the distress and away from the harsh reality of airport arrival is the actual realisation the trip has begun. For some it doesn't take very long. Quick learners like me find it sitting on a pint in the departure lounge, uploading a photo we just took of our drink in the airport bar to give scale or context to the impersonal goodbye we've attached for anyone who cares. For others, realising they are present in an untold adventure of their own design takes time to mature — for retentive thoughts and reservations to soften in the clamour and colour of a jour-ney. This can propagate new misgivings. But the enchantment of embarking on a new journey of unknown opportunities and encounters prevails.

It resurrects itself gradually upon stumbling into a hostel and being told at reception you're in luck and there's one spare bed due to a cancellation. You're escorted upstairs where your packs slide off your arms and drop on the pristine made bunk bed. The heat and stout pressure of a shower massages your aching back and hydrates your flightdry skin. You saunter back downstairs five minutes before reception closes and order an unknown label of beer. Sitting at a communal table in the kitchen with baby pink feet and toes tingling from the fresh shower you open the front page of your guidebook and stare down at a map to decide where next to go next. Precipitation from the mayhem of arrival disappears without you realising. Hearing destiny call you champion and cheat you're once again scolded by the certainty that this is exactly where you're meant to be. In that moment you exist without the word *no* in a universe of unlimited possibilities.

It's all relative I guess is what I'm trying to say. Shit happens, or it doesn't. The idea is to enjoy the ride regardless which I know is often easier said than done — or in the words of the pantheistic granddaddy of quantum relativity Albert Einstein:

*'Reality is merely an illusion, albeit a very persistent one.'*

If the aim of Zen is to lead a thoughtful practitioner to a direct experience with life itself then a traveller must remain blissfully diligent *(or failing that)* diligently blissful. So don't go looking for adventures. You can only have adventures. True adventures, like love, lost luggage and good times find you, or they don't. And thinking you've found it can be the kibosh that causes you to lose it. After all, why look for happiness when it's the natural state of the self? I'd like to think Einstein would agree *(and didn't take shit too seriously either)*. In a letter to his son Eduard he likened people to bicycles saying only by moving do we maintain our balance.

Christian Mysticism also echoes the core values used in Zen practice to attain self-realisation. *The Cloud of Unknowing*, an anonymous text written by a Christian monk in the middle ages immaculately reiterates the cardinal idea of incorporating everyday life with mindful mediation. Instead of prescriptively searching for a spiritual truth with intellect and study, the book instructs a pupil to seek God through intense contemplation, stripped of thought and inspired by love. Only through surrendering all preconceptions, beliefs and desires to a 'cloud of forgetting' is the student able to peer into the unknowing cloud of God.

One who sees travel as a literal and spiritual journey is one who understands every unplanned backpacking odyssey and bold new venture is one extended mediation session, one spontaneous mantra, one epic yoga class or Hare Krishna chant, and one symbolic breath — where the delay between your trip commencing and the salient feeling it has begun is the pensive inhale — to then be complemented by the long exhale where you still feel like you're tripping on the road months after it has ended. Personally, I find it hard to predict when I'll intercept the euphoria from casting myself out blind onto another adventure abroad — to be embalmed in the equanimity of being right where I want to be. I'd like to say it comes in stages a bit like *jhana,* the meditative states one passes through on one's way to the perfection of wisdom. But I identify more with the evocative awakenings from the obsession of drinking tea which Lotung, a Tang Dynasty Poet conveys in *Book of Tea*:

> *'The first cup moistens my lips and throat, the second cup breaks my loneliness, the third cup searches my barren entrails but to find therein some five thousand volumes of odd ideographs. The fourth cup raises a slight perspiration — all the wrong of life passes away through my pores. At the fifth cup I am purified; the sixth cup calls me to the realms of the immortals. The seventh cup – ah, but I could take no more! I only feel the breath of cool wind that rises in my sleeves. Where is Horaisan? Let me ride on this sweet breeze and waft away thither.'*

With the end of her final semester and graduation looming, Rosie was starting to sound more and more like me. I knew she was seeking an emotional enema to the psychological rot of college. She had already threatened to be reckless and crash my road trip after graduating. And while living together she prefaced a litany of expressive gestures to commemorate her impending freedom. Her unwavering desire to do any number of things changed daily like a horoscope — spread her nascent travel wings and go see the world, live in another city, woof around Europe, become a yoga instructor, qualify as a natruopath, relocate to Atlanta to live with her brother, attend graduate school, train to be a chef, move to Greenville to live with her other brother, take photography lessons, surf and paint every day, learn another language, and never stop moving. I felt partly responsible, or at the very least an influence, which was a shitty-proud feeling because all of them sounded like they were to the exclusion of me.

Although I didn't admit it to Rosie, I would have broken two fingers to have her say she was coming on the road trip with me. I didn't tell her this because I wanted her to make up her own mind, which is why if asked I would only admit to two broken fingers when in truth it would have been a lot more. Instead I tempered Rosie's fantasy of freewheelin' it across the USA. I warned her not to expect the *Beat Zenness* expounded by gurus and travel veterans to grace her as soon as the trip began. It took daydreaming time to fall into the rhythm — to swoon at the diamond voids of roadmaps and speculative spaces between places; be engulfed by the silent roar of alien tongues; and hypnotised by the cadence of countryside, ocean swell, and your own footsteps that dare to speak to a land that's not home.

On my maiden venture to Europe it took time for me to truly appreciate being in the moment of where I stood. I remember this because I can still vividly recall the feeling — and the feeling had a name called Rachel. The first two weeks of the trip passed by like a job. I spent it on the French Riviera with Joel, my old university compadre. Each day we cussed up and down Nice's laddered labyrinth of alleyways to the HI hostel perched high above the city on the edge of Mount Boron Park. We blagged it on the local line along the coast to Cannes where we attended the International Film Festival, the impetus for the trip. We bickered about fluctuating fractions of French francs we owed one another, and after we worked out we were fighting over pennies and cents we continued to argue. We met Fabien, the quintessential Parisian, who chainsmoked Gitanes, lived on *baguette de pain, fromage* and *œuf mayonnaise*, and refused to say *'th-eh'* when he spoke English because he was scared he would bite off the end of his tongue. We became lifelong friends and he offered an open invitation for us to stay with his family in a small village outside Paris.

We skipped across the border to Italy after that. We arrived in Florence, where we were forced to sleep in an open recess outside the dubious Santa Maria Novella station because every dorm bed in the city was fully booked. As the night wore on, with back and bones pressed on hard concrete, other shoestring backpackers and independent families in the same predicament joined us to seek refuge in numbers. I was enlivened by the communal strength of travellers — and the idea that night times are made for talking them away. So when Joel announced two days later he didn't want to journey south with me to Rome I bade him a curt farewell. I couldn't think of any sane reason not to gander at the Colosseum, Vatican City and all the other ancient relics of the Eternal City.

On the train ride down to Rome I fretted over thieving gangs of Romani gypsies. From tall travelling tales I heard they swept through train carriages in Europe. And when you stole a wink of sleep they robbed you down to your boxers. I locked my over-loaded pack to the luggage rack above my head with a leaden bike lock I carried from home and tried to stay awake. Rome goaded me like Florence with an accommodation blackout. I doubted my *savoir-faire* and cursed my independent flair. I regretted coming to Rome but did what any self-respecting backpacker would do — I lumbered my packs around the frenetic metropolis in a bid to see as many tourist sites as possible in a day. Rome sweltered and the burden of luggage drew my life in pints of sweat. I chewed up the hours in the day traipsing between places. When I got anywhere significant I found the crowds and lines too unbearable. So I levied the transitory satisfaction of ticking a checklist box and chuffed to the next archaeological treasure.

With shelter in doubt I employed backpackers' *modus operandi* and decided to catch an overnight train to somewhere faraway. As the hours passed I started to wonder why I was doing this — waging a masochistic vendetta against European exoticism and antiquity — all for the small, voluble contentment of seeing ancient rubble. I eventually ceded to Rome, and to the infernal traffic and vile heat, chalking it up as an utterly wasted trip. As I retreated to Roma Terminus station I wondered if I was travelling right. I knew I was well suited to a budget backpacking lifestyle. I was stalwart and thrifty, ecumenical, amenable and adaptable. The only real difference to my student incarnation was my campus was now a city, which altered with my movement every few days. So why didn't I feel right?

At first I wondered if this was what homesickness felt like then realised it was quite the opposite. The queasiness came from an abundance of fear — fear of failing at it all, at backpacking, at finding work in the UK, at life in general and being forced to return home prematurely. Everyone I knew who came before me to Europe with a UK work visa stayed a year or more. I had the same intention — live a life and graft in London to afford short Eurail excursions around postcard European destinations. I appreciated this was a contrivance of both internal and external forces, but to do less felt like a failure of sorts. Fear of failure was a stowaway in my backpack — taunting me with reminders of the shirt, slacks, ties and work shoes I'd packed — which now seemed stupid and superfluous, and added to preposterous weight and size of my pack.

I did take respite from the stillness cast by a burnt sienna sky. Passing under the Colosseum in the blue dye of twilight I marvelled at the anachronistic vision of the ancient structure against the cityscape. I realised I loved Rome for what it represented and reviled it for what it was — an epileptic city of adoration encased in the chaos of everyday living. I now saw how a cosmopolitan Rome reconciled its reincarnation from past grandeur and decline with an excess of éclat and elegance — an enviable balance which on a personal level I struggle each day to get a smidgen or sip of. I was jealous of Rome — I could at least admit to that. But darkness didn't assuage the city's madness — and the night air replaced the daylight mayhem with expectation and folly set to burn.

I sat on an empty platform and waited for the late night service to Bologna, to seek Joel out in the tranquillity of northern Italy. As I soaked up the nocturnal hours I felt glad to be leaving Rome. From choices I made to be here, I knew *(at least for now)* I wouldn't quit on my wending ways. However, I still wondered how many hours in my life will be spent waiting. How will I reflect upon it when all is said and done — will I see the excess of time spent in departure lounges, train station and terminal buildings, or on benches, docks and desolate roadsides as something substantive and worthwhile?

My seesaw shrug is mimicked by the wheeze and bellow of my train arriving. It releases an *oh-well* sigh as I quickly board ahead of other passengers and scout along the carriages to claim the prize of an empty second class compartment. As the train gradually withdraws from the city centre two youthful American backpackers burst into my carriage sharing the same design as me. It turns out Rachel and Kim also suffered under the high season blackout of budget accommodation in Rome. They too decided to use the train ride to Bologna as a cheap place to spend the night.

Bologna was an obvious choice. It took just over five hours to get to, which would put us in the regional capital just short of sunrise. A longer journey would have been preferable, but a couple of hours more and we would be in Switzerland or Austria. Kim soon falls asleep while Rachel and I swap stories the way young people do — relentlessly as if everything and nothing mattered all at once. I now see the symbiotic beauty in the swift changes of fortunes on the open road — how a day hemmed by constant frustrations can fall away to a magic night of chance encounters. Fatigue and mental catharsis embellish the tantalising fantasy of it all. And I have to keep reminding myself:

*'Yes, I am on a train rollicking through the Italian countryside sat next to a girl with soft blue eyes and dirty-blonde hair whom I've known for 10 minutes but feels like 10 years.'*

For the first time I realise home can be found in the distance between places. We talk through the night as the rustic Tuscan countryside slips by the window in a whisper. Intermittent trackside lights accentuate the gnarled landscape of grey in lulls of silence when our eyelids flutter in contemplation of sleep. The augured sense of change in my travel fortunes isn't hurt by Rachel's corruptible expression and womanly body, both which appear new, and as if she was treating them with care. We lay out across the narrow knee-gap with feet up against the vacant seats opposite us to maximise the leg room. The rhythmic lullaby underfoot... *clunk,* **clunk**, *clunk* ... *clunk,* **clonk**, *clonk* ... *clunk,* **clonk**, *clunk* ... makes a nest of our bodies — her arm on mine, legs together in gentle contact from vibrations of the train on track. We talk to fill the silences *(so they won't sour and turn awkward)*. Talk through Terontola, talk through Sienna, talk through Florence. When we pass through and around mountains the cart rocks and sways Rachel's legs back and forth into mine — the left bringing us together ... the right sending us apart. The touch and pressure makes me appreciate how quickly we miss human contact. We talk until we we're too tired to open our mouths and turn sounds into words. Even then I keep talking in my sleep — and pray to the ghostly grey mistress of the landscape:

*'Please make another left turn again soon – a long oblique left turn. Gratefully yours in advance and always – Dave.'*

Bologna is a rural expanse still slumbering when we arrive. The hostel is a long hike away and an incomprehensible challenge in the insomnia of daylight. Outside the train station we lump our backpacks together and sit on the steps, shivering in a predawn prayer of silence. Who knows how long we would have remained contemplating our situation in a drowsy stupor. But it turns out the solicitude of travel has no time or grace for the sleep deprived. Two affable shift workers exit the station house and offer us a ride in a bedlam of gestures. The men are smiling chatty souvenirs of provincial Italy — complete with olive complexions, shadows for beards and black helmets of hair. Made to sit with the luggage in the boot space of a tiny two-door Fiat I consider whether our two samaritans are motivated by something other than good intentions. Maybe they fancy the Americans. Maybe they do this all the time. Given Rachel and Kim's Italian was nonexistent and I was surviving on two years of compulsory lessons from way back in high school I couldn't actually recall how we managed to convey where we wanted to go. Who cares — we were getting a free ride. Italian men were just doing what Italian men are meant to do. One for all and all for one, right?

The hostel is still closed when we arrive so we drive to a nearby cafe and drink espressos. We get back to the hostel for the start of breakfast, at which point our gracious chaperones bid us farewell. While we check in I spot Joel sitting by a window of morning light. We hadn't communicated since Florence — there hadn't been enough time. I knew he was heading to Bologna but thought he may have moved on by now to Venice. I should be floored by the staggering coincidence but I'm so heavily sedated on sleeplessness. I watch Joel blow on a steaming bowl of coffee *(a penchant we had both picked up from our short time in France)* while gazing over an impractically large foldout roadmap of Europe. Maintaining a parody of composure I approach.

'Hey Joel – fancy seeing you here.'

Joel looks up with a reflection of my own disbelief.

'Dave – Fuck! How?'

I flop down on the seat opposite him and recount my abject detour to Rome, along with the sparks of good fortune which rose up from the doused ruin. In turn Joel describes the pleasant yet mundane feel of Bologna. I say that's exactly what I'm looking for but Joel is in a hurry to find something else. He explains that he's departing shortly for Padua, a dignified and charming town in its own right and host to one of the oldest universities in the world. Padua also acts as a gateway town for budget backpackers with cheap accommodation for those exploring the Venetian islands. Joel asks if I want to join him. I glance across at Rachel and Kim at reception. I've already paid for the night. Joel understands so we make vague plans again to meet up again in a couple of days.

I spend the day with Rachel and Kim wandering the streets of Bologna. The city is subdued and serene and pairs perfectly with our somnolent languor. Kim decides to head back early to write postcards and take a nap. While walking back to the hostel in the late afternoon Rachel and I agree to see out the day's gloaming together. We pass by the hostel and continue beyond the city limits to where the sky and land are fully fed. A cumulonimbus eruption rises like a cauliflower on the horizon, eclipsing the sun to form a blinding halo. Overhead an aircraft slices the sky with a saffron incision. In my head I play the game I always do when tracking an aeroplane cruising high in the blue ethers — I try to assign aspirations and background profiles to the seat numbers of 300+ souls on board. I never even make it into the teens, but I guess it's because human desires are like literary tropes — when you reduce it all down there's not that many of them.

I feel tipsy on a sense of timelessness. A weekend spirit of lazy acquiescence has hold of me — charmed me groggy and jubilant with a day, empty and free, swaying at my devising. It's all so fucking simple. All that's required is the new light of today and the ability to get up, walk onwards embracing everything from now on both in and out of my control. I now see the gift of it all

— a riveting expanse of unknown possibilities hovering beyond the hostel's walls. I'm invincible. I start to feel the unstoppable momentum of travel.

We find ourselves at the steps of an old farmhouse by a busy country road. Fields of grass sway in front of us. We sit down and I see the steeple of an old church rising from the woods in the distance. We talk through the sun setting and cars turning their headlights on, talk through the quarter moon rising, talk through the accompaniment of constellations which twinkle decorously against the falling night sky. Time with Rachel is timeless, or maybe it's just my chronic fatigue stirring up delusions. I want to kiss her with my hand locked in the warmth between her thighs. I think she wants me to as well but she's not giving me back that look I need — a clarity in the eyes that turns oblique with a blink. She has a youthful chastity that I had no clue how to leaven, and I'm young and much too prudent and patient with love. I hesitate and it's lost. Eventually, we walk back the way we came. We don't talk much. It's like the end of a holiday. We walk hand in hand along the side of road occasionally bumping bodies, which neither of us mentions but feels deliberate. Rachel is leaving for Milan in the morning and lives a galaxy away. I don't know what's left to say.

At the Magnolia Bar inside Charleston's small international airport, Rosie finds me waiting for her sat on an imperial pint of Palmetto Pale Ale. It's where I always wait for her because she's always late. Would I have wanted her to be at the gate, arms open with her dimpled, thin-eyed smile? For a change it would have been nice. Now that I think about, in all my years of travel I've never had someone waiting for me at the airport. It's all part of a backpacker's life — the feeling of leaving is superior to that of arriving.

When Rosie arrives she makes up for her lateness — sliding her arms around me and hugging my face with a soft kiss as she whispers, 'Heyyy' into my ear. I can't recall if Rosie ever said she was coming on the three-month road trip, or if I asked her. I think the understanding was osmotically conveyed, which is the way when you're living out of each other's pockets. For the next two weeks we gorge ourselves on each other's company at every new bar top and food joint which has opened since I've been away. But it's getting harder to tell what part of it is an arrival or departure ritual. Without a plan I'm set to leave again with Rosie intent on joining the road trip after her graduation.

I did accomplish some practical stuff. I got the O-rings and timing belt in my Subaru Legacy replaced. I bought a road atlas and books on the top scenic drives in the USA. I fixed the cigarette lighter in my car and purchased an inverter to charge my mobile and power my laptop. I had the oil changed and got a five gallon jerry can and 28 quart ice cooler from Wal-Mart. Then I'm breathing in the chai honey scent of Rosie's skin as I rest my head against her neck. I cap it in a vial in my memory as we say goodbye again in the carpark of Five Loaves Cafe where she worked. By now it was fair to say I was winning the Goodbye Contest, which wasn't the only reason Rosie was dark about the whole situation. Distance like nostalgia is its own kind of aphrodisiac but it was wearing off. We'd become so familiar with goodbyes the choruses of sweet platitudes didn't hold the gravitas they once did. I too had grown weary of the repetitive visa restrictions the same way a professional gets ground down by the rotations of packing and unpacking their life between temporary contracts and homes.

We both wanted to be leaving Charleston together for all the reasons companionship and road trips make sense. But Rosie's graduating ceremony was still two weeks away. And given the time I'd already spent in Charleston, which was eating into the limited timeframe for the road trip, she knew I couldn't wait any longer. I also knew how vital it was to bathe in the rhetoric of silence when travelling. Just like with traditional meditative practises, silence of solitude is revered for it is often the best answer when facing the ineffable nature of the world. But it can also get really fucking loud. From past experience I knew it took time to let the noisy fetters in my head fade into calmness. It would take time before I felt the *p'u* of the wind blasting through my open Subaru as I coasted along desolate plains. Rosie also expressed her own need for personal time following a lifetime of brick-walled learning. So we did what we do best — we formulated a plan. While I drove solo cross-country to California, Rosie opted to fly out to San Diego. To coincide with my arrival in three weeks she planned to depart two days after graduating, to embrace the gift of her own solitude in San Diego before I arrived by car.

I drove down the short stretch of US 17 to Wholefoods where I bought organic coffee and a cheap bottle of red wine. Shuffling alone around the aisles I already felt utterly lost. Together Rosie and I owned grocery shopping. We lived off Wholefoods and Trader Joe's free food samples, and spent hours circulating a store while deliberating what to do next — which invariably led to margaritas and free chips 'n' salsa. Now on my own I couldn't think of where to go to next, even though I knew precisely where I was heading — West! *(like so many pilgrims before me)*. But I guess these sorts of complications are bound to arise when your path becomes glued to someone, and no longer aligned to a route or destination.

I soon found my way onto the I-26 on a familiar path of least resistance through Columbia en route to North Carolina and the Appalachian Mountains. A cheap USB cable to the iPod Rosie loaned me caught fire so I turned on the radio. The playlist of country and western classics cheapened my grey mood — parodied by a pathetic fallacy of foul weather, despondency and heartland romance. In the end I turned the radio off in preference to the rap of heavy rain and pulse 'n' squeak of the windscreen wipers. After crossing the North Carolina border I stopped at the welcome centre outside of Columbus and read my two-star rated horoscope in the back of a free local rag:

*With the moon and Mars conjoining in your sign*
*you may feel irritable today,*
*and struggle to maintain your usual cool.*
*So try to avoid people and situations you may find vexing.*

No shit, I thought — thanks for epitomising every day of existence. As I got closer to Asheville, houses and structures soon give way to turbid hillsides of russet and green. I start to recognise landmarks from my last visit with Rosie when we camped in the Pisgah National Forest. I find myself automatically following the same route and exit the I-26 at Hendersonville. I pass the petrol station where we stopped and asked for directions to the Pisgah National Forest Ranger's Station, and bought a six-pack of Dales to feed the ice in the cooler. Then I spot the Rodeway Inn where we spent a cheap comfortable night after a cold, wet weekend camping.

I spend the afternoon driving through the rain and soft light on an aimless circuit around the Nantahala National Forest while deliberating whether to overnight it in Asheville. Through mist and mizzle I spy idyllic hamlets by rivers and sculpted lakes. But navigating the tight, winding route along the US 64 then back up on the US 74 on my own, without Rosie is empty and absent of reward. The irony is not lost on me that while solitude fosters a reflexive clarity when embarking on a new trip, being alone fixes you to nothing. In your head past, present and future turn into chunky wintertime soup. It takes time for aloneness to simmer down, and to get control of the flow of thoughts through your head. Memories of Rosie and Asheville are all too near and within reach, and in the sopping gloom I find myself climbing up the Great Smoky Mountains towards Tennessee. Pellets of rain hammer the roof and bonnet in clots following strong gusts which dislodge them from the dense sodden tree line. Bandages of mist curl over the car as the four cylinder engine whines up the Parkway on US 441. Rumours of fog and darkness take purchase.

They spread out in the dwindling light, as headlights of oncoming traffic turn into orange eyes of nocturnal spectres. Night has fallen by the time I reach Newfound Gap on the Tennessee border — not that I could tell. I couldn't see shit.

The world is gone. Either I'd surpassed it crossing the Appalachians, or it had been swallowed up in the rear vision mirror — and I am the only person in existence, left by grace or damnation to drift in limbo through the empyreal belch of a wet fog. As I crawl along the scenic road to Clingman's Dome, a panoramic lookout and highest point in Tennessee, I imagine myself driving on the only remaining earthly ley line. Protected by Tog, my magical Subaru Legacy I watch an apocalyptic mist entomb my alien module — quietly snuffing out the last miniscule memory that we, the world was ever here. As possibly the best and also worst place to ever spend the night alone I park up at Clingman's Dome — looking out over the mourning void of existence. In the deserted tourist carpark I decide to save money and sleep in the car. I want to phone Rosie, to hear her sweet, gentle voice but I have only one flickering bar of reception which refuses to make the call. So I fold the back seat down and lay out. I strap on my headlamp to read and drink wine from my plastic camping cup while listening to the soundtrack of howling wind and torrential rain.

As I fall half asleep I think how funny it is the paradoxical ways we view water and mist, like the way we perceive form and formlessness. Water, like the god Kali is both destroyer and life giver. Despite its sense of infinitude, it has form so we give it character because we connect with it. Water can be a brooding ocean with its plangent spume and crashing; an imperturbable lake under moonlit glow; an ungodly carnage of Kraken wakes; a carefree crossing from the gentle tug of a light breeze; an invigorating downpour; a duplicitous flow with secret undertows; a riverbed lullaby from the soughing lips of a bountiful stream; or a tranquil calm from the heavenly seclusion of a hidden cove.

Conversely, mist shows few redeemable features, or somatic properties. And yet an enveloping fog holds its own dimension of ashen terror because it represents an inescapable and intangible void we cannot contain within our minds. It makes me think how the attachments of connotations to words dictate our perspective, and not the other way around. The woe of words and tongues I suppose. It is the same with *never* and *forever* — words of similitude when used in the context of love:

*'I will love you forever...'*
*'I will never stop loving you...'*

And yet, never has strength and veracity over forever because our mortal nature comprehends never. Never is form, whereas forever is formless. But never is easier to sell so it's thrown around like sports equipment. The fact that forever is harder to give away makes it special. I hope I expressed some sense of form to my love when I said goodbye to Rosie — but I can't recall precisely what I said in the Five Loaves carpark off Johnnie Dodds Boulevard. Something about how it all really sucked and I wished she was leaving with me. I realise I have drunk way too much wine right before I sink into a dreamless sleep.

The world is slate vapour when I wake and the rain follows me down the mountains into Tennessee. I can't help but be impressed by the Smoky Mountains in that they far exceeded their namesake because I saw none of it. I spend the day snaking along water-logged foothills on back roads to Cades Cove. Without purpose the dismal weather directs me back onto the interstate and by day's end I find myself in Chattanooga. Lured by its small-town charm and exhausted by the doleful weather I decide to spend the night at the Crash Pad, an exceptional hostel which welcomes me with offseason perks of low occupancy and onsite parking.

In the morning I make an indecisive plan to head to Nashville because people had told me a new hip had taken over the old hip. Being back on the interstate I get a real sense of chewing up distance. And the rest stops bring a civility to road trips, which can turn feral pretty bloody quickly. In daylight they are fairytale garrisons for the road weary — with immaculate amenities, fresh water, maps and pamphlet information. There are also grassy picnic areas, occasionally housed under bizarre concrete teepee structures, an obeisant reminder to the Trail of Tears. Part of me however, feels like a cheat being on a six-lane freeway. And I am somehow dishonouring my literary and cinematic heroes of yore, who inspired as much as embellished my childhood fantasy of road tripping around the USA. Like any mode of travel I've always preferred less obvious, less travelled cursuses for all the rewards which come along with being somewhere undiscovered. I'm trying to reclaim the *śūnyatā* of movement, the vast sense of emptiness I get when travelling between places (*which allows me to lose my sense of self in the unobstructed void*). But in my desperation I feel I've acquired a desultory and tortured flavour of aimlessness.

Traffic, billboards and exit signs build in frequency to signal my arrival in Nashville. I start to ponder the pragmatic limitations subject to the liberty to having four wheels under your feet and no particular place to be. It's an enviable predicament I know — but I can't help thinking about the chore and cost of parking; the cheap hotel which will invariably be off an interstate junction on the outskirts of town; how I'll have to watch what I drink because wherever I go I'll have to drive myself back to my overnight abode. I can't even think of what I will do with a car in a big city. I was used to bopping around cosmopolitan centres on foot and using public transport — enjoying the inchoate ambulation with my eyes and mind set to wander as I strolled between places of interest. Considering how long I've dreamt of owning my own wheels on an overland trip, right now I have no iota what I'm doing or where I'm going.

I make the impulsive decision to head for the Nachez Trace Parkway instead. So I circumvent Nashville and make my way onto the I-40. It's funny how I now see the caveat of having a car is there is possibly too much freedom to bear. Compared to other modes of travel, it still does nothing to alleviate *(and if anything it accentuates)* the ultimate curse of independent travel — the fear of missing out. The Natchez Trace Parkway is a scenic route covering over 400 miles across three states. From Tennessee it slices the left ear off Alabama before cutting diagonally down through the state of Mississippi. I must have driven clear of foul weather because the day is now filled with sunshine and is free of traffic. Sailing along through thick wooded corridors and sunlit curtains I should by now feel like I'm in *vacilando*. In Spanish, being in *vacilando* is to wander without any particular interest in the destination. It's artfully noted by John Steinbeck in *Travels with Charley* as being 'as much a state of mind as an action'. But as I coast left to right around gentle bends carpeted with wide shoulders of green grass I'm still too preoccupied with where I'm heading next.

While *vacilando* has no precise English equivalent, it's funny how people still grasp the concept — most notably my Mum, who cannot comprehend the notion of me never quite knowing where I'm going. But they're our roles. My Mum's is to worry, and mine is to make her worry. And to her credit she's slowly got used to it over the past 15 years, or she's better at pretending, or she's just given up — it's hard to tell. It makes me think of how limiting words and language are. Another achingly beautiful word comes to mind, *komorebi* which in Japanese describes the ephemeral shower of sunlight through leaves. Under dappled light I imagine myself following the original traces of migrating bison as the Native American peoples once did. But there is something too landscaped, too artificial and ultimately monotonous about the profane greenery of the commemorative parkway, which also avoids the welcomed interruptions of townships and quirky roadside Americana. In the end I exit halfway and make my way across to the Mississippi River to the join the MS Highway 1.

As I pass through sundry towns of Winona, Indianola and Leland I realise I'm only doing this because of a prevailing pressure to make the most of every moment. And in doing so I'm fucking up my road trip. I'm searching too hard for something that can't be found. Online research and books I bought made it worse. I'm fixated on traversing every scenic roadway between South Carolina and California. When I put my mind to a picturesque onward route and stare down at the broadsheet maps in my road atlas I become lost in the possibilities. I scry the mass of pink arterial byways and blue-vein freeways, trying to divine the most spectacular yet expedient cross-country route. At toilet breaks and petrol stops I second guess myself — uncertain of my stitch work navigation I repeat the process of pulling out all my books and maps to formulate a new alternate path.

A Romanesque sense of failure taints the day. It briefly lifts as I hit the ancient flow of the Mississippi River and follow its turgid waters north back to Tennessee, to complete a mindless day's detour. Against a custard-baked sky I recall childhood daydreams of being Tom Sawyer and Huck Finn — skiving off school to go fishing, catch frogs and frolic in backwater eddies. But once the smouldering Mississippi sunset is snuffed out by an evening blanket of grey I grow tired of where I am heading and cross Big Muddy into Arkansas. From there I make my way north back onto the I-40 where I sleep again in the car at a rest stop outside of Little Rock.

In the morning I carry my cooler, camping stove and pot of water over to a concrete picnic table to brew a coffee. As I wait for the water to boil I shuffle inside to the restrooms to wash my face and brush my teeth. I look down at my dew-grass covered feet and thongs and think, *'This is it Dave. This is life!'* I begin to feel the flow — and sense my resistance to the preliminary beginnings of my own journey dissipate. A precipitative atmosphere of new opportunities settle around me. I now succumb to the unknowing road ahead.

Back on the interstate I open myself up to a kingdom of straight lines and smoky mirages. I start to feel my mind go as the distance of crossing spaces invites a cacophony of silence. All the retroactive micro-moments when I almost got it flood my memory — a spring day, Bob Dylan singing *'I'm on the pavement, thinking about the government'*, a dusty road, university days, afternoon jugs of beer and pub pool, Chorlton Water Park on a Wednesday, reggae on a Sunday, beachcombing on Sullivan's Island, future abounds. Reality sunders. I think of Rosie mostly — constructing the most ardent and tender emails in my head, which I then scrap and rewrite then scrap again. It's a game because I know I will never send them so they'll stay perfect. I conceive grandiose gestures of romance on our road trip together — the expensive meal or hotel room I can't afford and let them play out like memories — reliving the glow in Rosie's eyes when I announce I'm taking her out for dinner, the sight of her ricocheting from bedroom to bathroom with the undisclosed zeal she has for upscale accommodation. I recreate our playful conversations of a future together — eloping to Hawaii, making babies, how we'd make great mums and dads. But just like in ordinary life reality seeps in and spoils the edges of the fantasy and my mind replays all of Rosie's talk about her own future.

I stay on the I-40 into Oklahoma and when I've had enough of the interstate I head north into Kansas. I continue using rest stops to sleep — and witness the fall of night bewitch carparks with nocturnal dog walkers and rendezvous with dodgy goings-on in heavily thicketed perimeters. On a whim I decide to head to Dodge City because I enjoy saying it in my head — sounding like a cowboy returning home on my trusty white Japanese steed. Churning up enfilades of wind turbines, reeking fields packed with livestock and belts of wheat and oil drill rigs I know I should be feeling close to where I wanted to be. But from personal experience I know this process doesn't just rest on the hooks of a prescient traveller, or the purity and mode of their voyage. It's also affected by what we've left behind and what we hope to find on a fuzzy horizon. I didn't declare it on arrival in Charleston but I could feel the phantom weight of emotional baggage dragging anchor. It wasn't just the sense of Rosie breaking free into a new chapter of her life. It was also the years that separated us, which despite her unwavering love I couldn't help but imagine one day soon she would wake up, examine my laugh-lined face and wonder why the heck she was with this silly older man.

To be fair I could have been out plying the scenic highways and byways before now. But Rosie, Charleston and me fit. I survived rent free on contract work from back home and meagre royalties from my first book. In between 90-day visa-free visits I initially flew down to Ushuaia in Argentina — to plant my feet in the southern most inhabited spot on the globe, and romp around the rucksack-infested wilds of Patagonia. After that the timing was perfect for a belated trip home to see my younger sister get married. Now I'm left to wonder why I'm endeavouring to drive around a continent — to chase a ghost, prolong an inevitability of sorts, succour a long-held ambition, find some flavour of redemption, or reconnect with something which I don't know yet what it is I've lost? It's not my home, but man Charleston and Rosie's family did a good job of convincing me otherwise.

We stayed with Rosie's parents from time to time. Her father was an ex-clergyman with an arm span as wide and reassuring as airplane wings. He'd pace about with studious steps and talk with a curious gaze while Rosie's mum sassed about the kitchen preparing dinner. She was a savant of Southern flavours which she served up with an excess of Pickwickian mirth and trimmings of sharp wit. Meanwhile Rosie's two brothers were imagoes of fraternal love and support, who drifted into town on holidays and spare weekends for spontaneous mini-adventures. Had all my contradictions and nonsense and sense of self-sabotage finally caught up with me? Had I proved myself wrong and found my Shangri-La after all this time in the tranquil magic and regional charm of the Lowcountry?

Breaking my Kansas introspection is Dodge City. It turns out heading towards Dodge and getting the hell out of Dodge are the only redeemable aspects to the city. I head west on US 50. A black-on-sand horizon signals another day's end as I cross the Great Plains into Colorado. I stop to get a six-pack of Ranger Imperial IPA and park up on an access road well after dark to sleep. Through the windscreen the Great Divide is a frosted moustache on the face of a midnight sky. In Colorado I feel my aloneness settle — I fall into a comfortable groove on treacherous back roads through sleet and snow between Cañon City and Cripple Creek, then criss-crossing the I-70, threading mountain and sky; joining peak to peak against a blue and white bannered backdrop; getting kicked out of Estes Park by the local cops for sleeping in my car; and being turned around at high passes and camp sites still closed due to adverse weather.

Tog becomes a transportable vessel for isolation therapy. All the sacrifices I've made to live the way I do rise up like a sounder of puppets in my head to debate their self-worth. While driving I adjudicate their diatribes like a prime-time presenter hosting a presidential debate. But no matter how skilfully I extinguish one wretched voice, two more sock-heads spewing self-loathing take to the lectern to shitbag me some more — peeling away my insecurities — of being a seed that won't sow — picking at my anxieties — of being in my thirties still without any tangible proof I ever existed, except what's in my car. I am haunted by regret. It is my liege, my confidante, the drunken life of the party at the soirees hosted in my head, the piñata I cannot break to spill.

Music helps. I DJ to the landscape. Descending from the Rockies, through Telluride and Durango into the charred expanse of New Mexico it's Explosions in the Sky. Exploring Monument Valley and Valley of the Gods is The Flaming Lips post *Soft Bulletin*. Entering Utah under a blue-plated sky chipped by wind-worn buttes I let Conor Oberst's existentialist musing take over my own.

I soon get good at ignoring the unhelpful figments in my imagination, because they're part of me and I know them too well. I traverse the Colorado Plateau, airing my tent out in the Canyonlands and Capitol Reef, kept company by blistering winds and star-lit skies. I keep myself entertained moderating bouts of fisticuffs between my ego and id, my flaws and strengths, peccadilloes versus what makes me worthwhile *(or at the very least redeemable)*. I feel close to something I can't grasp driving down UT-12, like a high plains drifter along the dizzying rimrock of Escalante's Grand Staircase. I find the local alcohol agency selling booze out of a hidden booth at the back of the outdoor store in Escalante. But a drunken lady is engaged in a deranged and lengthy debate over a half bottle of vodka. So I abandon the shop for the nearest gas station. I get a mid-strength tallboy of Bud and drive three miles out of town where a National Forestry map indicates a campsite by Posey Lake.

That night I sit on a small jetty casting a small silver lure out into a cool green lake surrounded by a parapet of pines. The surface of the water is alive, zinging with zigzagging dragonflies and plops from airborne fish. I work the lure while sipping on a beer. A low-circling bald eagle swoops down to scratch the lake and snatches a trout clean out of the water. With a sharp follow-through it banks left and rises to glide directly overhead, deliberately almost as if to say, 'That's how it's done, boy!' I get a desperate shallow bite and frantically reel in a small brook trout then another in quick succession. I watch their scarlet bellied bodies jounce on the wooden decking before I quickly get a handle of them and whip their heads off to give them peace. The forest sighs with thunderous silence. It carries shivers of night across the lake:

*This is it — this is what I seek — this is my dream — this is me — this is everything — this is the apotheosis of travel — the present-mindedness of being exactly where I should be.*

The utter simplicity of what makes me happy is staggering. It obliterates the looming storm of suspicion and doubts about Rosie and me — and with a tremble of cold I feel resident anxieties of impermanence and perpetuity fade into calmness. I dress the fish and hurry back to my campsite where I fry the trout on my camping stove using olive oil from a sacrificial can of tuna. This is where my trip begins.

Two nights later I'm burning along the Extraterrestrial Highway. A velvet frosted glow decorates the Nevada sunset. By nightfall I'll hit California. I'll camp for the last night on my own in my car against the fetlock of the Sierra Nevada Mountains. I feel a readiness in my body and mind to welcome all the new experiences and encounters awaiting me. By morning I'll be back in the thick of it — in traffic on the interstate balling down the I-15 to meet Rosie in San Diego. It's the life of the living and I'm ready. I can't wait.

# CHAPTER 16

# THE VEGAN ENIGMA

I'd been vegetarian for almost 10 years when I first arrived in South America. It was 2003 and half that time I'd spent hooked on the abandonment of crossing borders over mountains and bridged rivers. Chasing down the mutable awe of meeting new people and encountering new places made me flexible about my eating habits just like I was about everything else in life. Vegetarianism after all isn't a religion — not in a Western sense of the definition anyway. I prized the heady elixir of distance, self-reliance and solitude above all else. And I welcomed the heavy thirst and appetite from foraging the gamut of beguiling rituals, mannerisms and incomprehensible tongues. I also didn't want any predisposition preclude me from new tastes and sensations — or prevent me from collecting a new tome of experiences.

Belief generates experience and experience generates belief, and all that. In other words I was sold on the idea that what you get out of a trip is intimately related to how much of yourself you put in, and how much you're willing to relinquish. It can still be a challenge for the undergraduate backpacker to let go, or for a gap year graduate to blast out the cognitive cobwebs from a life-time of academic teachings. However, it's hard to make it sound too difficult when the planet is your home and you're beholden to no one and nothing. I'd also just arrived in the kingdom of *pollo con patatas fritas*. My Spanish was woeful, and eating meat seemed inevitable. In no way did I see this as any kind of failure. However, it turns out there's a lot of vegetarians and vegans who would disagree.

Years later I recounted the details of my South American trip to Daisy, a good friend who recently became a vegetarian. She chastised me immediately for being lazy. I told her I embraced my own hypocrisy a lifetime ago because nothing good ever came from it — especially with regard to eating habits. When hypocrisy and reductive labels enter debates, backs stiffen up against walls. Everyone wriggles into their own defensive onesie to protect against what people fear the most — being called a fraud or a phoney. Hypocrisy is for people who prefer opinions over understanding, and as such ensures nothing pertinent ever gets addressed. I parodied Tom Waits from Jim Jarmusch's *Coffee and Cigarettes*:

> *'The beauty of me not eating meat is now I can eat meat whenever I like... cos I've quit eating meat.'*

Daisy looked as confused as Iggy Pop, but she did appreciate food and drink is a major part of what connects us when we're away. Daisy had just returned to Australia from a study abroad program in Guilin, China and admitted she ate meat in a region I consider a wonderland for vegetarian cuisine. Like many back-packers, Daisy conditionally suspended her guiding beliefs in lieu of the experiential value of an overseas trip. She recalled eating the first batches of freshly steamed dim sum at three in the morning after nights out with her student exchange friends. It reminded me of a similar ritual Maccas and I shared in Beijing after long nights on the *píjiǔ*. Daisy explained how she would have missed the rich connectiveness of such experiences *(along with the rich char sui in gravy)* if she didn't eat meat. Maybe it's because she just called me lazy, but I felt an erroneous whiff abetting Daisy's justification. Yet, it's something I fully appreciated — yearning for immersion in authentic experiences. Also, I thought no differently when I flew into Caracas and spent the next six months journeying south to Santiago.

As a monolingual backpacker who lacks the enviable gene or talent of a polyglot, taste and smell are my second language. Sampling new flavours from a banquet of unidentifiable and sometimes questionable food dishes on long trips anchors me. The complex and contrasting aromas, from detestable to delectable anodise memories with an incorruptible quality. As supreme architects of nostalgia and teleportation, tastes and smells thrust you without warning into the past, rendering photographs kitsch and impotent by comparison. I've since travelled through other regions such as Central Asia, where maintaining a vegetarian, let alone vegan diet crossing the kingdom of yak and mutton is commendable, pig-headed, culturally insulting and also nutritionally irresponsible. I agreed with Daisy that at least in Latin America being vegetarian or vegan isn't difficult to maintain. Self-catering is a prerequisite. It also complements budget travel in much the same way as staying in shared accommodation and taking punishing local transport. It's why budget backpacking has become such a popular travel trend regardless of whether you're skint, on hiatus, or enjoying semi-retirement — it offers unlimited opportunity to connect and share in sincere moments at no extra cost.

The local *mercado* is always a free highlight of any town, and self-catering tasks you with purpose while canvassing the diverse richness of regional cuisine. Pallets of fresh produce dazzle the senses as you discover the fecundity of endemic fruits and vegetables. Slowly you feel the heat of the day rises to warm the cool maze of shaded laneways and indoor pavilions. The tropical stench of melons and stone fruit from platoons of juice stalls ripen and lift to mingle with the visceral odour of slaughtered meat. You embrace your foreignness and become lost in the fruit-punch parade of everyday life, joining the repartee between purveyors and locals while gathering supplies for an evening meal.

Aside from self-catering there are many facets to how international cuisine and gastronomic indulgence curate the trip we're on. And these don't always come with vegetarian options. Travelling south along the Andes I tasted Colombian ants that were surprisingly good — oily like peanuts but with legs that got stuck between your teeth and an enduring nutty aftertaste only mouthwash could remove. In Peruvian *chifas* I treated myself to mounded plates of special fried rice with dyed cubes of mystery meat. I ordered *anticuchos*, kebabs of ox heart at Bolivian street stands because I was told it was a local delicacy. Oh yeah, I almost forgot. From Venezuela to Chile I also consumed a slaughterhouse of rotisserie chickens with sides of fried plantain and potato chips.

My last stop before Santiago, where I had a scheduled flight to Easter Island was San Pedro de Atacama. It's a vibrant little town of mud-plastered buildings with flat roofs, and colourful doorways and window frames adorned with rustic decorations. One could easily be mistaken for thinking they were in a beach town on the Oaxaca coast in Mexico, or some quaint new Santa Fe progeny in New Mexico. However, where San Pedro is was hard to disguise. We were just inside the Chilean border on the northern edge of the Atacama Desert, one of the driest places on the planet. I was staying at a cheap cabañas on the rough edge of town with others from the tour group I'd crossed the Altiplano with from Uyuni in Bolivia. It was midafternoon and we respected the hour by lounging in the el rancho patio area. We sipped slowly from fat bottles of local beer we bought one at a time from the corner shop nearby because their refrigerator was colder than the one where we were staying. We let the deposit on the king browns carry over to the next one, and whenever the inclination struck, we slowly rose from the unstable plastic outdoor furniture and hammocks and shuffled out the back gate and down the dusty road to get another one. We talked in spurts, punctuated by long spells of silence like a Sunday comedown. It coalesced with the recumbent torpor of San Pedro, the result of which made us all want to do precisely nothing much at all.

An intermittent stream of new arrivals slowly complemented the courtyard loiter of backpackers — some joining forces with conversations of what to do next, while others seemed disposed to sweet nothing like us. A shriek lanced the haze of lazy palaver.

'Are YOU a vegAN?'

A second squeal of equal merit responded from the portico on the opposite side of the courtyard, which had all of us conscientious objectors twisting in patio chairs and hammocks.

'Yes! Oh my GOD, are you VEgan too? Ahahahaha.'

The two vegans ran at each other and embraced like long-lost lovers on a cinematic screen. We all laughed. They spun around the courtyard in the form of a flapping, slow moving hurricane to consecrate the moment before bunkering down at a corner table with daypacks out and notebooks open. It brought to mind the hackneyed joke about vegans:

> 'How do you know if someone is vegan?'
> 'Don't worry – they'll tell you.'

The two vegan backpackers were like carrot and parsnip mash. One had just travelled down the Andean route, while the other had started in the Patagonia region and journeyed up through Argentina and Chile. As the day turned to night they kept at it, feverishly exchanging all the vegan friendly eateries they had encountered on their respective trips.

'Ruddarudda*Baños*raddarudda... oh my god, you have to go to the cafe there. It's on...'

'Blah, blah, blah... it's not on the menu but you can ask for it without cheese...'

'... shut up! They have nutritional yeast?'

'Raddaradda*Bariloche*ruddarudda... and did I mention Puerto Natales? There's a pizza place there in the main square with wooden benches and...

'... but be careful there are two. So make sure...'

'Blah, blah, blah... vegan yoghurt and in-house roasted museli...'

'Sucre! Whatever you do, don't miss the Sucre fruit market...'

'Ruddarrudda*Quitos*raddaradda... hahaha... I completely forgot about the tofu burgers at...'

Much to the general amusement of us less stoic travellers, the zeal of their conversation soon transformed our evening blather. For most of us the single-mindedness of the two semi-sexy vegans in San Pedro seemed counter-intuitive to the openness of travel. We all felt very sure of ourselves because we all followed the maxim attributed to Mark Twain and didn't letting schooling interfere with our learning. But this didn't necessarily mean we were listening. Twain also famously asserted:

*'Travel is fatal to prejudice, bigotry and narrow-mindedness.'*

Today, the satirist, humorist and original aimless vagabond still sounds like the wisest bodhisattva in the West. However I dare reduce the father of American literature and standup comedy further to say any experience with life injures ignorance. I guess the struggle on the open road, like I said before lies in how much of yourself do you volunteer — because the quality of intellectual and emotional clarity on a trip depends not only on the nature and motivations of a journey, but how much you're willing to open yourself up to new experiences and foreign cultures. I think my Mum tried to instil this in me when I was 12 and wanted to quit karate but I wasn't listening. That's because I didn't even want to learn karate. The only reason I was there was because it was late eighties — and karate and dental braces were the penance for Western kids back then.

The ultimate conundrum to all this holistic betterment of mind, body and spirit is what you let go of is often apportioned to what you pick up. Prolonged trips have a propensity to discard and wear thin prepacked partialities and prejudices — but this provides extra room and weight to fill up on souvenirs of knowledge and new opinions. The problem with opinions is they are very collectable. And as symbols of who we are and our sense of free will we take special care of them — showing them off on occasion and at other times keeping them to ourselves, quietly revelling in their company while we make fun of those who expose theirs. But just like hypocrisy and arguments which profit from opinions, they're all a bit useless. They achieve very little as they agitate and elevate notions of right and wrong. And opinions aren't much help if you don't know the answer to what you're looking for. Again, I lean on the Tao and Lao Tzu:

> 'Learning consists in adding to one's stock day by day.
> The practise of Tao consists in subtracting day by day.'

I'm not suggesting independent travellers swan around expressing a degustation of valued judgements regarding the place we're in or about to visit. But an unfortunate side effect to travel is seeing the fallout of bad shit done to humans by other humans. A natural reaction is to scrutinise host countries over present or past transgressions — and condemning governments' deplorable actions or despicable inaction is a common pastime. The travelling community is even more voluble and outspoken in contentious places like Tibet and Eastern China where the overt and systematic suppression of Tibetan and Uighur people is disgraceful and deeply upsetting. Political debate overtakes beer table banter as everyone fights to be heard, to broadcast their opinion which varies little from everyone else. It's not that anyone's necessarily wrong or ill-informed. And it would be wrong to package it as a fable of sinners throwing stones — because leaving Tibet I got arrested for minding my own business as I hitchhiked on my lonesome *(which it turns out is illegal)*. But what country could claim their shit didn't stink?

Similarly, there's nothing wrong with an economics student wearing a t-shirt made in Turkey with a slogan "No to Sweatshops". It's just that it doesn't actually help the sweatshop worker in China who is made redundant because of consumer pressure forcing contractors to relocate to a more clandestine or politically correct territory. I guess this is why for so many people who embark on a backpacking adventure to jettison themselves into an apogee from all they know, it's hard to truly leave yourself behind. You take so much of yourself with you. I guess it's why so many of us feel the need to keep moving — trying to outrun a sense of who we are on an epic round-the-world marathon. And while we might find a temporary escape in the void between places, the faint sense that the omphalos of the universe is under our feet settles like shifting sand whenever we stop for more than a moment on our journey.

This is why the mystics and mantics warn us against hunting for truth and answers on the trail of reconciliation and understanding. It's a dangerous game because it invites a platter of vices, disrupts natural intuition and massages egos — erecting tenements of pride, intolerance, stubbornness and rectitude around the ideals we deem important and right. After all, it's easy for people who start to think they're smarter than they are to turn into bombastic and righteous tools. Like Twain I'm cognisant that books won't delineate all the incoherent and unutterable contradictions and conundrums of being me. Books help but from a young age I felt certain I was going to have to go out in the world and live it to find shit out. To quote an ancient Zen proverb:

*'Do not strive to seek truth; only cease to cherish opinions.'*

Maybe it's why all of us wandering fools who haven't yet felt the tractor beam from the Mother Ship of life's grand plan find affinity with Zen and oriental philosophy. Like us it's hard to define. It's not didactic and preachy and all about books or study. And it doesn't get all messy with deisms and theisms, anthropocentric rings around theocentric circles, mortification or celebration, ritualistic legalisms and fistfuls of memes and neologisms. It's also encouraging that even Chuang-Tzu finds spiritual merit in the merry drunkard:

> 'When a drunken man falls from a carriage, though the carriage may be going very fast, he won't be killed. He has bones and joints the same as other men, and yet he is not injured as they would be, because his spirit is whole. He didn't know he was riding, and he doesn't know he has fallen out. Life and death, alarm and terror do not enter his breast, and so he can bang against things without fear of injury. If he can keep himself whole like this by means of wine, how much more can he keep himself whole by means of Heaven! The sage hides himself in Heaven — hence there is nothing that can do him harm.'

Back in San Pedro it seemed fitting that we embraced the beer in our hands while sat in the outdoor arena of our hostel. We honoured the desert chill, the two rapturous vegans, and the silliness of it all by facetiously challenging one another's moral stance over what animals we would refuse to eat if given the opportunity.

'Would you eat mono?'

'What?'

'Monkeys-'

'Yeah, I would – I mean if the locals are why not?'

'I saw two men in a village in Peru with half a dead monkey, but they were feeding it to the dogs.'

'What about turtles?'

'No way! They're sacred dude.'

'I would if I was in an indigenous community that traditionally hunted them.'

'Is it true you eat kangaroo in Australia?'

'Yep – and they're on our national coat of arms.'

'Shit.'

'I ate snake once.'

'I ate beaver tail and bear in Canada.'

'I've eaten alligator.'

'What about dolphins?'

'Even the Japanese don't eat dolphins man.'

'How about an elephant if it had just been killed by poachers?'

The discourse continued in this manner, degenerating into semantic farce and humour as we listed all manner of blessed, sentient, noble and cute creatures to test each other's ethical pliancy — orangutans, giraffes, dogs, zebras, horses, penguins, frogs and gorillas, before we predictably concluded with a life-or-death scenario of justifiable cannibalism. However, a common theme did emerge as to how accepting the majority of the group were to eating animals so long as it was served up as a traditional and authentic experience. It also turned out no one gave a fuck about eating camels.

On the backpacker's road I've witnessed this phenomenon of moral dexterity often, especially pertaining to food, as well as drug use *(both recreational and ritualistic)*. It's not uncommon for moderate backpackers to carry a libertine check list, much like the adjunct list of monuments and museums when they embark on a round-the-world trip of a lifetime. We want our line of marching powder coming from Panama into Colombia; seek out an *ayahuasca* experience while rescuing a sloth from a refuge in Peru; get hooked on coca leaves then mate in Argentina before flying to South East Asia for ayurvedic retreats, magic mushroom shakes, opium dens and make-it-happy everything; head to India to down bhang lassis and chew on *pann* while finding sanctuary in a locus of meditation and yoga; upon departure stock up on brain-jarring pharmaceuticals because currency supplants subscriptions then go woof around Europe; a final flutter in the continental red light districts; a brief sojourn to the hashish origins of Morocco, and finally flying home, feeling like phew, that all got a bit crazy.

In terms of eating habits, our flexibility is no different. It's just as dependent on our beliefs and individual preferences. But whether it's personal taste, concern for the environment, a protest against animal exploitation and cruelty, an act of supplication or a more encompassing pantheistic view demonstrated in Eastern philosophies, everyone has their boundaries. This includes even the most impulsive and daring wayfarers. I admit I'm the sort of dickhead that if challenged to eat something exotic I probably won't refuse. I've eaten whale nigiri in Iceland, jellyfish sushi in America, Japanese eel in Australia, sacrilegious reindeer celebrating a Swedish Christmas, and crudités of poly-legged bush tucker. I've also tried yak, crocodile, kangaroo, snake and haggis. Who knows what kind of varmints I ate skewered on roadside grills in Laos or lacquered in a tarry Asian sauce. But from the great Aussie tradition of backyard barbeques I'm certain I've consumed a childhood of earlobes, eyeballs, lips, gizzards, trotters, tongues, tails and other viscera neatly disguised in charred sausage sangas, party pies, cocktail hotdogs, and diced polony and cheddar *hors d'œuvres*.

Regardless, I refuse to eat frogs' legs because frogs are sacred to me. I don't need to be *fugu-ed*. And given the sentient mystery and marvel of octopuses, the thought of *sannakji (live octopus tentacles)* repulses me. I don't think I'll ever be struck peckish enough on a bus in Thailand to chug down a chicken foetus from a runny soft-boiled egg. And while I support diversifying our food habits to aid sustainability, I'm wary of animals served as novelty cuisine to tourists. So I eschewed the insect market when I was in Beijing. And I distanced myself from tourists in Cambodia looking to get the *fuerte* back in their loins at the cost of a live cobra's heart served still beating in a shot of vodka. On my Latin American odyssey I also had no intention of trying the regional delicacy known as *picante de cuy* AKA hot 'n' spicy guinea pig.

It wasn't that I was grossed out at the thought of eating an oversized hamster. The Spanish conquistadors weren't. In fact they respected, or at least tolerated local Quechua customs enough to let *cuy* and *chicha (fermented drink derived from maize)* on the menu of Marco Zapata's *The Last Supper*, which is displayed in the Cusco Cathedral. I was even assured *cuy* was virtually free-range since they ran around in the back gardens behind small-town restaurants until an order came in. But I was the son of a farmer's son. As a kid growing up on the remote west coast of Australia I'd trapped, killed and eaten my fair share of rabbits and other critters that walked or crawled at one time or another. So eating a rodent held little appeal since like most people I'd come to the conclusion it all basically tastes like chicken anyway so what's the point.

In 2003 there was also no Facebook, Instagram or smart-phones pestering to get a selfie with a roasted guinea pig. In an age of glorified distraction it makes me wonder how much of our behaviour is now predisposed to the documentation and self-promotion of our online identities — choices made not as a result of our sensibilities, but to aid our latest status update.

Take the self-publicised metanoia of a backpacking acolyte, who by way of travelling starts to identify more of themselves with the surrounding culture. They downsize their rucksack for a satchel; give up eating meat *(except for seafood)* loudly and proudly; discover yoga and meditation as a new expression of who they are; stalk dietary movements and herbal cures; become activists in expressions of pacifism; are outspoken advocates for vitamin supplements, superfoods and universal harmony; turn strict vegetarians then vegans; tweet inspirational quotes from Vedic teachings; instagram daily headstands, health shakes and yoga poses; and take hostage of the super moons, celestial eclipses the and ebb 'n' flow of the tides. Once fully converted they discard their deferred college future for a life of travel — and they may well do that *(at least while in their twenties)*. I jest because we all do this when we find something new we are passionate about and learn from the experience. Aldous Huxley addresses this process in the introduction of *The Perennial Philosophy*:

> *'Knowledge is a function of being. When there is a change in the being of the knower, there is a corresponding change in the nature and amount of knowing.'*

Just like with travel, the reasons I started off as a veggie are not the same as they are now. This is what I tried to explain to Daisy. At 17 years of age when I first decided to become a vegetarian I was in my first year of university and surrounded by all these super-hot alternative looking vegetarians and vegans. I was shit with chicks and was really into dreadlocks, tattoos and body piercings so becoming a vegetarian, or at least saying I was one seemed to make perfect sense. There was also a convenience to it in the beginning. Without a political agenda I enjoyed having no allegiance or team — because I tend to agree with Royal Tenenbaum in the Wes Anderson film classic. 'There are no teams,' he exclaims from the rooftop perch of their summer home on Eagle's Island before shooting Chas, his son and ally *(and owner of the house)* between two knuckles on his left hand with an air rifle.

By default my decision was also a personal embargo against factory farming, so yay to me because I championed the survival of our planet. I could support local farmers who promoted organic and ethical practices. And if persuaded I defended the civil rights of hunters to kill and eat animals. But I didn't go around commandeering sedate backyard barbeques and friendly get-togethers with pontificating arguments. And I didn't make a fuss when there were no vegetarian options at catered gatherings. There was always beer and wine — and that was vegetarian right?

That's why I giggled at the two vegans in San Pedro, along with the other backpackers because we all thought they were being silly and missing out on way too much due to their rigid stance. However, as my knowledge grew it expanded and strengthened my outlook. I began to see the cultural hegemony of what we eat and why isn't natural, historical or vaguely nutritional. It's a false construct invented by industry long ago, commercialising bad eating habits along with cute advent calendar stories about turkeys, pigs and chickens to fuel consumerism. And milk and dairy were just as complicit, manipulative and malevolent — to the cancer-causing free radicals in our bodies and methane emissions feeding greenhouse gases. Then there's our anthropomorphic dial which we tune into the special animals we deem conscious or clever enough to be like us. We admonish Asian countries for eating dogs but ignore the eco pawprint of a pet dog is arguably larger than an SUV. And we protest Japan, Iceland Norway for whaling *(and feel good about it)* while overlooking the cataclysmic decimation of ocean fauna through our own fishing practices and eating habits. It's easy I guess to get swallowed up by the hopelessness of being completely fucked — especially given our unremitting stupidity and persistence using inequitable and unviable resources. But we can't save the world all at once. At least that's what I came to realise.

From time to time I thought about the two vegans from San Pedro de Atacama. I no longer considered them sedulous and too blinded by principles to understand the true point of travelling. On the contrary, I now thought of them as being progressive and way ahead of their time. Part of me felt bad that I had laughed at them even though they were pretty funny. So I gave up milk in morning coffee, cheese *(except on pizza and free samples in supermarkets)* and sushi *(except on special occasions)*. After a while I preferred a long black to a flat white, I no longer craved pizza every day *(which I thought was inconceivable)*, I still ate free cheese samples in supermarkets, but special occasions to eat sushi stopped being every second lunch and dinner.

Through a progression of personal taste, awareness and conscience I realised the more I invested the more positive I felt about the world and my place in it. My attitudes changed without feeling like anything had changed. In an incomprehensible way everything just got simpler and clearer. As I developed a more encompassing outlook which respected the interconnectedness of all of us, I stopped contemplating my reasons for not eating animals. And from what seemed like a fairly insignificant decision the best version of me started to glow. I guess this is what it's like for people who put their faith in religion. The benefit of a book and manmade rules said to come down from the holiest of holies is they can help guide us to make us believe in the best of ourselves — a dogmatic instrument of *do's* and *don'ts* inspire us to be better, or at the very least behave ourselves because let's face it we can all be shitheads. I was fairly sure I would continue to fuck up my life and personal relationships for reasons I would later try really hard to frame as being out of my control. But my choice not to eat animals was something I could take ownership of. It became an inadvertent centrepiece of who I am, forgiving my faults and contradictions, letting my flawed and good intentions shine. And the *ahisma* of Zen Buddhism, which I once considered radical for viewing consumption of any flesh as a sort of cannibalism, now made perfect sense.

Nine years had passed since my Atacama encounter with two vegans. It was the end of 2012 and I was about to embark on a return trip to Chile and Argentina. Over the last decade the vegetarian and vegan movement had come a long way. We even had science joining the fundamental principle of non-violence to all living things, imparted for thousands of years by Buddhism, Hinduism and Jainism. In 2010 the United Nations Environmental Programme made international headlines when it released a report stating a vegan diet was environmentally and economically vital to save the world. This followed a publication the previous year by Lord Nicholas Stern, former advisor to the British Government on the economics of climate change who also claimed the planet needed people to stop eating meat. However, science has been saying this for a while. Almost a century before Einstein demonstrated his extraordinary vision wasn't limited to theoretical physics and maths when he advocated a vegetarian diet:

> '... it is my view that a vegetarian manner of living by its purely physical effect on the human temperament would most beneficially influence the lot of mankind.'

I had also just read Jonathan Safran Foer's *Eating Animals* and seen him talk at College of Charleston where his book was selected for the 2012–13 College Reads program. I was inspired and decided to make amends. I would follow Foer's advice and not play the role of the pedagogic vegan. I would be a vegan who avoids labels and confrontation. But I would still chivvy every meat eating backpacker by simply asking people to question what they are eating. It was an ambitious challenge. I was travelling to arguably the world's premier destination for the finest cuts of butchered bovine barbequed to mouth-watering perfection. Even idle talk about visiting Argentina could make the staunchest vegetarians salivate over their holiday concession to eat beef steak at bargain prices.

Driving overnight down the I-95 from South Carolina to Miami, Florida to catch my flight I could have been questioning my mission — wondering how much the vegetarian message penetrated the shoal of activism and global awareness which backpackers cultivated and hid behind like it was a religion. If it was anything like the cloistered bastions of liberalism at tertiary institutions there should at least be enough independent travellers pretending to be vegetarians and vegans. I mean, what are backpackers if not lazy students of life? Would I at least avoid ridicule when queuing at hostel barbeques to order sides of grilled mushrooms and zucchini?

However, all this seemed of little consequence when Tog, my newly bought Subaru Legacy started spewing smoke from the engine block. Faint emissions started licking the bonnet driving on Highway 17 shortly after leaving Charleston. Toxic fumes washed in through the air vents. With a solid 10-hour drive ahead I realised a simple breakdown would completely fuck my master plan before it began. I even remember the smug sense of genius when I devised it. The idea was to road test Tog out on the red lanes of the USA in lieu of the massive road trip I had planned early in the new year. I also saved approximately $150 against the cost a return flight from Charleston to Miami.

I made it to the I-95 connector, churned through Georgia and four hours later I was in the top end of the Sunshine State. As rain and darkness fell on a cold December night the smoke took on a baleful grey tone as it billowed from the front of the hood. What the fuck was I thinking? I had not contingency whatsoever. I had a non-refundable return ticket, no travel insurance, the legal minimum of car insurance and I was on the final day of my 90-day visa-free stay. I had not even thought about what I would do if my car broke down. Would I abandon Tog or my trip?

My reasons were sound enough when I made them. From what was essentially a glorified visa run to get another three months in Charleston with Rosie I'd constructed an elaborate vegan crusade. There was also symmetry to the trip. It completed my 2003 visit which was curtailed when I broke my left foot on Easter Island three days after leaving San Pedro and the two vegans. As it got late and traffic faded away I started having delusional thoughts. Who cares about vegans and vegetarians and all this baloney? All that matters is the bees — bees and beer and frogs and Rosie. Why do I keep leaving the one girl who matters? Why aren't we drinking downtown cocktails, staying in a hotel to celebrate whatever, and having loving drunken sex where we wake up in the morning still stuck to one another? Why didn't we just run away from custom regulations and go live in the Appalachians — live happy long lives together in the mountains making hooch and furniture and instruments from wood. She understood why I was leaving but still had to ask.

'Why are you going when I have three weeks off?'
'The stupid US visa regulations baby.'
'I hate this,' Rosie groaned.
'What are you going to do when I'm gone?'
'Mmmm...
go for bike rides...
get runny noses...
learn to play a lot of really sad songs on the guitar...
read myself to sleep...
make savoury snacks...
'Stop it-'
'... make myself look really pretty every day so I don't get so sad...
paint my nails different colours... annnnd...
take a lot of pictures.'
'Please don't go falling in love with any other boys while I'm gone.'
'I won't.'
The five-disc compilation soundtrack Rosie ripped for me as a parting gift didn't help. In the dark cabin lit by the blue LED lights of the stereo I listen on loop to the jaunty finger-picking rhythm and kick-drum beat of *Just For Now* by Cloud Control. It makes Rosie present — like the song was written with us in mind:

*'And I gotta leave in the morning light*
*Got a book to write*
*Leather-bound in my feathered hand*
*To make you understand*
*To make you understand*
*That's it's just for now*
*It's just for now'*


Passing Melbourne I submit to the conniving temperament Tog passed onto me. I get a cheap room at the Budget Inn using a hotel coupon. I eat a cold tin of Trader Joes' vegetable and lentil soup I packed so I didn't have to survive on vegan-friendly junk food at gas stations and fast food outlets. I sleep a few nervous hours and get back on the road a little after 2 am. The frigid night and rest appear to do Tog some good. I keep her in the right lane hovering on the minimum speed limit. Three hours later I'm taking the Miami International Airport exit as dawn breaks on the interstate with an epileptic surge of downtown commuters. I find the shonky garage I booked online, take their complimentary airport shuttle with a surly Mexican driver who pretended not to understand English until he realised I was a customer. I check my baggage, get my boarding pass, make it through customs and with an hour to spare I sit myself down by the departure gate.

Hit by fatigue and hunger I'm still struck by the prodigious shudder that always accompanies the climactic emptiness of departure lounges, night-time campfires, mountain summits, and staring into the infinite green and blue oblivion — how the heck did I get here? Well, in case anyone asks — yes, you can conceivably buy a car, get it licensed and registered in South Carolina, drive it 580 miles to Miami and have it securely parked for a month while you go to South America. Should you — well that is something altogether different and much harder to answer.

I get a complimentary Starbucks coffee using the promotional coupons Rosie's mum collected. I chat to Rosie on Facebook before the plane boards, conceding I can't quite figure out how I ended up creating such a convoluted and painful plan to catch a flight.

> This sucks so much!

> I know - i hate it to!!!

> i hate you

> I love you so fucking much - miss u already!
> Wish you were coming with me :):)

> I wanna travel with you so bad

> Promise - love you more than...
> hot sauce, pizza, sushi, fishing, raw oysters,
> the ocean... um... camp fires, camping...

I didn't get a chance to express myself beyond the prominent themes of food and the sea because the plane started to taxi. And I didn't want to get blamed for my Nokia 6120 breaking the plane. Ordinarily I avoid eating on planes. I feel like a force-fed cow with a grain bag strapped around my muzzle. I do respect the Monty Burns "Tartare Sauce" philosophy to make amenable all of us smelly anchovies in economy class. I also love the distraction of food and I'm mindful of evading extortionate airport meal prices on extended layovers like I had coming up at Ezeiza International Airport. That's why regardless of appetite I always preordered vegan meals because they were typically the lightest and healthiest option. The other benefit of special meal orders is they get served first and if the host is on their game they'll offer you a drink which means you're up for a refill by the time the drinks cart comes along with main meal service.

Despite making my meal request when booking my flight, Aerolínas Argentinas *(I renamed Aerokakka Argenshitas)* had no meal options. They didn't even have regular meals. For the nine-hour flight I was handed a paltry lunch box with a cellophane wrapped *jamón y queso* sandwich, a juice box supersaturated with sugar, and for desert an *alfajor*, a cookie sandwich filled with *dulche de leche* and coated in white chocolate and nuts. I feel the empowerment of hunger as I hand back the untouched food and instead of requesting a coffee refill I order 'un cerveza nacional' *(for medicinal purposes to suppress my appetite)*. My connecting flight down to Ushuaia is part of a plan to spend the following five weeks overlanding it back through Patagonia, the Lakes District and Mendoza to Buenos Aires to catch my return flight. But the flight via Trelew departs early the following morning so I've got 12 uncomfortable hours at the airport. By the time I arrive at Ezeiza International Airport I'm exhausted well beyond the point of caring too much about my appetite. The trick to overnighting at an airport is not to be hasty. Don't settle for the nearest row of empty seats that could get disturbed by late night arrivals, zealous security guards, or the premorning clamour of kiosks and shops preparing for the day's trade. In my experience the flagship terminals are best for finding quiet nooks where airport luminance is dimmed short of a headache. I follow my instinct and transit to Terminal A where I find a sweet, darkened spot on the deserted upper level and try to sleep.

The next morning I head to Terminal C to get my 7.25 am departure to Ushuaia. I'm a French breakfast minus the cigarette man. In other words black coffee — the rest I'm pretty philosophical about. This is convenient since it appears the Aerolínas Argentinas curse of *jamón y queso* has followed me off the plane. Every savoury snack and pastry sold at convenience stores and early morning takeaway shops has an unappetising mat of cheap deli ham and cheese. And no matter how innocuous or veggie friendly other options are, they're all glued together by a thick layer of butter or mayonnaise. I buy two apples while waiting for the plane to board which stokes my growling stomach.

The three-hour flight is slow to taxi. After ascending to cruising altitude the loud clatter from the aft galley is equally slow to produce the meal service carts. They parade down the aisle displaying the same style of snack boxes that were on the international flight. Tracking the crawl of the meal service back through economy section depletes my vegan fortitude. Finally, I'm handed a meal box. I open it to find an exact replica of food items from my previous flight. I'm defeated. I take a coffee from the drinks service but I know the trick of liquids won't work. Reading the Blanco *alfajor's* dairy enriched paragraph of preservatives, I rationalise that it's more chemistry than husbandry. I eat it and feel like shit in a way that is guaranteed by processed snack food. Less than 48 hours into my vegan mission I've failed. I'm now starving so I pop the sandwich wrapper, discard the suspicious flap of cheap meat and scoff down the cheese roll, which is as unfulfilling and tasteless as eating a leather shoe.

Like everything in life I'm a big believer in balance and moderation — matching head with heart and eyes with feet. To set your inquisitive gaze both to the ground and to the drink in your hand — and whittle yourself away until you're a glorious little pipe which breathes in adventure and temerity and exhales compassionate quietude. Debating these competitive internal forces, deciding when to be reckless because you're missing out and when to be wary and stay the course is commonplace in budget backpacking — whether it's ordering a snack from a dubious street vendor, or accepting an impromptu invitation. I guess this is because while faith and trust lay the foundation of hospitality, we don't find it as easily in a good samaritan as we do with frail paper notes of currency. And it's unfortunate for women that the covenant of hospitality carries a stronger caveat of hesitancy and reticence. But what you eat is your own doctrine. It is a blend of faith, allergies, beliefs and tastes you can choose to modify or not, like ordering your own signature sandwich. And just like every other slice of our personality, as we change, so too does the type and mode of our knowledge. This in turn affects how we perceive ourselves in the world around us. It's why vegetarians gravitate to other vegetarians; people who drink mingle best with others who like to drink; and those who mind drugs rarely mix with those who don't mind drugs.

This is why Mr Twain and I agree that travel shits on institutionalised learning for the way it engages all your senses. For backpackers the art of travel is so potent in this regard by the measure it broadens perspective and stretches our vision from the point of departure. Travelling abroad is a *tour de force* of sights, sounds, smells and flavours, which continuously confront and confound — conditioning a deeper yen to explore and understand the foreignness of faces, places and novel situations. Show, don't tell. It's the 101 tenet of film and writing schools. It's also how Bill and Ted managed to pass their final history exam and restore the future's history of being excellent to each another. Again, this process of change comes down to what you keep and what you leave behind. In the same manner, my rejection of orthodox theology and religious hegemony in favour of a personalised portmanteau of precepts and beliefs is supported by all I've seen, done and experienced. It's not that I don't think there is no value in rules and books. But I don't believe doctrine and books will get me much closer to understanding myself in the unitive knowledge of divine reality.

In *Eating Animals* Safran Foer discusses the loss of choosing not to eat meat in respect to his Eastern European heritage and the decision along with his wife to raise their children as vegetarians:

> *'Changing what we eat and letting taste fade from memory creates a kind of cultural loss, a forgetting. But perhaps this kind of forgetfulness is worth accepting — even worth cultivating (forgetting, too, can be cultivated). To remember my values, I need to lose certain tastes and find other handles for the memories that they once helped me carry.'*

On the open road, the choice not to eat meat can accentuate this sense of loss and gain — especially when encountering so many rich cultures linked to land, where hunting and killing animals make up so much of the art, history, social fabric of everyday life. And you don't want to self-cater all the time! Going out for a drink and a meal is the perfect end-of-day reward for the contortion and torture of overland routes, where you're a pillar and post for all the sweaty locals to lean on for hours on end. A restaurant or bar also offers a meditative spell of quiet after an exhaustive day of travel. They provide sanctuary from streets crowded with relentless peddlers and touts, and they punctuate long solitary journeys. They're the venues where we can unhook ourselves like accordions and relax and elongate, and make some noise with new comrades and other solo backpackers.

Descending beneath the clouds on final approach into Ushuaia International Airport revives my outlook. Maybe it's because I'm about to set foot on the southernmost city in the world. I know I will reboot and start over my vegan agenda. I peer out over the Tierra del Fuego archipelago — the stark, uninhabited rock and snow-splattered landscape cut by the icy waters of the Beagle Channel. As sure as I am that I will not quit, I am equally certain I will fail again — and I'm okay with that. I can't desecrate the sanctity of hospitality by refusing a charitable offer of milk tea or a plate of gristle from someone barely able to provide for themselves. I also can't think of practical vegan alternatives to eating light weight protein-packed tins of sardines and tuna on solo treks *(and yes, I know if choosing to eat animals, I should at least eat the ones that eat vegetables).*

Five weeks pass quickly. A lot of time is taken up on multi-day hikes around the lush, granite-fingered mountains, glaciers, lakes and rivers of Torres del Paine, Los Glaciares and Nahuel Huapi national parks. Days and nights are otherwise lost crossing the barren steppes, grasslands and desert of southern Argentina and Chile. The new year is feeding on January when I arrive back in Miami. The afternoon is setting as I pull Tog out of the garage by Miami International Airport. Heading back north under a gilded firmament I reflect upon my trip.

I achieved everything I set out to — which in my head sounds satisfying without being remarkable. The hiking was superb but came with a heavy set of conditions — protective rules and regulations guarding the high volume of tourists. The overland journey itself was exhaustive and uninspiring. I had no consideration for the desolate enormity of the Patagonian region — which I guess made the angel-fingered mountains at Torres del Paine and Fitz Roy all the more exquisite and rare. But most of the long, expensive bus trips up the Ruta 40 were conducted overnight anyway so it didn't really matter.

During the trip I continued to champion the vegan cause. Sat beside backpackers enjoying juicy steaks and chicken breasts from *asados* operated by hostels, and in self-catered kitchens I questioned their eating habits. Everyone was receptive and appreciative enough to nod and understand the cause but everyone was on holiday. Even the few self-confessed vegetarians were on a gastronomic holiday too. They used ductile labels like *flexitarian* and *pescetarian* which I loathe because they sound daft.

Patagonia also has all the frugal hallmarks of a true *frontera*. The cold, dry region doesn't produce anywhere near the rich abundance of produce and cuisine found in the central and northern parts of Argentina and Chile. As such I didn't go out much to eat and stayed in camping grounds where possible, living out of my single-person tent. In fact I only had two standout food memories for the entire trip. The first was treating myself to a gourmet funghi pizza and cerveza in Puerto Natales after completing a gruelling, rain-soaked four-day circuit of Torres del Paine. The second was Christmas Day lunch at a campsite by the shores of Nahuel Huapi Lake, just outside of Bariloche. I cooked pasta with a tomato and basil sauce on my camping stove while listening to the background revelry and boisterous politics of a tour bus full of Aussies and Brits who started celebrating well before midday. In solitude I enjoyed the meal. Accompanied by a bottle of Mendoza cabernet I sat watching the cold wind brush endless patters of sun glitter across the cerulean lake.

Burning the breeze back up the I-95 I turn on the stereo and Rosie's mix CD plays from the point when I left the car — the same song, the same band I tirelessly listened to on the way down.

Through the decaying amber glow of another typical Florida sunset I know *Just for Now* will forever fuse the interstate, Tog and me to the feeling of coming back to Rosie:

*'20 years on a steady slope*
*I'm all out of hope*
*Never thought we'd come this far*
*Oh I'm telling you that when I go*
*There's something you should know*
*There's one thing that you should know*
*That's it's just for now*
*It's just for now'*

Mindful of the lack of memorable food experiences, I wonder if this has contributed to how ambivalent I feel about the trip. Maybe it's because it was the overdue conclusion to a previous trip — or maybe I miss Rosie too much. I've never travelled before with someone waiting for me to return. I guess regardless of what you pick up, let go of, or cherish enough to carry with you on any journey through life it's getting to a point of contentment. To stand at the end of a rainbow, see nothing but the simple palette of reality around you and not be disappointed. In other words after trying so hard to be lost, you would still be happy if you were found.

Tog is behaving and there is only a faint waft of oil through the air vents. I am certain I will make it — a highway that first led me to Rosie would continue to do so with the faithful magic of a rainbow bridge. Eleven hours later, just before six in the morning she will open the door to our Cannon Street address. With a voice soaked in sleep she will say, 'Heyyy,' and nothing more. She will hold my body which trembles from anticipation, cold, sleeplessness and energy drinks and kiss me softly before rubbing her tired eyes and lead me into the bedroom. She will peel off my travel clothes and whisper, 'I'm so glad your home.' She will tell me about a new Mexican restaurant that has opened since I've been away and I will say we should go there later. She will draw me on top of her and kick up the covers and say, 'Kiss me.'

# CHAPTER 17

## SEARCHING FOR THE RABBIT IN THE MOON

It's funny how after all the supplicant phone calls to papa bear, the scrimping and scratching and savings, sleeping on couches and hard floors, living between missed meals on ramen and stale bread, livers full of booze, arteries swollen with liberty and MSG, the fight to stay adrift in the world weakens. The instability of it all starts to rot your transom of clarity and resolve. Your non-conformist pride to fit in anywhere wanes. All the *Zenness,* real or indulged stymies. Conniving over a feast of stilted insights and semi-enlightenments in hostels becomes beleaguered and repetitive — as travellers spew their life stories out over one another in one desperate breath to be heard. Through the hedonistic veil of uninhibited freedoms you start to notice the inevitability of routine. Or in the words of F. Scott Fitzgerald from *The Beautiful and the Dammed*:

> 'Travel, which had once charmed him, seemed at length, unendurable, a business of colour without substance, a phantom chase after his own dream's shadow.'

Travel, it's fair to say can be downright unhealthy and tiring. And when the mantle of enthusiasm, determination and indulgences shift, the palisades of home creep into your thoughts. You start thinking of your parents and their big, bulging parents' fridge and pantry. You envisage your old bed with the laundered smell of clean sheets. You're reminded of new nieces and nephews you're yet to meet and greet into a world you're still not even close to comprehending. You look forward to seeing old friends who don't require the timeworn introduction you're forced to give everyone you meet because everyone is a stranger. And you get more and more thrilled about the prospect of returning home — of being still *(at least for a while)* and not having to think about where you're to sleep each night.

While writing this final chapter it's hard to deny a sense of cosmic irony when considering I'm in the same situation, doing the same task I was doing when I completed my first travel book three years ago. I'm at my sister's house, keeping an eye on the front lawn through the window of the study. The reason I'm doing this is to get a little change for my back pocket by charging $15 for a set of axles to park on my sister's verge during the Perth Royal Show. The realisation that I'm in it, for life, doing what I think I'm supposed to do — write this book to illuminate the eschatologies and esotericisms driving budget travel, scares the shit out of me.

The Showground which hosts the week-long agricultural event is just around the corner from my sister's house. Coinciding with school holidays the cultural legacy of our rural heritage is celebrated with the carnivalisation and commercialisation of a shitty fun park. It's also insanely popular. I calculate if I can turn over a minimum of two vehicles per day in the four spots on the front lawn and the additional driveway space, I stand to make in excess of $750 for the week. It's not bad considering I've struggled to find work since returning from Charleston six weeks ago. My home state wants miners and builders — not Beat Zen wanderers who juggle with words.

Some would say I'm winning. When I'm back in town old friends married with kids and mortgages reminisce about our youthful indiscretions — romanticising heartbreak, hookups and adolescent insouciance as if it were some kind of elusive childhood witchcraft they lost yet I retained. Then there are the young idolaters of "no regrets" inspired, or at least impressed by my foolhardy *daveness* — because I'm still putting myself out there while the rest of the ageing figureheads around them telling them what to do are ensconced *(contently)* in terminal domesticity. But you can't put yourself in the flow, you can only be in the flow — just like you're not supposed to weigh the sacrifices of an adventure before you embark on it otherwise you may never leave. In other words don't look back on empty fear. It's easier said than done and I'm doing a shitload of that lately. It turns out trying to find the *Middle Way* while pursuing a life on the open road is really fucking hard. Without paid work I signed onto the dole. When asked to declare my assets as a gross sum I floundered:

*My laptop — how the fuck am I spose to remember what I paid for that? What's a computer that's 108 years old in human years worth anyway? — I have clothes! A few sets of clothes I can fit into my backpack — clothes so old even my Mum complains and insists on taking me shopping so I can look different than how I look in photos over the past 15 years. What do clothes even cost nowadays? Reminder! I need to go clothes shopping — talk to mum — there's my hiking boots — didn't I buy them in the UK? I must have spent over a hundred quid cos your feet are the second most important thing to look after — household stuff from my time in Melbourne — I couldn't even give away my household stuff in Manchester to freshman students — what about my Bose speakers? Remember to get them out of storage — cos after your feet sound quality is the next important thing...*

'Is it more than two thousand dollars?' the dole officer asks growing impatient from my silence.

'Fuck no – sorry, I mean no way!'

I remember my guitar, a gorgeous Larrivée dreadnaught. It's the most expensive possession I own and accounts for half the 2K, which in hindsight still feels somewhat inflated. Degraded by the audit, I'm prompted to do a retrospective tally. I don't have a home — I'm not even sure where to look for one. And if I did find it I'm scared I wouldn't recognise it and move on. I don't own a car. I sold Tog to a lovely hipster Christian family in Charleston to pay for my airline ticket back to Australia. I have no family, no kids. I have no discernible superannuation. No private health cover. All the personalised cool crap I've accumulated over the years resides in packing boxes in my childhood room at my parents' house — which I'm reminded of like shoebox memories each time I visit. I live on happy hours, handmedowns and pre-paid phone credit. And I still look forward to Xmas for the cash handouts from my loving family which helps me limp fiscally across the line into a new year.

Don't mistake me with being resilient or fearless. I never set out to be part of a bohemian vanguard. On the contrary, all the places I've been and crusades I've embarked upon in solitude are because of my own shadow — chasing it with trepidation and impertinence because it's holding a big grand question mark on the blind road ahead. I'm hooked on the feeling of being lost in the *ma* and the sonority of foreign tongues and landscapes — determined to keep searching *(without concerted effort)* for what I don't really know. If you asked me right now what is my default everyday motto to get me through life I'd quote Charles de Mar, the underachieving, mature-age high school friend of Lane Myers in the cult eighties coming-of-age movie, *Better Off Dead*:

*'Go that way, really fast. If something gets in your way – turn!'*

Actor, Curtis Armstrong AKA Booger, encapsulates the veracity of a Beat Zen master with his crazy-perfect advice to an insecure John Cusack, who's trying to win back his ex-girl-friend in a death-defying bid to ski the K-12. Perhaps if I was a little camper growing up in France *(away from the influence of a chemically dependent life coach)* I'd say, '*Le mieux est l'ennemi du bien.*' In other words, don't rock a boat that's not broken. To add gravitas to a lifetime ideal I could adopt a dead language and say, '*Carpe noctem; carpe vinum.*'

I guess the danger of being the carefree pilgrim lost in the world is you can easily fall into a liminal limbo. And when you've been adrift for so long you might not have any friends close enough to notice — to call out and see if you need rescuing. I don't necessarily believe in putting yourself in extreme positions to find your true potential, but to go the furthest distance often require one to forget about the idea of returning — to be a jellyfish — to surrender to the tug and tow of the universe. So you keep going with abandonment — because if you're having so much fun lost in the maze why the fuck would you want the reach its end — to be struck with aimless despondency as you contemplate what the fuck are you spose to do next?'

I doubt I'm winning. Winning is not my thing — but I never really looked at life in contrasts of black and white. I'm a Virgo for what it's worth — who cares. Blame it on the crescent moon and tides if it makes more sense. I'm mercurial, autumnal — I like green and shades of grey clouds. I must admit if I think heavily about my interloping lifestyle and continuing belligerence to eschew society's conformist ways I find it utterly terrifying because all of it is not unreasonable — get a wife, have a family, pass on my genes and knowledge to an already overpopulated planet, buy a home, or at very least have enough for a rainy day scenario. I would have made a great hypochondriac. I would have made Freud proud if he hadn't ignored one of the most creative mental disorders. Crudely put, when mortality sets in no one wants to die alone with regret. In the words of Don Dawson from *Dazed and Confused*:

> '*Well, all I'm saying is that I want to look back and say… that I did it the best I could while I was stuck in this place. Had as much fun as I could when I was stuck in this place. Played as hard as I could when I was stuck in this place… Dogged as many chicks as I could when I was stuck in this place.*'

Travel, like any other part of life comes down to choices and commitment. And sometimes you're too stubborn, or feel you've gone too far to retreat or turn around. So fuck it or fuck it all. The cycles of travel make it very easy to reflect on where you've been and where you're going. It's also really fucking easy to gauge your life's direction when you're sat parking cars thinking, 'Holy fuck, where's all the time gone?' I guess what I'm trying to say is living on the kerbside of life I've gotten weary of waiting — not just waiting on the universe for a wrong turn from a shooting star. I'm also talking about the all the waiting in life and travel … waiting in lines … waiting in crowded terminals and departure queues … waiting on empty highways for your next ride … waiting on overnight trains, long haul flights, slow boats and overloaded buses … waiting to get to the next destination … waiting for the tour to start … waiting for the rain to stop … waiting for the fog to lift … waiting for the sun to come out for the perfect photo … waiting on the next round … waiting to save for my next trip while living back with my parents … waiting on friends … waiting for the girl I love to message me back.

All this introspection makes me think what else have I done in the three years it's taken to write this book? What have I achieved? What abstruse revelations have I gleaned from the absurdity of it all? Well, I travelled through Central America and the USA. There I met the most gorgeous and kind-hearted girl, who projected a love so heedless and trusting she jumped on a plane to

Australia to come find me. Two years later, after living together in Australia and the USA, Rosie still dug me enough to join me on a 17,000 mile road trip circumnavigating North America. To say Rosie was *it* is putting it mildly. She filled up my weaknesses and never failed to let me know through truth of words and touch how much she loved me.

The trip wasn't full of perfection and fun. Her purse of 'mmmhmmms' and shruggy-shoulders could mean a season of things. Feeling sexy came and went like ocean rain. And her mulish pride belted her heart and mind into shape on things like anvil harder than iron. It came from resoluteness buried deep in her marrow and that I was sure one day I would face — and that I would lose. Rosie also hated decisions beyond those posed by cocktail and restaurant menus. They were her kryptonite. She built them up in her head with giant, unstable Jenga blocks of apprehension over what she felt expected to do versus what she wanted to do — as if her entire future rested on each and every single choice. She'd just graduated college which also means graduating from the part of your life where you've spent the majority of time doing what you're told. I implicitly understood how uncertainty can be downright frightening. As a traveller I live in this world. And in the conservative South the antiquated gravitas attached to college graduation is still alive and well — a defining moment of adulthood from which point you're supposed to be productive, contribute to the national GDP, settle down and procreate to set the whole cycle in motion again.

Completing college turned Rosie into a briar of anxiety and irritable quiet. At the start of the road trip she'd developed body image crisis while maintaining a super-sexy and healthy appetite. So driving up the Californian coast along Highway 1 into Oregon, careening over the Cascade Mountains, crossing the high plains of the Columbia Plateau into Washington State then pinballing up the neck of Idaho heading towards Montana, Rosie ate at every quaint brew pub or diner we stopped at. She ordered salmon burgers with sweet potato fries, fried pickles, huckleberry pie, and *(at my insistence)* every gastronomic peculiarity of locality served as a side order. While driving we snacked on trail mix, chocolate pretzels, fruit and salmon jerky. Then in the afternoon Rosie would snuggle into a complex of guilty contentment and joke about it while blaming me partially for encouraging her *(which is true)*. And what became fun and easy and simple again by evening time was no guarantee it wouldn't go back to being hard work in the morning light.

Rosie was also petrified the entire time that Tog wouldn't make it — and my unquestionable faith in Tog only seem to exacerbate her fears of us getting stranded out in the serial killer middle of nowhere. Crossing Montana and Glacier National Park I could feel the endless highways and byways doing their job — chewing up Rosie's fraught tensions concerning her future, and slowing the pendulous sway of her heart and moods. At Polebridge Mercantile and Bakery Rosie bought a slice of apple strudel that took two days to make. We then sat outside the Northern Lights Saloon, under a bluedome kingdom of green grass, suspender belts, billycocks and mason jars of craft beer. We talked about where we should go next, without care or concern about how we go there — or if indeed we even made it because we might get sidetracked along the way. It is the perfect conversation. This is it, I thought — I never want to return from this orbit.

Travelling down the Great Divide, and winding up over Beartooth Gap into Wyoming, I saw Rosie relax even more. As we passed through South Dakota, the Badlands and Devil's Monument then up through the trout-popping, mosquito-droning lakes of Minnesota Rosie finally got it — the spontaneous joy of life on the open road. And the sense of freedom she fretted over now excited her. When we fell back into unison, as we always did, it was so blissful it made all the ghost-grasping worthwhile. But the point in the trip you feel the climax of emptiness often occurs right before you start running out of time or money. Then you're fucked because from then on you can't shirk thinking about the end. It's the crescendo of reaching a summit on a heinous uphill hike — the brief caesura in which you take in the magnificence of it all before thoughts of the knee-crunching return splinters the serenity.

It's a bit like holding onto an airport goodbye with a love you feel so strongly you're scared you'll snap it in half versus a love so pure you know you're supposed to set it free. Did I spend too much time with Rosie walking the line between the two? On the trip I started to fear I came across as too methodical and apathetic. I reminded myself I'm a fucking maniac, a truthsayer, a profaner, a provocateur, a raconteur, a nihilist, a god-fearer, a larrikin and a lover. After all, travel like art and love, and any kind of fetish or faith are really good ways for a lot of people to pretend. I guess the trick of it all is to pretend not to pretend which hopefully leads to not pretending at all. When this happened Rosie and I hit Canada and rain. We crossed the dull, endless plains of Ontario around Thunder Bay. In peripety to a journey that was now locked on a homeward dial, it rained for the next two weeks.

We stopped in Montreal where Rosie tried to practise her French and refused to eat *poutine*. We passed through a remote upstate border in Maine where we were interrogated for an hour and a half. Reliving fond childhood memories Rosie bought us so much lobster in Maine the mere sight of lobster trucks and their signs made us queasy by the time we reached New Hampshire and the White Mountains. Crossing into Vermont then down to New York State was a grassy-green heaven with dairy cows, apple orchards, farmers' markets and white picket fences. When we hit the Adirondacks we were running out of daylight. We got pulled over by a cop for a faulty taillight but found a cheeky off-road camping spot on Raquette Lake. With a rare break in the clouds the sunken sun spilt a sundae of orange and pink across the sky, and lit a galaxy of votive candles across the altar of black water. We spent a dreary day at the Finger Lakes wine tasting then cut down through Pennsylvania and Maryland. We camped on the Chesapeake Canal and fished for sun fish under a mellow tangerine gloaming. We got on the Skyline Drive through Shenandoah National Park before we found ourselves once again on the Blue Ridge Parkway, heading back to Asheville — the solar plexus of our Carolinas connection. We spent one final night camping on the Tennessee side of the Smokies. I splurged on a posh hotel in Asheville for our last night on the road and Rosie treated me to dinner at one of her favourite vegetarian restaurants. Before we knew it we were driving Tog back on the US 17 through North Charleston to Rosie's parents' house — and into a wrack of uncertainty about our relationship with my visa about to expire.

The road trip, like all our escapades and ventures presented a future of sorts. We co-funded an Emirates ticket for Rosie to come back to Perth. I had lined up two months worth of house-sitting gigs so we talked about it as a holiday between holidays — a stopgap of sorts while I worked on finishing this book and secured a more permanent work visa for Rosie and me to return to the USA together for Christmas with her family. I know it's not stable ground. But ground isn't stable — like faith, popularity and wealth we believe in it because we have to; to have certainty in some areas of our lives to make sense of all the shit. So I've been doing what people do when they are patiently waiting for someone they love to arrive — devise exotic and expansive cinematic clichés of how they hope their time together will play out. I guess that's why a lot of people think they're romantic — because a lot of romantic gestures go on in our heads.

To coincide with Rosie's arrival I got tickets to The Breeder's *Last Splash* tour. I researched all the isolated and halcyon coastal camping spots where I planned to take her and act out a fantasy like a couple of Beat Zen lunatics. I also bought a tower of herbal tea to add flavour to the grand welcome. When we lived together Rosie exhibited the cutest little compulsive streaks, which is why she got really narky at me when I drank her herbal tea. For the most part this was a sincere gesture to reciprocate all that she had selflessly given to me. Call it regret but I was also so happy to have the opportunity to usurp the difficult time Rosie had when she first arrived in Perth — and seeing her fractured look of withheld tears as she bought 70% cacao chocolate in Bozeman because I'm drinking too much *(and being an arsehole)* and chocolate always cheers her up.

The last time Rosie and I hung out before I left we went fishing at Breach Inlet on Isle of Palms. She did cartwheels in the sand and goaded me into being filmed which she then instagrammed with bawling emoticons about how I was about to depart.

'I love you more than…

Staying in hotels…

Fish…

My iPhone…

Games apps – my Rdio playlist which I worked really hard on and am really proud of…

A new spring day…

Cartwheels! – Sleeping in fresh sheets…

Nuts – Pine nuts…

Sneezes…'

I was going to miss Rosie's face, her mouth, her voice, her accent, her whimsical impulses, her flair for concocting impromptu cocktails in tea jars before we drove somewhere, her hand on my leg while driving, being between her legs, the perfect bites constructed for me on a fork from her breakfast stir-fries and lunchtime salads, the way she put avocado on everything, her kimchied breath, slapping her butt for good luck, her sexy underwear, taking off her underwear, showering together and drinking beer in the shower, the salted melon of her lips, the crazy beautiful lists she rhapsodises on about, her chipmunk laugh, her feisty stubbornness, her rubble of nerves when trying to make a decision, her addiction for watching Australian cooking shows, a sticky face from smooching her morning facemask of honey and

BEAT ZEN AND THE ART OF DAVE

cinnamon, her neurotic collection of vitamins, her fearlessness in emergencies, her consoling glow, her delight in winning, the way she clings to me when we walk down the street, the way she looks in a poncho, the notes she leaves me around the flat saying how much she loves me and how she wants to make trashy American/ Aussie babiezzz with me. However, I didn't say any of this. I've overreached and went all poetic.

'I'm going to miss you so much baby... you're my coastal highway-'

'Owwwww... You are so talented and say such amazing things. Most of the time I think there are a lot of girls way cooler than me that you'd like more.'

'Now that I've gotten to know a thousand of you's I know I'll never know anyone else like you.'

'Tell me again how much you're going to miss me?'

'You're my moon and I'm going to miss you like the ocean... misses the moonlight.'

Rosie gushes in a quiver of embarrassment. She talks in giggles with shruggy-shoulders about how we could go get married at city hall so I didn't have to leave.

'Should we get married?'

'Yep.'

'Really?'

'Yeah – why not?'

'Cos I'm crazy?'

'I love your crazy.'

'And go to Hawaii-'

'Or Fiji!'

'You know how you first like a person cos they're a mystery – well I like you more now that I know you – but you're still a mystery. You have both.'

On the way home we stop at the supermarket. As we exit I put a quarter in a toy vending machine. I tell myself if the universe gives me a ring from the multitude of plastic trinkets I'll propose. Rosie lets out a funny little ugly noise of joy when the plastic capsule revealed a cheap, shiny gold ring.

'I want it – Can I have it?'

'Of course beautiful – I got it for you.'

It fits snugly on her little finger but I stop short of proposing. I know the pregnant talk of hearts on the beach was a dizzying moment full of loose implication — and the moment had passed. Given the mind-blowing future of choices ahead of Rosie I know she would think twice, brood over it and say no. What am I to do then? What do you do with a *no*? Won't it just metastasise into a terminal case of *can'ts* and *no's*? My journey with Rosie has gone far, to such wonderful places I'm nowhere close enough *(or prepared enough)* to see it end.

In contrast, my travelling spurs feel more and more comfortable hung up on the hat rack the longer Rosie and I have been together. Is it a symptom of getting older as I watch age engrave my skin and pepper my temples and beard with quicksilvers of wisdom? Or is it Rosie and the glimpse of another life? I have no fucking idea. She wants to travel with me to all the places I've been and I want to take her with me to all the places I hadn't yet visited. I feel a bit like Kerouac on his mountain top in *Desolation Angels*:

'... I'd rather undo the back straps of redheads dear God and roam the redbrick walls of perfidious samsara than this rash rugged ridge full of bugs that sting in harmony and mysterious earth rumbles ...'

The point of being a Beat Zen travelling bum is surrendering yourself to the flow of life, confronting everyday moments as they happen, opening yourself up to uninhibited vulnerability. This makes it easy to become intoxicated by serendipity and the provocative notion of letting the universe decide for you. The problem is you can spend too much time waiting for a sign to tell you what to do and where to go next — to give your life direction and meaning.

So when do you stop? It's a simple question for a backpacker who runs out of money thus time. But I'm referring to the life-long vagrants like myself — aggregators of worldly experience, heretics of conventional living, kerbside scholars, and castaways who got caught in the outbound swell of it all and lost interest in finding solid ground again. Once the inception of uncertainty over lifestyle and career starts to fester, it can quickly turn into a full-blown existential crisis. It's not unlike the peons in service to a higher calling of creative expression — the global commune of obscure and unemployed painters, writers, dancers, sculptors, architects and musicians. When do you give up on a labour of love or work in progress — when to sell out for the path of least resistance?

It breeds a quiet hysteria as you panic more and more about what the fuck you're doing. Even worse is when you start to question your talent, or worth *(which is purgatory for the freeloading free-roamers and creatively minded)*. Have you been kidding yourself? Is everyone around you *(even your closest friends)* fraudsters and phoneys who've been lying to you the entire time about how great you are? You descend into a sceptic's worldview. The paralysis of melancholia can make the idea of when to quit on what you are most passionate about, or feel you were born to do impossible to contemplate. The good fight is to stay upright in water that is becoming more and more unstable, but it's fucking exhausting sometimes.

Whatever spiritual, hedonistic or basic corporeal instinct con-vokes us chameleonic outlanders, sun seekers, moonlight dancers, campfire catatonics, dusty dreamers, fringe dwellings, and drift-wood artists onto a new place, an undeniable force underpinning our motivations is the sense of the grass being greener. Is it part of our "spiritual calculus" or the work of doctrines, scriptures and sermons to make our hearts beat with discontent — forever on the lookout for something... well something better I suppose. To live in fear and doubt, grappling with some kind of fantasy or faith everything will eventually work out okay?

Even Zen, which tries *(and struggles at times)* to avoid the entire debate of divineness, everlasting souls and an immanent god comes under criticism for making the practitioner "mind-drunk". But every religion or belief system could be accused of being self-intoxicating. Travel is susceptible to the same accusation since it too endorses a process of disillusionment and open-mindedness to the see the clear light of the void. In *The Perennial Philosophy* Huxley describes the danger of 'no-mind' is avoiding both the carelessness of the average sensual man and over-eagerness of the zealot wanting salvation — uncaring quietism versus egocentric austerity:

*'As always, the path of spirituality is a knife-edge between abysses. On one side is the danger of mere rejection and escape, on the other the danger of mere acceptance and the enjoyment of things which should only be used as instruments or symbols.'*

So, again I wonder when do you stop — when do you give up on a myth, a dream, providence in the world — when do you stop looking for connections and patterns — when do you put down the unfinished prototype that is yourself — when do you stop searching for the rabbit in the moon if you can't see it already? I sure as heck don't know. I'm back in the waiting game — waiting for my girlfriend to arrive. Actually, Rosie is supposed to be here right now. She got so excited when I told her we'd head down the coast after making bank on parking cars at my sister's house. She wanted to go camping, fishing and wine tasting and live the dream. But she cancelled her flight to Australia ten days ago. I found this out because she then wrote me a message on Facebook telling me so:

*I have very very sad news, maybe the worst news, and that is that I'm not going to fly to OZ. I just can't afford it. So, the ticket has been cancelled. I'm so so sorry if this breaks your heart. I wish I had all the money in the world so we could go everywhere. There are other factors involved on my part that have fed into the decision. I'm as lost as ever about what my next move is, but going to Australia doesn't feel like the right one anymore. As far as taking steps that allow me to build on and discover what I want to do and where I want to live. I really really need time where i'm excited to do things for myself.. i've never ever had it and it's so important right now and i'm sorry that fucks you up too, but i don't feel like any other decision would be the right one. Perth seems more like a procrastination, and I feel pulled to make more solid decisions that help me narrow down on these questions, even if they might be selfish ones. This sucks, I know, but I hope there are consolations and happy results in the long run. You have all my love.*

The "Dear John" message hoisted a red flag of notification on my Facebook profile page three days after my birthday. It was during a week in which Rosie ignored me on Skype and Facebook. The fact that Rosie was dumping me I guess was implicit in the action. However, I was confused and felt compelled to ask, 'Are you breaking up with me?' which made me feel pretty foolish in hindsight. The shock was compounded by a premonition I had two days earlier foretelling a similar outcome. But I suppressed any misgivings over Rosie's lack of communication and resurrected my optimism that everything was fine by remembering how awesome she was — that she wasn't like the others. It's happened to me before on the eve of arrival — being told not to come, or conversely that the person I was waiting for had changed their mind. Does it make me socially relevant — getting dumped after a two-year relationship on Facebook? I am in my mid-thirties and have never been dumped in person. A drifter's curse I suppose. I've also spent most my life drinking for two so I guess that's another Beat Zen cursling. I wonder if this even makes me culturally relevant — in a digital age where our empathetic axis is withering away, ironically by the nexus of connectivity and our opposable ease to unfriend, unfollow, block and ignore? I want an old-fashioned Shakespearian apothecary's potion to make it all go away — numb this reality with marshmallow waves that spill over my head as I lie on hot beach sand.

After all our competitive jokes of keeping scores of our goodbyes Rosie complained when I left Charleston that I was ahead. Now I feel like she shat on the finishing line after an emphatic victory. So what the fuck am I supposed to do now? I could look on the lighter side and appreciate that timing has now made my birthday bottle of Glenfiddich 12 year single malt Scotch whisky all the more pertinent and defilable. But it doesn't help much when I've lost my lover, my best friend and my life's direction in one deal. The tungsten glow of a lighthouse, narrow with warmth and affection has swung around abruptly, without warning and left me lost, rocking in treacherous swell in the dark void of life. I'm being dramatic — I know. I've had a dram or two already. Worse still is the realisation I've got to start all over again. I can't work out what's more unfair — that my girlfriend *(sorry ex-girlfriend)* broke up with my Facebook, or during my detox month *(which seemed prudent while waiting for Rosie to arrive)*. I can hear Lloyd Bridges's character, Steve McCroskey from *Airplane* in my head saying:

*'Looks like I picked the wrong week to quit drinking.'*

Through the venetian blinds in the study I spy a family return to their Subaru Forester, laden with show bags full of rubber candy, comic books, balloons and fluorescent toy windmills. They pack the car like it's a military operation before vacating their spot on the lawn. I head outside with a makeshift cardboard sign to tout the free space and earn another $15. As I stand there watching vehicles crawl by in repetitive circuits, deluded into thinking they'll find a magical free car parking spot I question what I am supposed to do with all this love. Who's going to put it in a sling? Hearts are robust but avoid pain and conflict like the plague. If it's love in its purest form I should just go on loving right? I got to be like Osho:

*'It may look paradoxical to you, but it's not. It is an existen-*
*tial truth: only those people who are capable of being alone*
*are capable of love, of sharing, of going into the deepest core*
*of another person — without possessing the other, without*
*becoming dependant on the other, without reducing the other*
*to a thing, and without becoming addicted to the other. They*
*allow the other absolute freedom, because they know that if*
*the other leaves, they will be happy as they are now. Their*
*happiness cannot be taken by the other, because it is not given*
*by the other.'*

I battle against a fever, hard and true to preserve the florescent memories of an unforgettable two years because that's the point right — to retain the ultimate gift Rosie gave me? I mean, if we're supposed to learn anything it's the greatest challenge and sacrifice in life is to love unconditionally right? The problem is love sutures love, and most of us aren't strong or bold enough to be like Osho and give it when it's not reciprocated — less we poison the existing well or turn into weird creepos. It's also tough to maintain an egalitarian heart when it's been dumped on.

Given all that I've seen and done am I disappointed, disrespected, hurt, angry — from someone who treated my heart like a feckless school girl playing with a dollhouse? Fuck yeah! By the end of the week I've made $1050. So I spend the weekend wallowing in the limerence of love. I medicate *(annihilate)* myself with a copious consumption of *The Essential Leonard Cohen*,

Elliot Smith's *Either/Or*, Blur *13*, *The Best of Bob Dylan*, Ben Kweller, Low's *Things We Lost in the Fire*, MGMT, Radiohead's *Pablo Honey*, Teenage Fanclub, Beatles Anthology *(disks two and three)* and Galaxy 500's *Today*, along with a shit tonne of whisky, rum, tequila and fags:

> *Baby, my head's full of wishes*
> *Baby, my head's full of pictures*
> *Baby, my head's full of colours*
> *Baby, my head's full of pictures of you*

It turns out this rather clichéd methodology I successfully employed to douse past relationships won't wash away heart-ache of this magnitude — which fucking sucks. Even booze has forsaken me. I guess it's because punishing your body, trying to obliterate your sorrow with liquor and cigarettes is a placebo of martyrdom. Maybe that's why Mark Twain wrote:

> *'Martyrdom covers a multitude of sins.'*

I turn to even more clichéd strategies. I write really bad breakup poetry and seek out long lost ex's on the internet with a heavyset tumbler full of ice and booze. I try to spike the love with injections of all of Rosie's little imperfections — her pixi-lated twists and unresponsive turns, her conspiratorial silences and reclusive spells, her jury of chiding looks, how she justified thoughtlessness with aphorisms and New Age crap, her forged apologies wrapped in effusive text messages which amounted to *'Sorry for not being sorry'*, how she would tell me what I wanted to hear rather than what she felt because it was easier to say. But my *Beat Zendaveness* steps in to call me a doofus — that I'm churlish and petty and just as flawed with my own slew of contradiction that are maturing like a fine calvados.

I message Rosie asking her to uncancel her ticket and treat Australia like the most amazing two-month holiday ever. She says

I'm being way too wonderful and that I should be calling her a bitch for breaking my heart, and how she's been totally unfair and a really really *really* shitty person. I tell her distance is an imagined reality. She says she still loves me and the silly things I say. I tell her I love hearing her say that and ask if it would make a difference if I got on a plane for the USA tomorrow. Five times that night I search for flights, get airfare quotes and almost book a flight direct to Charleston. Rosie messages me back saying she just can't do this cycle anymore, going back and forth because it's fucking with her way toooo much — and that she doesn't want to live in Australia, or get married. She says she's not ready to commit to anything big, she's too young and needs time alone to figure out all her fucked up shit. I tell Rosie I feel sick and that Scotch isn't helping — and I'm sighing a lot, which feel like the hiccups because they seem impossible to get rid of. She agrees, and says she's yawning a lot too, and that she's definitely going to be drinking whiskey later on too. Rosie asks if we still want to see each other before we die. I say I'm still thinking of coming back to the USA in the new year. Rosie tells me she'd love that but not to come because of her.

Monday morning comes around in a blur. I wake up late and try to write. An online article of the day is titled 'Takosubo Cardiomyopathy' AKA Octopus Trap Syndrome AKA Broken Heart Syndrome. I log onto Tumblr where every reblogged picture and quote from Rosie about freedom and love appears to be speaking both directly to me and in ignorance of me. I clean up my laptop and move all the pixelated memories into a stunted yellow folder icon. I religiously check Instagram. Five days later she posts a younger version of me with her dog lying in his lap. Then she blocks me from Instagram and deactivates her Facebook account. I feel like I'm taking all of this too seriously so I say to myself:

*'Don't worry Dave. We're the DuPre's. We're the seeds that don't take root. For us it's not supposed to get easier as we get older.*

*We prefer love in shapes that are handmade and awkward to wrap. Those around us didn't change — they just turned into the people they were meant to be. We're built to be alone — lone wolves occasionally riding in lone wolf packs — taking solace in solitude and knowledge we are all one. We're the light, travelling light to spread the light — part-timers in an intergalactic co-op.'*

However, when I leave the house my hometown is littered with memories from when Rosie spent six months here. I can hear Frank Sinatra's *A Man Alone* in my head. I convince myself I really do listen to the trembling of trees with sentimental ease. I also realise I don't have any stories that don't start with, 'When Rosie and I...' and the sheer number of songs I can't listen to right now is staggering. After Rosie reinstates her Facebook profile the penitent platitudes ping at odd hours of the night:

hey :)
whatcha up to?

Hi!

I had a really weird and sad dream about you :(

hey stranger

i hope you're happy
A lot

:)
hey there

i miss flat whites so much
what are you up to?

:
(

i miss watching movies with you

heya
what's news with you dear?

<333

I watched strickly ballroom last night. I made me miss australia lots

Sometimes i really wish i was in Australia

I miss you. I wish it was easier to see you

I'm sorry it didn't work out

In the postmortem of live chats on Facebook the reasons become irrelevant. Reasons don't change anything. In the end I think the answer was simple enough — Rosie didn't want *it* or *us* or me any longer. I was the sacrifice so Rosie could get something else, new or different — even if she didn't know what that was. I guess despite one-in-six-billion chances *(the sort they name stars after)* sometimes there's no beating the odds. It's still all a matter of... timing. Is it the legacy of evolutionary psychology, religious traditions, or something more fundamental that makes us feel we need to sacrifice to gain some sort of reward? I have no fucking clue. But how can I be resentful or mad at Rosie when I did exactly the same thing at a similar age — sacrifice that which I had for the unknown, possessed by a basic conviction I needed to experience whatever it was.

Whether it is Zen, Tao, Shinto, Hindu, Sufism, Science, Stoicism, Eroticism, Gnosticism, Animism, Kabbalah, Panthesim, Christianity, Mysticism, Zoroastrianism, Circles, Spirals, Stars, Spock, Kirk, Yoda, Unicorns, or Houyhnhnms it's all the same shite — liberating ourselves from attachments, misconceptions, dispositions, desires and sin — dedicating ourselves to vulnerability and compassion to selflessly connect me, you, us and them to *all-is-one* and peer in the great unknowing cloud *(in whatever face or form it may take)*. Chögyam Trungpa reduces it all down in a masterful fashion which makes all I've said sound like nonsense:

*'As far as I can see, there is no difference between theism and non-theism, basically speaking... Whether you worship someone else or you worship yourself, it is the same thing. Both theism and non-theism can by problematic if you are not involving yourself personally and fully. You may think you are becoming spiritual, but instead you could just be trying to camouflage yourself behind a religious framework and still you will be more visible than you think... We are not trying here to sort out which tradition, or which particular type of merchandise is better. We war talking in terms of needing to develop a personal connection with one's body and one's mind.'*

The eternal conundrum of dualistic tendencies is a bitch. Yet, on the battleground of happiness versus suffering, connection versus separation, travel like love is some kind of faith. The irony that as travellers we desert everything that's familiar — all the people we know and love to find a deeper connection somewhere foreign is some sort of fanatical, beautiful lunacy. Just before I left Charleston I met John, a *wabi-sabi* potter at the Smoky Oak Tap Room on James Island. Despite being sluiced on PBRs, John spoke a truth of a wandering bhikku. He admitted to being a voracious traveller when he was younger but stopped when he realised he was taking his home and expectations of the life he left with him.

I guess the ultimate seduction occurs when you become trans-fixed on something specific bringing you joy, or making things better — instead of doing the deep digging of who you are and where you want to be. In other words, why not let your inner self reacclimatise — pause to yawn and pop the ears of your psyche every so often while overlanding it through life. You can still get caught in this process — constant philosophical excavation where you're always reapplying a temporary dressing of self-healing. It's a bit like relocating each year to a new city because you're unhappy with your current station, or people who strive to get thin because it's a plausible answer of sorts to why they feel so shit about life. In the end, succeed or fail it doesn't necessarily change if the reality and perspective you carry with you remains the same. I guess Rosie needed to roll down the other side of the hill, cover herself in the pollen and fragrance of fresh new green grass — even though in time most of us come to realise all grass tastes kind of looks and smells the same.

It's late in the afternoon on Wednesday when I head down to City Beach. It's early spring and the chill has kept the numbers down to anorak tourists and the few regulars who surf and exercise here every day after work. My toes sink into cool, white sand that's soft and granular, reassuring and perfect — it's home and cannot be replicated. An ocean breeze is spitting at the waves. The words of Lisa St. Aubin Terán never felt more poignant:

'Travelling is like flirting with life. It's like saying, "I would stay and love you, but I have to go; this is my station."'

As I jog down into the surf I feel the vices of past and future that call me a faker weaken and vent into the bracing water and slush of waves. I swim out past the breakers and let the swell lift me up and down like a parent. Small sets of soft spilling waves come through at regular intervals. I catch a few, gliding down the face of the wave on my belly before I'm swallowed by the breaking water. I flounder around in the whitewash until I find my feet and leap up to run back into the surf to catch another one before the set ends. Growing cold I leave the water. Walking up the beach I spot a jellyfish freshly plucked from the tide and embedded in the sand. Its translucent skin glistens against the dying embers of daylight. I am that jellyfish. I want to throw it back in the ocean but it won't change anything. I know, no matter how far it travelled, its destiny was always to be here now — to get beached in this spot and die.

I dry myself off and walk back up to the grassy esplanade of pine trees where I salute the setting sun by cracking a traveller. Beer and sunsets make the best companions, I conclude as the climax of emptiness returns. It's a quiet roar only I can hear. It emanates right now from the edge of the ocean — from the infinity of the horizon. I know I'll leave again soon. I'll embrace the open road like a lover with no sense of future as to where I'm heading. How can I stop or quit after all I've discovered and vetted? Whatever intention, predilection, subjective validation or grand questions you set out with on a journey, I know they're not always appeased or answered. I shiver as the first stars appear in a purple sky. I welcome the magnificent insignificance of it all. The white tail of a jet lances the sky above. I visualise an empty seat, centre aisle at the rear of the aircraft — 39G. I recall *The Rum Diary* and Hunter S. Thompson's description of arriving in Vieques — the feeling of being less in reality and more in some kind of Hollywood film starring Humphrey Bogart:

*'I felt a tremendous distance between me and everything real.'*

I stare out over the Indian Ocean as it turns from indigo to black — knowing there's nothing between me and Madagascar. A new moon lifts cast with the ephemeral shade of a full moon. I picture the rabbit curled up in the cradle of the lunar's mantle and start to wonder where I will go to next.

# ACKNOWLEDGEMENTS

*Special thanks to my family*

I am extremely grateful to all the contributors who supported ***Beat Zen and the Art of Dave's*** crowdfunding campaign. With your help we successfully raised the target amount needed to print and publish my latest book. It can now embark on its own journey to bookshelves, coffee tables and rucksacks around the world. A special "thank you" goes to the following:

Rory Alcock
Stacey Bell
Juliette CampbellGolding
Robert Cappellin and Carl Freedman
Andrew Driscoll
Peter Driscoll
Ellison family
Warren Gibbs
Maredudd ap Gwyndaf
Adam Harris
Pauline Iles
Jane and Toby Jefferis
Nigel Jones
Beverley Martin
Anne McNamara
Kate McNamara
Greg Nairn
Frank and Julienne Prendergast
Melissa Osborne
Cindy Seeberger and Peter Waldie
Adam Snow
Varga family
Mitchell Wilton

I would also like to thank the vanguard of crazy wonderful beautiful Beat Zen wanderers I have met on my journeys – you are the architects who have helped shape the story of my life so far and for which I am eternally grateful. I hope to meet you and new amazing overlanders of life down the road sometime soon.

`ormation can be obtained
'testing.com
'JSA
130917
.00002B/3/P